A Brilliant Teacher

Lessons learned from one family's
journey around the world

Steve Rhine & Toby Abraham-Rhine

Sawtooth Press
Salem, OR

Published 2004 by Sawtooth Press

Sawtooth Press
2766 Weatherford Ct NW, Suite 207
Salem, Oregon 97304
www.sawtoothpress.com

Rhine, Steve & Abraham-Rhine, Toby
A Brilliant Teacher

ISBN 0-9654099-3-7

Books published by Sawtooth Press are printed on
recycled, acid free paper to limit their impact on the earth.

Printed in the United States of America.
First Printing: November 2004

DEDICATION

To my grandmother, Helen "Mama B" Burns,
whose adventurous spirit in her golden years
inspires me to live life fully in every moment.
To my parents, Arlene and Tony,
who raised me to believe
that I could attempt to do anything,
because there is always someone, somewhere,
who can help fix it if I mess up.
SR

To my parents, Geraldine and Richard Abraham
who never once said, "Are you nuts?!"
Special thanks to my mother
who taught me at an early age
the fine art of washing clothes in the sink
and instilled in me an ecological heart
and a deep appreciation for people from all cultures.
To our children, Clare, Bridget and Michael,
three amazing individuals
whose creativity and compassion
never cease to amaze me.
Continue to love each other as we love you.
TA-R

ACKNOWLEDGEMENTS

Many people marveled at our plans to take this trip with three children. Some felt it might be a strain on our marriage; all that 24 hour closeness. The trip was remarkable. The true challenge has been writing this book together. For ease of reading we have written our account of this adventure in Toby's voice which occasionally led to debates beginning with "I did not think/say that!" It has been an equal labor of love by the two of us.

During the trip, our trusty Grolier's Encyclopedia CD served two purposes. It came in handy because we always had a resource for educating the kids on the road and we were able to embed many of these obscure facts within our tale. We also relied frequently on <u>Lonely Planet</u> guidebooks for advice and trivia, which are often referred to in the text.

A number of people helped us with thoughtful comments about the book during the writing process including Felicia Cameron, Cathy Abraham, Barbara Blake, and Karen Egan. Special thanks to Sandy Luna for her moral support, and editing help and Kate Webster for her apple earth drawing.

TABLE OF CONTENTS

"The world is a brilliant teacher."

Unknown

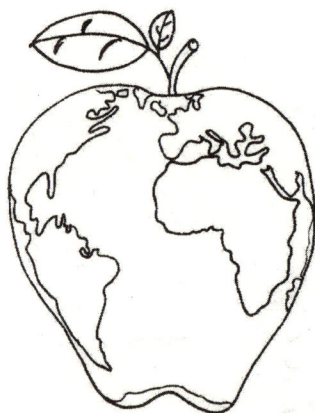

"Twenty years from now you will be more disappointed
by the things you didn't do than by the ones you did do.
So throw off the bowlines,
sail away from the safe harbor.
Catch the trade winds in your sails.
Explore. Dream. Discover."
Mark Twain, American Author

PRELUDE

Eighteen years ago I married my best friend. Planning for our lives together we decided to forgo any gifts for each other at birthdays, holidays and anniversaries in exchange for traveling. I haven't missed the gifts one bit. Instead I have years of memories from backpacking, bicycling, sleeping in the most unique of settings and sharing in the kindness of strangers. Working in the educational setting leaves summers available to explore. It became a lifestyle choice to live very simply in order to support our habit. We love to travel.

As our three children came into the picture, Steve and I saved money in an account for "something." We didn't really know what that would be, but a few years ago, when we started talking about a trip to experience other countries, the decision became crystal clear. Let's go see the world.

"We need to save for the world trip" was our mantra for years. It became excellent practice in delaying gratification-- something we can all find challenging. After selling anything that wasn't nailed down or already donated, the $15,000 we had saved was not nearly the amount needed to go on this adventure. At first, the estimates for a trip around the world for five were in the $20,000-30,000 range, but as the details became apparent, we were resigned to the fact that it would cost approximately double our first estimate to be gone for the full eight months. Thankfully, the timing worked out perfectly for us to rent out our home while we were away. Loans would have to cover the rest. Fifty thousand is two new cars, a college education, or a sizable down payment on a house. Could we afford that much money? Of course not! Would it be worth it anyway? Maybe . . .

Fortunately, Steve had the advantage of a sabbatical year at his university so his partial salary helped to pay the bills as we traveled. A number of stops in our trip revolved around him learning about education in different countries, connecting with colleagues who were working with him on mathematics education issues and piecing together something of worth. He would need to write furiously about upon our return. I, on the other hand, would be leaving a part-time counseling position and hoped I would still have a job when I got back.

Our three children were about to miss a semester of school. Would that be a problem? Michael was heading to first grade in the fall. Even though there are many important things to learn in the first semester we reasoned that our trip would balance out what he was missing.

Bridget was a budding poet facing the fifth grade. One of the major accomplishments in her young life was holding numerous jump-roping records at her school. She would be disappointed to not be there to defend her titles. For Bridget and Clare, our oldest, our former experiences teaching English and math would come in handy.

Clare's education was probably our greatest challenge as she prepared to enter her second year of middle school. She was just beginning to establish friendships at school, so the trip would be a social loss for her. Perhaps email with teachers and friends would be sufficient to fill the void on both fronts.

Our friends and family had mixed reactions to our plans, ranging from "Are you crazy!" to "Would you pack me in your suitcase?" Some were nervous about putting our kids through the ordeal of hostel hopping (hostels are a cross between college dormitories and hotels) and a lack of routine. Others were impressed that we would be willing to pour thousands of dollars into eight months of an education for our family. Not all of the countries we would be traveling would be the safest places to visit, so there was certainly trepidation about our choices. On the day before we left, two of the children's uncles managed to slip Clare and Bridget their business cards saying, "Call from anywhere in the world if **something happens**." Many recognized that travel without risk is travel without opening yourself to possibilities.

The children's reactions regarding our grand plan were varied. In spite of our incessant reassurance of "It will be great!" all of them were a bit nervous. Clare was probably the most enthusiastic, as she had recently studied ancient Egypt and Greek and Roman gods in her social studies class, and Spain in her Spanish class. Bridget was excited sometimes and hesitant at others. One of her best qualities is that she is willing to try new things, whether it is food or places, so that would be a bonus. On the other hand, she had enough understanding of the trip to know it would be very different from her day to day experience, which made her worry.

Michael cried. "I don't want to go!" became his constant refrain whenever the topic came up. He had just developed a friendship with a classmate down the street and they loved playing together. We tried to encourage him with stories of elephant rides, seeing lions and giraffes, and visiting the home of Robin Hood, but he was very skeptical that this trip would provide him with much opportunity to play. In the end, he wisely chose to bring his baby pillow and his favorite bunny providing a connection to home and a source of security. I constantly wondered what memories and perspectives each of them would take away from this trip.

When in our wildest dreams did Steve and I think that emptying our savings account, taking out loans, leaving behind our safe routines, friendships, and jobs and traveling around the world for eight months would be a sensible thing to do? Was it a stroke of brilliance or insanity? Was it courageous or foolishness to put our family in vulnerable situations?

Ultimately, it was, of course, all of that and more. We did not set out to escape the rat race, although it was nice to be away from the pace of life and work. We didn't have a specific mission to achieve enlightenment. Perhaps it was the same reason mountain climbers climb mountains: because it is there. "The world is a brilliant teacher." Our desire for this trip was to learn from that teacher.

We were not without objectives. Society bombards our children with the "buy this latest thing" mentality. A lesson in the value of simplicity was at the top of our list. Years ago we purchased Material World by Peter Menzel. It is an outstanding piece of photographic work and text. Menzel asked families around the world to put all their possessions in front of their homes so that he could take a picture. He also mixed demographic statistics with the family's answers to a few questions, such as "What is your most valued possession?" and "How many times has your family been more than 30 miles from home?" This book served as one of our main inspirations for wanting to make the journey.

Finally, our children are growing up so quickly. Perhaps our most important reason was that we love each other and really wanted to escape routines and spend time as a family.

We each packed only a small daypack so we would not have to check luggage and risk their loss. Keeping our loads light allowed easy mobility.

Our daypacks held:

3	t-shirts (2 packed, one on)	1	bathing suit
4	pair socks (3 packed)	1	waterproof parka
1	long-sleeved shirt	1	toothbrush
1	pair of jeans (worn or packed)	1	hand towel
1	Polartec 300 hooded jacket	1	bandana
1	pair of zip off shorts/pants	1	Sierra cup

4 pair underwear (3 packed)	1 spoon
1 pair walking boots	1 hat
1 pair sport sandals	1 pair sunglasses

Shared items: Soap, shampoo, tooth paste, brush, hair cutting scissors, first aid kit, Swiss pocket knife.

We planned to add layers in cold places or visit the local thrift stores if we needed anything else. The kids had a cheap digital camera and we had a moderately expensive one, along with Steve's laptop which, in spite of the extra six pounds, was a useful addition to our possessions and came in handy for downloading pictures, homework, and his work. We also decided to carry sleeping bags to save on lodging where we could.

On the 24th of June, with $2500 in traveler's checks, credit cards, passports, health certificates, shots in our arms and day packs in hand, we said goodbye to our family and friends and began the adventure . . .

"If you start now,
you will know a lot next year
that you don't know now,
and that you will not know next year, if you wait."
The William Feather Magazine

STAY LEFT!!!

<u>NORTH ISLAND of NEW ZEALAND</u>   26 June

K ia Ora! Greetings from New Zealand! "Aloha" from
Hawaiians is the equivalent of "Kia Ora" from the
Maori, the indigenous people of New Zealand. Our
jaunt through New Zealand would teach us much about their
native ways and relationship with the British as well as the
magnificence of their land.

Arriving in Auckland at 4:57 a.m., three hours earlier than
anticipated, we needed to kill a few hours in the airport
because everything was closed. Flying for the first leg of this
long trip, the children were too excited with the movies,
music, and food service to bother sleeping. After our twelve
and a half hour flight exhaustion reigned. Piling our gear in a
small mound, we found one of those plastic café tables and
rested our heads for just a minute. We were asleep instantly.

At 8 a.m., with matted hair, morning breath, and the look
you might expect from sleeping with your face on a table for a
couple of hours, Steve wandered away to get our rental car. He
had found a great deal on the Internet: 12 days of car rental
plus 10 nights of youth hostel vouchers for the five of us for
about $600. The only problem was, he had higher
expectations for the E.S.P. of Kiwis (New Zealanders.) His
instructions were to go to the information desk to get the car…

12

"Hi, I'm Steve. Can I have my car?"

"Huh?"

"I was told to go to the information desk to pick up a packet for my rental car."

"I'm afraid I don't have any idea what you are talking about. What company did you rent with?"

"Uh . . . . I guess I should have written that down." (This was not a particularly good omen for the beginning of eight months of travel.)

"I suppose so. Well, over there is all our information about rental cars and hotels."

Up on the wall was the usual airport conglomeration of one-foot square advertisements for about 50 rental car places and hotels.

"Now, what was the name of that darn company? I think it started with a 'C'."

Needless to say, after about an hour and a few calls to the wrong rental car places, Steve achieved contact.

"Go back to the info desk and tell them you want to pick up the packet for the Omega Car Rental Company."

Info Desk: "Oh, that packet!"

Since Steve was the one who had battled the info desk, I volunteered to drive. After all, in New Zealand the steering wheel is on the right, I was born in England and am left handed to boot. Working the stick shift with my left hand felt surprisingly natural but I was still very jittery, wanting to swerve into the right lane. Steve was impressed with my courage as we dodged crazy Kiwi drivers whizzing in all directions. He, on the other hand, was relegated to the noble role of navigator. Frantically he tried to ascertain what street we were on, while trying in vain to locate it on the map.

Our typical car conversation evolved on this first trip into a smooth running machine:

Toby: "I'll drive because I hate navigating."

Steve: "Okay, you look for streets as we drive and I'll try to find them on the map."

Minutes into the trip . . .

Toby: "There goes Westminster St."

Steve: "We should have turned right there. Should we double back or keep going?"

Toby: "I don't know! You have the map!"

Steve: "Oh, right. Well maybe we should just keep going. Why don't we try to find Shepherd St. and we'll turn there. It should be about a block."

Toby: "Okay, here is Shepherd St., I'm turning right."

Steve: "Stay on the left hand side of the street!"

Toby swerves to avoid oncoming cars.

Toby: "I keep forgetting that."

Steve: "When you get to the next major intersection, turn left."

Toby: "Is this a major intersection?"

Steve: "That was. Oh well, let's keep going straight and turn at the next street."

Toby: "It's a one way street. We'll have to turn at the next one."

Steve: "Darn, that one ends in a cul-de-sac."

Kids: "We're hungry!"

Steve and Toby: "Shush! We are trying to figure out where we are!"

With this sophisticated method, we usually reached our destination, although not necessarily going a direct route. There was one slight variation in this repertoire: the kids would yell, "We have to pee!" Otherwise, you basically get the idea.

One of the novelties of driving in New Zealand (and most other places in the world) is that the government likes to save money and electricity by not using stoplights. Instead, they have roundabouts. Now, if you have never had the pleasure of driving into one of these, I'll give you some insight: in England it's called a "circus." A roundabout resembles the hub of a wheel with three or more streets radiating out of the circle like spokes. Everyone supposedly knows who gets to go when. Once in the roundabout you must find your desired street to get out. If you miss your turn, you can go in circles (two or three times, if necessary). That little feature came in handy more than once. Big roundabouts even have extra lanes that add to the craziness so numerous cars can go 'round and 'round. Needless to say, this transportation strategy caused us a few anxious moments.

The roads in New Zealand are extremely narrow, as if former horse, cow or sheep trails were merely paved over. It's hard to say whether the cars are tiny to accommodate the roads or the high cost of fuel. Petrol was very expensive (about $4.00 per gallon). We drove a little Toyota Vista and it cost $50.00 to fill it. It's no wonder (and a welcome relief) that there were no Suburbans on the road. It was rare to even see an SUV, and when we did, it was a miniature version of the models in the States. Reaching the highway was always a relief. No turns and we got to stay on one side of the road for a while.

The kids were usually oblivious of our stress and merrily played and napped in the back seat. Billboards constantly implored drivers to stay awake and drive carefully. Even so, hundreds of white crosses dotted the sides of the road, marking the sites where reckless Kiwi drivers (or tourists?) met their Maker. Curious, I counted 150 crosses during a forty-five minute section. We also passed about 15 cars that were impaled on trees. Maybe renting a car wasn't such a good idea.

In spite of a few near miss collisions, we made it to the oasis of the very stylish Auckland Youth Hostel. For those who are not acquainted with youth hostels, they are a unique, relatively cheap way to see the world. Hostels exist worldwide with varying degrees of quality. Most have rooms or dorms with four, six, or eight beds to a room and provide a communal kitchen for guests to prepare their own meals.

Having just flown from Los Angeles we weren't ready for a big city, so as soon as we got settled we decided to head to the countryside. The hills surrounding Auckland were lush, green and dotted with sheep, the fresh winter air crisp and

15

rejuvenating. Along the way, we found the Pohuehue forest and had a refreshing walk to a waterfall. Fern trees, long vines, and the peaceful sound of running water surrounded us. Cool and dark, the leaves and plants were so thick we couldn't see any soil at all. It was very unexpected to be in New Zealand in a place so tropical. Over eighty percent of the country's native plants are found nowhere else in the world. That fact tells you basically two things: 1) this country has a long history of isolation and 2) uniqueness doesn't just apply to the Kiwis.

Driving up to the small town of Mahurangi, we found a staggering panoramic view of the islands, ocean and forests. At dusk we enjoyed a long walk on the beach collecting shells as the waves of the South Pacific Ocean gently crashed against the shore. June is winter in New Zealand and it was dark by 5:00. Hunger kicked in, so we found a Thai restaurant nearby where we ate "burritos", which amounted to canned baked beans in a tortilla. Mysteriously, it took 30 minutes for them to make (my guess was that they had to go out and buy the beans.) This was to be the beginning of our continual quest for food that the kids would eat. One treat we certainly agreed upon was kiwis. Formerly the Chinese Gooseberry, a whim of marketing changed its name and altered its fate to become one of the most popular fruits in the world.

Our next stop was Rotorua, the geothermal wonder of New Zealand. Everywhere we looked there was steam emanating from something; manhole covers, street or sidewalk grates, ponds, creeks and sewers. Thermal fields with boiling pools of mud and water abounded. Even the youth hostel boasted of a piping hot thermal mineral pool in which we swam several times. The landscape looked otherworldly or prehistoric in nature. It was as if someone put the whole town on top of a boiling teakettle and the steam was just itching to escape. The result was a pervasive sulfur odor. I wondered if residents ever got used to that rotten egg smell?

The first night we treated ourselves to a visit to the Tamaki Village, including a walk through a recreated, living Maori village and a hangi. A hangi is a cultural feast with traditional dancing and a concert. A shuttle bus picked us up at the hostel then toured the city gathering fellow travelers from France, Uruguay, Argentina, Australia, England, Germany, Holland, Wales, and Thailand. Tamaki Village was enchanting and had a haunting, sacred feel to it. At the village gate we were greeted with a Haka, the Maori war dance. Warriors wielding spears shouted at us in unintelligible phrases while sticking out their tongues and making their eyes bulge. This was especially popular with our children. The distorted face is meant to scare their enemies--conveying to them, "Your flesh looks delicious and will soon be inside my stomach."

Places like Tamaki Village are living tributes to the natives of this superb country. In the heart of Rotorua we saw a copy of the land grab treaty that had been fashioned by the British and signed by Maori chiefs. Ironically (or maybe not) the chiefs who signed the treaty were not from the tribes being displaced. What struck me the most on this document was that in the very center was a picture of Chief Seattle and his famous words: "The Earth does not belong to us, we belong to the Earth." What makes one people think they have the right to take over, enslave, kidnap or disrespect another? What is missing in a person's life that fuels the desire to own, conquer, build? I suppose it's a question for all time with no answer. Why are there wars? It seems to be the same story all over the world, only the names and locations change. The Australian physician Dr. Helen Caldecott said that we have all the resources we need and all the solutions to the problems facing this planet if people would just stop being greedy. Long hours of travel provided much time for reflection.

Steve turned 41 on June 28th, our first birthday on the road. After swimming in the hostel's hot thermal pool we explored the Rotorua Museum of Art and History. According to the exhibits, a huge volcanic explosion (the likes of Mt. St. Helen's in Washington) killed 120 people and forever altered the landscape and lifestyle of the Maori people. Foreigners moved in and started to capitalize on the thermal waters by constructing a grand bathhouse in the 1800's. Thermal waters were piped up into the baths as guests were lavished with care and treatments. The posh therapeutic spa later became a rehabilitation center for war veterans. This resort did not close until 1960. Now it has been restored and reopened as the museum.

It was a fascinating place to spend Steve's birthday but we still needed to do something to make it official. Following another simple dinner made in the hostel kitchen we went in pursuit of a "birthday cake." Hours of walking in the dark, wet night proved fruitless but we did get to witness first hand the sport known as "hoop ball" being played by women at the local park. I can't even begin to explain it but it appears to be a cross between basketball and Ultimate Frisbee. No dribbling and you can't move once you have possession of the ball. Cold and wet we returned empty-handed to the hostel and purchased a stale, overpriced muffin, stuck a candle in it and Steve was officially "fortysomething."

As we drove the roads down the North Island, it was clear that New Zealanders have considerable inclination to protest things. There were "no nukes", "no jails in my backyard", etc. posters throughout. On the other hand, there were no billboards anywhere to distract from the scenery. The Maori and Europeans seem to get along well here, which is a lesson to U.S. race relations. Everywhere in New Zealand signs had both the Maori translation and English. In schools, children learn Maori language as well as traditional dances. The Maori arrived in New Zealand about 900 AD and named the place "Aoteoroa" or "Land of the Long White Clouds." James Cook, however, spent three days here in 1769, claimed it for England, and named it New Zealand (I guess there must be an "old" Zealand somewhere in England). Hence, our brood had their first of many future lessons in imperialism.

From Rotorua we had a very long, cold drive down to Wellington, breaking up the trip with stops at Huka Falls, Taupo Lake, and Tarangiro National Park. The pouring rain felt like home but we were able to catch a glimpse of the mountains. Stretching our legs in the visitor's center we spent over an hour learning about what we could not see through the clouds. New Zealand is a glorious country and the Kiwis extremely welcoming. We were shocked, however, to see clear cutting of forests along the way. Beyond the few bald spots, the terrain changed from valley to beach to mountains. New Zealand seems to possess every land region except desert.

A summary of the children's perspectives after the first couple of days:

Michael: "I don't like the city I am in because it smells gross! Like rotten eggs."

Bridget: "I miss home, but am getting used to the outdoors. We have been learning a lot. It is difficult to get used to the time changes. We lost Monday!"

Clare: "It is difficult changing to the different time zones. When we first got here we slept for three hours. There is an 18-hour time difference. The best thing has been watching the Maori people."

STEVE'S PHILOSOPHY 101: *Extroversion*

Well, what began in my journal on our first day as a highly detailed account of our travels has very quickly turned into occasional philosophical reflections upon lessons learned and insights gained.

There are great people in New Zealand. One of my objectives for this trip is to hook up with people from different countries, particularly at the youth hostels. My style is to hang back and wait until I get a sense of people before I dive in and develop a relationship. I know I need to stretch myself and be a bit more outgoing if I am going to be able to experience people as well as sights. Toby is wonderfully able to bond with people instantly. Obviously, my style is not conducive to this type of travel if I want to learn about the people in each culture we enter.

Is travel only for outgoing personalities? Actually, it often seems quite the opposite. There are many reflective, hermit types traveling alone and reading their books. Most people, however, travel in at least pairs. I'd imagine, that if you are a bit outgoing on your own, or even with one other, many opportunities for entering into people's lives around the world await. When I traveled with my friends Paul and Ken throughout Mexico years ago, I certainly relied on their gregariousness all too often. Due to their jovial natures, we often stayed with people we met along the way. I knew that I could easily rely on Toby's nature on this trip. Yet, I truly want to initiate some interaction with people where I can. For me this trip is not just about sights to see, but about immersing myself in other people's perspectives and experiences of life.

I know that if I remain true to my nature, many opportunities for learning about people will pass me by. With three kids in tow, I am sure that the times we are invited into people's homes will be few and far between, but I am hopeful nevertheless! I hope our large group size doesn't isolate us from opportunities to interact with people. It will probably be all too easy to stay focused on each other rather than seeking companionship. Then again, the kids may be an entrée into other cultures as well. We'll see!

Even without entering people's homes and daily lives, I pray that we will have more to tell about our trip than beautiful buildings and majestic mountains. We will have gained greater understanding of how people around the world experience life similarly or uniquely from ours.

SOUTH ISLAND of NEW ZEALAND   30 June

Wellington, the capital city of New Zealand, is at the base of the North Island. Between the North and South islands are the Cook Straits, famous for the many boats that were shipwrecked as they attempted passage. Clare has a children's magazine with a story about a white "ghost" dolphin guiding ships through the straits in the 1700's. When ships entered the strait, the dolphin would show up and swim in front of their bow, leading the way past the treacherous rocks. Recalling this story made Steve a bit nervous as we crossed the straits in our ferry. He didn't see any dolphins. However, the captain assured us over the PA system that we would have a lovely voyage. The weather was agreeable and we made it safely to Picton.

Whereas Wellington is a grand city, Picton, on the north tip of the South Island, is a cozy village. Walking off the ferry we found a little park for a picnic lunch next to the water. There was a miniature train operated by local train enthusiasts (older men and women offering the local children and tourists a thrill). It runs on a track around the park and across a tiny bridge over a small pond. We couldn't resist and let the kids have a ride around for the $0.50 per child fare.

Setting our sights on Christchurch, we spent the next four or five hours driving winding roads and rolling hills. Despite complaints of queasiness from the back of the car, no one lost lunch. Hundreds of sheep ate the countryside as we passed. Sheep actually outnumber people in New Zealand about 13 to1. The trip was gorgeous, but we were nowhere near our intended destination when the sun set. Making one of our many spontaneous decisions we stayed on the coast in Kaikoura for the night.

As serendipity would have it, Kaikoura was a splendid place; a tiny village set in a quiet bay at the foot of rugged, snow-covered mountains. Despite the late hour, we decided to take a walk along the beach in the ice-cold evening air. Numb toes and fingers were rewarded with exquisite shells and polished rocks found along the way. The hostel in Kaikoura was one of our favorites with an extremely congenial host and a million dollar view of the mountains across the bay. It was a fine example of typical New Zealand hostels; cozy, organized, great information at our fingertips and recycling bins in place for just about everything.

Everywhere we looked were advertisements noting that Kaikoura was internationally famous for its whale watching. Steve and I agonized about the hit on our budget, but finally relented in favor of a potentially exciting and educational experience.

"Hey, do you kids want to go out on a boat and go whale watching?"

Clare: "Sure!"

Bridget: "I guess."

Michael: "No."

Such was the first of many split decisions on what to do. Steve and I lobbied hard for an hour and eventually convinced Michael and Bridget that they would be safe from the whales.

Rising at 6 a.m. for a quick breakfast we packed up and headed for the office on the beach.

"Sorry, we need to cancel all the trips today due to rough seas."

Great, 6:30 in the morning and nowhere to go. Time to learn about our adaptability as a family. It was the dead of winter so temperatures were down to –5 degrees Celsius. In our foul weather gear for the boat ride we managed to stay warm enough to go out to the point to seal watch. Snow-capped mountains glistened as we witnessed the breathtaking sunrise and the gradual awakening of the seals. The children had great fun climbing all over the rocks and walking within a few feet of a group of small seals.

Here, around the southern 45th parallel, the sun seemed to rise and set in about the same place each day and never got very high in the sky. Waves crashed into large rocks at the head of the point, while the seals enjoyed the resulting spray. Ocean water crept through the cracks and crevices in the rocks all around us. The morning was a success in spite of its auspicious beginning.

Christchurch, our next stop, was a bustling English town with Tudor style architecture. People use paddleboats to travel on the river running through the city. In spite of our children's pleas, we opted for frugality and walked. During our stay we enjoyed the Botanical Gardens and an evening of jazz at the cathedral. Before the concert, the minister of the church advertised their next event that was a prayer service with "Elvis style music." Disappointed our timing was a bit off and eager to go further south, we headed to Queenstown the next day.

Queenstown is very much a Kiwi version of Lake Tahoe, California with magnificent mountains surrounding a picturesque lake. It is certainly in danger of overdevelopment, as is Lake Tahoe. The hostel was right on the lake and had an unobstructed view of the water. Perhaps it is most famous as the birthplace of bungee jumping. A video playing in the lobby thrilled the children by showing all manner of different approaches to bungee jumping: in a refrigerator box, in a kayak, in groups of 10. One couple even got married as they, literally, took the plunge.

Steve: "May I go bungee jumping?"

Kids: "Yeah. We want to see Daddy jump off the bridge!"

Toby: "NO! I hate to have to be the grown-up here, but you don't need another MRI. You've already had your quota for the year."

It happened to be a national holiday for New Zealand that week so the hostel was completely booked. We were assigned to a room with a chap who snored so loudly it kept us awake until he left at three in the morning. I've no idea where one goes at three in the morning in Queenstown but it certainly was not to the hostel kitchen. As we headed there to make breakfast the children had an unfortunate lesson in human nature. The kitchen had been left a filthy mess from the night before. Some people had simply walked away from meal preparations and dinner dishes! We had never seen anything like it. Suddenly it was obvious why the hostel staff had posted a notice on the wall: "In protest we are not cleaning up today." Home schoolers talk about teachable moments and this was a classic. After eating our breakfast we rolled up our sleeves and dove in to clean the entire kitchen. It was a disgusting job but a good lesson for the kids. Many of the world's environmental problems likely stem from the fact that some individuals were not taught the basic rule "clean up after thyself."

23

Early the next morning we drove to the top of Coronet Peak, where we walked in the snow, dodged skiers, and feasted on a spectacular view of the lake and valley below. If there is something to be done that will get your heart racing in fear, the Kiwis in Queenstown do it. One of the latest crazes is to roll down a ski hill inside of a clear plastic ball. We decided it was not a place to hang out too long, not knowing if we could contain Steve's inclinations to risk his life doing something insane, so we pressed on to Te Anau, at the southern end of New Zealand.

Te Anau is a hamlet set alongside another mountain lake. The youth hostel there is a charming, peaceful place. This was our southernmost destination, well below the equator. Here we were about as far below the equator as our home in Oregon is above it. Our major objective was the pearl of New Zealand: the Milford Sound. Like our Yosemite, the drive to Milford was filled with sudden breathtaking scenery. They say that at one point in their lives, every Kiwi walks the Milford Track. The five-day walk meanders through some of the most stunning scenery on earth. It finishes at the end of the Milford Sound, which is where we began our escapade in one of the most famous fjords in the world.

Wanting to get an early start so we could explore along the way, I was very impressed that we were up and out the door in the dark of the early morning. Thirty kilometers later…

Steve: *"Uh-oh. I don't think we have enough gas to make it all the way to the sound and back. Should we risk it or head back?"*

Toby: *"Are you kidding? Be stranded in the middle of nowhere in the heart of winter? Let's get gas!"*

Steve: *"Right."*

Sometimes my brilliant husband lacks common sense. Te Anau is the only place to get petrol so we drove back 30 km, tanked up, and retraced the 30 km for the third time. So much for our early start. We had to scratch most of the exploring in order to get to the pier on time for our morning departure. Foggy mist and low clouds accompanied us almost the entire way, causing Steve to worry that we would not be able to see anything on the tour. Instead, as we reached the Sound, we were blessed with an outstanding day.

The Red Boat takes you on a terrific cruise through the glacier-carved Milford Sound. Clear blue skies accented majestic peaks rising hundreds of feet from the ocean floor. Waterfalls cascaded down throughout the trip. It rains so much that there is often up to 5 feet of fresh water on top of the ocean saltwater. In spite of the wind and cold, the whole family managed to brave the weather and stay outside to enjoy the tremendous view for almost the entire trip. The tour included a trip to an underwater observatory to see the unique flora and fauna of the Sound. Most impressive was the 100-year-old black coral, found nowhere else in the world.

When we reached the entrance to the Sound, we rode for about 10 minutes in the Tasman Sea through very deep swells. As the boat rose and fell brutally against the ocean, the sea mist splashed into our faces. Fresh sea air was probably the only thing that kept me from losing my lunch. The constant rocking, rise and fall of the deck made me as nauseous as early pregnancy; not something I ever wanted to experience again. More than once I thought the boat was sure to be inundated with water, submerge, and that would be the last of us. In spite of a few fearful moments, it was exhilarating. Having witnessed all of this spectacular scenery, if you ask the kids what their favorite part of the trip was, they will respond: "The bouncy boat ride once we got out of the Sound!"

PHILOSOPHY 101: *Seeing is not always believing*

There's an overwhelming urge when I travel to see things. I find it difficult to read on a train, car, or bus because I want to soak it all in and see everything I can. Yet, this morning on my jog along Te Anau Lake, I ended up at Wilson Park and was in awe of all the different bird sounds. The squeaks and squawks, chirps and warbles as I wandered through the misty forest were magical. These were sounds that are very different from my experience in Oregon. We seem to be dominated by what we see. I know my focus is almost exclusively on the visual aspects of my experience. It is easy to pass the other senses by. Mental note: be more cognizant of all my senses in my experiences this trip. What smells, sounds, and touch will I encounter that will make my trip richer?

Another night in Te Anau then a farewell to our favorite hostel thus far as we headed north. While New Zealand doesn't seem so long (about 1000 miles from the top to the bottom), it takes a while to drive it.

> You think you own whatever land you land on.
> The earth is just a dead thing you can claim.
> But I know every rock and tree and creature
> has a life, has a spirit, has a name.
> *From Colors of the Wind, by Stephen Schwartz*

Peaceful miles passed by as this song's refrain repeated in my head. I spent long stretches of time praying, singing and marveling at hundreds of miles of untouched, undeveloped forests, lakes, rivers, beaches and mountains. It was strange to consider someone owning this land; it was so wild, so free. Four million people live in New Zealand (based on the 13:1 ratio, that means about 52 million sheep). Nearly half of the four million live in the two cities of Auckland and Wellington. The rest appear to be very sparsely spread throughout the terrain. Seventy percent of New Zealand is mountainous and three fourths of the population is in the North Island, so it is no wonder that we seemed to be the only ones around now and then.

On the way back up the south island, we drove as far as we could manage, which turned out to be Haast, a small town on the coast. The coastline was rugged. Outside our car windows endless lakes, forests and mountains were blanketed in snow, ice and crystals. A full moon rose shedding a dazzling light on an already heavenly scene. Everything looked untouched and pristine. In contrast, we were greeted at the Haast Youth

Hostel with the coldest welcome we had ever encountered, in both temperature and atmosphere. The place was freezing and the manager inhospitable. Our teeth chattered as we prepared a late dinner.

The next day's destination was the Franz Josef Glacier. The kids had a memorable hike giving us glimmers of hope that they will become the nature lovers I pray they will be. It is funny how the same scenario seemed to play out almost every time Steve and I suggested a trek . . .

Steve introduced a topic: "Tomorrow let's go hike up to the Franz Josef Glacier!"

Kids' initial response: "No way. We're not going! We hate walking!!"

We tried to win them over: "It is pretty impressive. The glacier is miles and miles of ice flowing down a valley. It looks blue and is hundreds of feet thick in some places. The huge sheet of ice is actually moving down the valley up to three feet in a day. Anyway, every time we go somewhere, you end up loving it."

Michael: "It will be boring!"

Bridget: "My knee hurts!"

Clare provided a silent scowl.

Steve opted for the authoritarian tact: "Well, we are going, and I know you'll enjoy it."

The kids moaned and probably wondered what they did to deserve us as parents.

We began the walk with a bit of whining here and there. This gradually receded in the first 10 minutes, at which point we started playing word games like "Pico, Fermi, Bagel" and Twenty Questions. About halfway through the hike, the games died out, and they started noticing the surroundings. By the time we got to our intended destination they were enthralled and loved every minute. We were hand in hand telling silly stories as we headed back. Happens every time. Why can't they simply skip the whining part?

Following our hike to the glacier we drove up the coast to Greymouth. This youth hostel was an old Marist Brothers provincial and school. It was just charming with artistic woodwork and an inlaid glass door entrance. There was an old piano and guitar in the common room. Bridget enjoyed the piano while I sang and played the guitar. After a fun evening of music we traipsed up to bed.

However, at about 4 a.m. ...

Boom, boom, boom.

"What the heck was that?"

"I don't know."

Boom, boom, boom.

"Someone's at the door. Should we go down (three flights of stairs) and answer it?"

"I think the manager of the place is..."

Boom, boom, boom, boom, SMASH!! *"Argrgoual glorious England is AOWinobi!"*

A British man, who had been out at a pub celebrating a soccer victory, couldn't work the security code to enter the front door. After pounding for a while and breaking a glass pane in the door he managed to remember it. The furious manager verbally berated the penitent man in the morning. The one small pane he will be replacing was $60. Just one of the many thrills you get when you travel on a tight budget.

I suppose another is never knowing when a dryer is going to function as promised. Early on the morning of our departure I did the laundry then put it through the dryer for three full cycles. It wasn't working. Even after packing up and checking out of our room the clothes still weren't dry. Long past checkout, the hostel manager graciously let us hang out in the common room to stay warm, but we really needed to move on. Taking the wet clothes to the car, I dried them a few at a time over the defroster and floor heater. It was quite a sight as we drove down the road, but worked more efficiently than the hostel dryer at $2.00 per load!

The next day turned out to be Sunday, July 8 th, Michael's 7th birthday. When we were still in Oregon, he was very disappointed to learn that we would be in New Zealand on his birthday. He knew he wouldn't be with his friends. We had a celebration before we left, about a month before his birthday, and invited a couple of friends. However, it is just not the same as your official day.

We celebrated by going to church at Holy Trinity Anglican in Picton (although Michael didn't think that was much of a celebration). It is a tiny church and the service that day was dedicated to sailors. People were thrilled to have us and gave us a warm welcome. The reading from St. Paul that morning was very appropriate: "It is better to give than to receive." We had quite unintentionally been giving all over this country as we packed up each morning to leave. We hoped that travelers were enjoying the food we accidentally left behind (often brand new and untouched.) It was tough to keep track of five of us, five sleeping bags, five backpacks and a few bags of food. We tried though. If what goes around comes around then we were due for an excellent meal or two somewhere in the world. If not, I hope we helped to feed some poor souls during their travels. At least we never left a child!

Later in the morning, we managed to fit in a miniature golf game and a kid ride at the park next to the bay. This appeased Michael a bit though the last couple of holes were rushed to catch our ferry to the North Island. We safely crossed the Cook Strait once again, with Steve still looking for the navigating dolphin.

During the ferry ride, we took advantage of one of the tools brought along for our world schooling effort: an encyclopedia on CD-ROM. It often helped us fill hours like these. An interesting tidbit from Grolier's: The two major islands of New Zealand can actually be considered parts of two different continents. The North Island is on the same continental plate as India and Australia, while the South Island is on the Pacific plate. The two plates slide past each other now and then, giving New Zealand a bit of a shake. Fortunately, we did not witness this natural phenomenon, but it was an exciting possibility.

PHILOSOPHY 101: *Simplicity and appreciation*

What do we want to teach our kids this trip? Certainly I hope to develop within them a desire for simplicity, a desire that originates from an understanding of the simple lives of others in the world. If nothing else, that would be a great achievement. Beyond that, I want them to gain a sense of themselves within the world on two levels. First, of their privileged status living in a first world country. But second, that they have a sense of their culture in relationship to other cultures in the world. They have much to offer as well as much to learn. That is not too much to ask, is it?

They enter this adventure with much nervousness about experiencing different cultures and interacting with people who don't speak their language. What a remarkable accomplishment it would be to transform that uneasiness to wonder, curiosity, appreciation and valuing cultures unique from their own. I am already at the point at which I appreciate and value other cultures, yet I realize that it is at such a superficial level. Only experience brings depth and intensity of understanding about the richness of a people's way.

Several stops were built in to our trip around the world where we planned to meet with friends. Wellington was our first opportunity to do just that. Donald and Lynn have three daughters, a bit younger than our kids. We lived near each other in California quite a few years ago. Donald got a fellowship for six months to learn the Maori justice system and work on victim's rights issues, such as involvement in the penalty phase of a trial. Lynn is Bridget's godmother. They were the first of many oases in the midst of our travels that helped us feel not so far from home.

Coming to the end of six months in New Zealand, Donald and Lynn had learned a tremendous amount about the people and country. Listening to them gave us much more insight into the Maori--European New Zealand conflict because of Donald's work. Apparently the government is struggling with the 1940 treaty that was done to/with the Maoris. Naturally, there are two different versions to the historical document and it has been very complicated trying to reconcile the whole situation in the best interests of all concerned. Just giving the Maoris billions of dollars isn't helping them. They need assistance with education, financial management and their traditional ways of dealing with anger. Historically, the tribes used to attack and eat other tribes not for land but because someone may have insulted someone's relative. It was a bit reminiscent of the modern LA gang rationale- "You dissed my bro."

Our final adventure in New Zealand was in Waitomo, about halfway up the North Island. There we stumbled upon Woodlyn Park and Billy Black's Pioneer Show. It was an educational and humorous one-man show highlighting "Kiwi ingenuity" through the century. Billy Black gave the audience a clear insight into the early bushmen who cleared the land for farming and grazing over 100 years ago. He demonstrated how, with only human power, they cut logs and sheared sheep with manual shears. His exuberant personality carried the show as he conveyed pride in the Kiwi inventions that were used to manage nature. I thought it was a very important balance to the history of the indigenous Maoris with the New Zealand pioneers. We gained a much broader perspective and grew to appreciate the gifts and talents of both cultures.

Our Waitomo experience was topped off with a visit to the Glow Worm Caves. The 3 million year old caves were indescribable, surreal, awesome, mysterious. The glow worms create thousands of blue pinpoints of light that dot the ceiling as your boat gently coasts on the river that runs through the cave. It is as if you are seeing all the stars in the sky on a cloudless night inside the cave.

The glow worms are actually fly larvae or maggots but, as our guide said, "glow maggots" just doesn't have the same appeal. From egg stage to larvae they have a mouth at one end and the glowing tail at the other. The light attracts bugs and mosquitoes. The larva puts out a fishing line or silk

31

thread to catch its food then reel it in. During the next phase it forms a cocoon from which the adult fly will emerge. The adult has no mouth and will starve to death in three days, just enough time to mate so the female can lay 150 eggs a day. They exist in only two places on this planet: New Zealand and Australia.

The caves are uniformly warm (60 degrees F) year round. Dripping water formed limestone stalactites (downward drips) and stalagmites (upward stacks) as well as columns. A deep river, running through the cave, carved out smooth hollows leaving the grand cathedral area with a 45-foot ceiling. The acoustics are astounding and when our guide asked if anyone wished to try singing in there I couldn't resist. What a resonant sound! It was magical. As we walked out, Bridget said, "Is that it?" Hard to impress a 10 year old, I guess.

As evening approached, we zipped up to the Auckland Youth Hostel once again for our last night's stay in New Zealand. Given the ominous introduction to Kiwi driving at the start of our trip, we considered reaching the hostel in one piece a blessing. Early the next afternoon we returned the rental car in plenty of time to make our flight.

One of our main strategies for world travel was to never check our bags so we wouldn't lose anything on planes. With tickets in hand we walked straight to the gate…

• • • • •

Security check.

"I'm sorry sir, but you need to pay the New Zealand departure tax before going through."

"Okay, where do we go to do that?"

"Downstairs and to the left."

"Toby, why don't you stay here with the kids and gear and I'll run down and pay the tax."

Steve runs down. Thirty minutes later…

"The tax people say we need to have our boarding passes. The airline says all of us need to be at the counter when we check in. She relented on the kids, but you need to go and show your face."

32

I run down, show my face, and run back up to get Steve.

"She says that now you need to go back down and do something about visas."

"Huh? Okay, I'll go see what the problem is."

"I'm sorry sir, but you need to have a visa to enter Australia."

"Are you kidding? I thought you only had to get visas for countries like China or something. Do I need to go to the embassy or what?"

"No, sir. You can just go over to our customer service desk and pay the $40 per person and they will help you out. Here are your boarding passes. You can go pay your departure tax first over there."

I suppose that no amount of planning can truly prepare you for a trip of this magnitude. Despite all Steve's countless hours of research, phone calls and inquiries the request for visas to enter Australia caught us by surprise. First, $22 per person to the tax people, then he wandered over to the New Zealand Air Service desk.

"Hi, we need visas to Australia and our plane leaves in 15 minutes."

The New Zealand Air employee enlists the help of four colleagues who make the thirty-minute process take only five.

"We are going to have to run for your plane." Literally.

Steve meets up with the rest of us and the gracious New Zealand Air woman personally runs us to the already-boarded plane. It is the first of many planes (trains, buses) we will run for in the coming months.

• • • • •

It was one thing for Steve and me to run for planes and deal with unexpected craziness. However, as much as I wanted our children to really appreciate this adventure they are just kids. We had pulled them away from all they knew to be familiar and secure. They now faced many months of daily uncertainties, often in languages they could not understand. Perhaps that is what was really on their minds the first weeks.

I often wondered if this journey was something we were doing *for* them or *to* them. They had no idea how significant some of these sights and places were: the tallest, the oldest, the deepest, one of the natural wonders of the world, etc. Maybe they will some day. All things considered, they were extraordinary little travelers and we really couldn't complain.

AUSTRALIA   11 July

When people vacation in Australia, they typically head to the east coast. This is understandable, because of the Great Barrier Reef, rainforests, and great cities like Sydney and Melbourne. Budget constraints and Steve's work dictated that we go to Western Australia instead. Due to the miracle of the Internet, one of his primary sabbatical tasks was to meet with Dr. Thelma Perso who works in the Western Australia Department of Education. Over a year ago Steve was trying to find information through different web sites about students' algebraic misconceptions when he found out that Thelma was interested in many of the same ideas. He contacted her, and they have been communicating ever since via email. This was their moment to meet and develop their relationship and common projects.

Australia is a big country and simultaneously the smallest continent in the world. The flight from Auckland to Perth took about seven hours. The four-hour time change confused our body clocks, but our weary eyes were greeted at the airport by the gentle smiles of Thelma and her friend Ross. They helped with our packs and bags, gave us food, and brought us to the YMCA where we stayed for the next four nights. It was not the best lodging in town, as our feet stuck to the floor and carpets because of the caked in dirt, but it served as home for the week. With abundant knowledge and love of their country Ross and Thelma quickly became our tour guides while their gracious, loving hearts made them our friends. After a drive around Perth to see the city lights shining on the Swan River we crashed into bed.

Due to the gold rush of the 1890's over a million people now live in Perth. James Cook managed to get over to Australia and claim her for Britain in 1770, the year after he was in New Zealand. Australians in general are oddly proud of their history as a penal colony of Great Britain beginning in 1788. It seems that all the long-time Australians have an ex-convict in their family history, which perhaps accounts in part for their thirst for adventure and carefree attitude about life. "No worries, mate!"

On the other hand, they don't have a particularly good historical relationship with the aborigines who have been here for 75,000 years. Recently, however, as highlighted by the Sydney Summer Olympics, there has been a greater emphasis on valuing the aboriginal culture. The aborigines are nomadic, with about 300,000 people in 500 tribes distributed throughout Australia.

The next day, Thelma and Ross were back early in the morning for a fun-filled day with Ross' nieces. We played in the Indian Ocean; hiked in state parks; explored a well-manicured cemetery with wild kangaroos; and walked through a wildlife park where we petted kangaroos, watched a koala baby, held a wombat, and saw many more of the fascinating animals of Australia. Everyday we found a new and interesting corner of Perth. Downtown Perth is easily walked, with a nice park just on the outskirts for morning jogs along the estuary. The Perth Natural History Museum includes interesting information about the aborigines. The highlight for us was the skeleton of an 80-foot long blue whale.

Ross generously lent us his car to visit the south coast of Western Australia for a few days. It was touching how he was willing to ride his bike to work every day so we could go enjoy Australia. He was a powerful role model for our family about kindness to strangers.

Towards the southern tip of the continent we purchased a tour pass to visit three natural caves that provided guided and unguided walks. Each cave had its own unique characteristics. Mammoth Cave was a gigantic cavern with stalactites and stalagmites all around. Lake Cave had the same exquisite crystal formations with the addition of a small lake inside which created a shimmering reflection of the artistry on the ceiling. Huge pillars of crystal hung over the water. Jewell Cave sparkled with gems of nature everywhere you looked.

One morning, walking along the coast of Augusta, we could just barely make out the tops of a whale and its albino calf floating close to shore. This inspired us to try again to go on a whale watching boat trip. Now, Steve has always been skeptical of these excursions. He **expected** it to play out something like this:

"Oh, look a whale is over there, I can barely see it blowing water into the air through its spout!"

"No, that was just a wave breaking."

"It looked kind of different than just a wave, it sprayed upward like it was shot up."

"Naw. When the wave breaks, the wind blows the water up in the air."

"I could have sworn it was more like a fountain squirting out from a whale." *That argument would continue for a half hour or so...*

An hour and a half of roaming the seas later . . .

"On your left, a whale tail!" *"Are you sure?"* *Run to the other side of the boat.* *"Yeah, you just missed it!"*

In other words, after four hours of rolling around in a boat, trying to stay away from people who were puking over the side railing, we would have seen about four or five things that somewhat resembled whale activity. He fully expected that we would be frustrated by the usual cry of "Oh, you just missed it!" Does National Geographic send armies of researchers to sit on the ocean for days in order to get photos of whales breaching?

All of Steven's presuppositions were dashed. This turned out to be one of the most spectacular experiences of our journey. The captain gently coasted the boat out into the middle of the bay for an unbelievable display of nature. He informed us that there were about 40 humpback and southern right whales in the bay at the time. Four whales breached simultaneously within a few hundred meters of the boat. They usually make three jumps in a row before settling down. It was unreal to see that much mammal leaping into the air and come crashing down repeatedly. We were speechless and quickly ran out of film. Multiple dolphins and whales swam next to and right underneath our boat throughout the morning. You got the distinct feeling sometimes that they were the tourists and we were the sights. Occasionally, whales would peek their heads up at us and whack their flippers against the water, as if they were waving. It was a stupendous three-ringed circus. We didn't know where to look because there was so much happening at once.

By July 18th we were back in Mandurah, Ross' home. We stopped to wash his car at the local self-wash to repay a bit of his kindness, but the car was dirtier afterwards. (What was in that wash water?) Back at his flat we just managed to wash it again before he came riding up the drive. Two days later we shared a farewell picnic with Ross and Thelma, walked along Mandurah's serene waterfront and prepared for departure. I marveled at how close we had grown to these two strangers whom we now call friends. Was it just typical Aussie hospitality or were they exceptional people who felt such joy in giving? Over the months of traveling around the world we were to learn that the kindness shared by Thelma and Ross was a glimpse of experiences to come. And something else: when asked, "what was your favorite country?" we find it impossible to separate the people we spent time with from the place itself. Western Australia will remain a favorite, not just for her natural wonders, but mostly due to Thelma and Ross.

"The real voyage of discovery
consists not in seeing new landscapes,
but in having new eyes."
Marcel Proust, French Author

STINKY FRUIT AND
ELUSIVE TURTLES

SINGAPORE   20 July

S tepping out of the air conditioned airplane and airport,
sweat instantly started seeping through our pores. It is
quite an understatement to say that Singapore was hot
and humid. Due to its proximity to the equator (about 1 km
south) it was 32 degrees Celsius (over 90 Fahrenheit) and 100
percent humidity. Never having lived in a place with high
humidity, I felt conscious of my breathing and wondered if I
would drown. With an average 100 inches of rain a year even
Oregon seems dry. Rain, however, did provide a brief and
welcome respite from the heat each afternoon.

Tiny Singapore is about the size of Lake Tahoe, in
California--a bit over 600 square kilometers--and four million
people vie for that space. Every area that is not occupied by a
building looks tropical, lush and green. Huge tenement
buildings and malls have taken the place of most of the
tropical rainforest. Picture New York and Hawaii combined.

Singapore has only been independent from Malaysia since
1965. Although three-fourths of the people are Chinese, they
form an interesting cultural blend with the rest, who are
mostly Malay and Indian. Everyone we met seemed driven to
turn his small corner of Asia into paradise. The government's
take on that goal is "create as many rules as possible." The
Lonely Planet guide describes Singapore as a "fine

country"—they fine you for anything from spitting on the sidewalks to not flushing the toilet. Forget about chewing gum, it's not even sold. Of course, there are the infamous penalties for stealing or doing drugs, which include caning or execution. In spite of the clear environment of regulations, we wondered how Singapore gained a reputation for being such a clean country. Truth be told, having walked miles of it, Singapore is just as clean/dirty as most places we traveled. Overall, however, Singapore was an intriguing place with a frenetic pace.

Our home for the week was the local YMCA, where we were met by two charming school principals. Lawrence and Bin Eng were Steve's connections for the conference at which he was keynote speaker. He would be talking about the culture of United States' mathematics education. In a switch from the U.S. perspective, schools in Singapore pack children in classrooms during the early years and have smaller class sizes for older students. Primary schools average 2000 pupils, 40 per classroom.

That night Lawrence and Bin Eng took us out to a typical Singaporean dinner. The East Coast Seafood Centre proved to be quite an outdoor dining experience where our children had their first close personal encounter with their meal. We visited long rows of two-story tanks that held the live, swimming, unsuspecting menu items. Watching a gentleman scoop up a net full of prawns, one in particular kept trying to swim away. It didn't succeed. Sure enough, a little while later, it landed on our table, eyes still bulging. The children and I just couldn't bring ourselves to eat the epicurean delights that stared up at us. Fortunately, we loved the green vegetables, different tofus, and noodles.

Steve bravely served as cultural ambassador politely sampling each item as the food kept coming... and coming. . .

Our host, Bin Eng: "Oh, you must try these frog legs."
Bridget: "Daddy, did she just say that these are frogs?"

Steve: "Yes. You are welcome to try some. They probably taste like chicken."

Bridget: "Gross! I'm not eating frogs!!"

Steve: (uneasily) "Sure, Bin Eng, I'll try the frogs."

Our host: "Oh, and these drunk prawns are delicious."

Bridget: "Daddy, what are drunk prawns?"

Steve: "See that bowl that looks like soup? It's some kind of alcohol. See the prawns that look like they are swimming around in there with their eyes looking up at you? Don't worry, Bridget, you don't have to eat it....Thanks Bin Eng," he says nervously. "I'll try some."

Bridget: "That's disgusting!"

So much for developing our children's cultural appreciation. It was nearly 10:00 p.m., but the food kept coming, and Michael was falling asleep in his chair. Bin Eng caught sight of Michael as his face was dropping down into the bowl of prawns and wisely suggested a walk on the beach. The children and I jumped at the chance. Walking past the chickens and roosters milling about the area, I pondered if they, too, were fair game for the dining tables strewn about the outdoor restaurants surrounding us. Sea mist and a light breeze woke Michael up as we watched the waves lap against the shore.

Steven spoke at the conference the next day leaving us to our own devices. That meant swimming to escape the heat and humidity. By late afternoon he returned and our hosts again surprised us, this time with a basket of local tropical fruits. After the previous night's culinary adventure, we were a bit nervous. Long, green, rubbery hair-like things were coming out of one fruit, which certainly piqued the children's interest (rambutans). One looked like a small purple apple with wooden leaves on top, but the apple had a hard shell that felt like plastic and was squishy (mangosteins). Another small, round one looked like it was wrapped in a snail shell (lychees). The last was the size of a coconut but had squarish bumps like a grenade (durian).

Not recognizing any of the fruit, we needed lessons in how to eat them, so Bin Eng gently guided us to the intriguing tastes inside. Mangostein is our new favorite fruit on earth. A brilliant white, segmented fruit about the size of a small orange sits inside of an inch thick purple velvety material. It tastes creamy and citrus at the same time. Most noteworthy was the durian. Smelling like Rotorua, it is no wonder that signs everywhere forbid bringing this olfactory disaster into buildings. We had to store ours outside the window ledge of our room to keep our eyes from watering and comply with the "no durian" rule. Despite the smell of sewers, it is a very rich custard-like fruit that is the love of many Singaporeans. Oddly enough, they don't even notice the smell. Do people acquire smell as they acquire taste?

In a constant display of hospitality, we were guests at a community picnic the following day. It was a celebration of a primary school's 22nd birthday and an excellent dose of culture as students performed on Chinese instruments, the choir sang, and we witnessed Chinese, Malay, and Indian dancing. The school's motto: "Service before Self." Their objective: every child will play at least one musical instrument. The master of ceremonies kept chanting, "Strong mind, strong body, strong Singapore."

Keeping with the strong body theme we spent an entire day walking around the city (country? I guess they are one and the same) in the extreme heat and humidity. Singapore has been described as a giant shopping mall. Not being shoppers, however, we couldn't appreciate the vast, high tech, big screens, lights, blaring music, and huge stores boasting of designer everything. Instead we sought out Little India, Chinatown, and visited a Hindu temple, which is a national monument. The children laughed when we had to buy a ticket for our camera to get in.

<u>Interesting facts about Singapore</u>:

1) Due to the aging work force and the desire to create more Singaporeans, the government is encouraging young people to marry and have children. It actually gives them a monetary "baby bonus."

2) To purchase a car, one must obtain a Certificate of Entitlement (COE) for $10,000 prior to getting on a waiting list to buy a car.

3) The price of a small car is $50,000 and up. After ten years one must purchase a new COE and scrap the car for metal receiving $10,000 back. (They send all their old cars to Indonesia, an apparent dumping ground for Singapore.) Waiting longer than ten years results in you only getting $1,000 for the car so most people are inspired to keep buying the new cars. The government regulates car sales per month.

4) Schools are torn down and rebuilt every twenty years.

5) Primary school: ages 6-12; Secondary school: ages 13-16; Junior college: 17-18; then on to university. A university education is free. For higher professional degrees such as law and medicine the student pays $6-8,000. Boys after 16 must serve two and a half years in the Singapore Army or pay $75,000 to delay service in order to study abroad. When they return they must still serve in the army or forfeit the $75,000.

6) Housing: There is a hierarchy of public, government subsidized apartments. You can get one of the free ones in a public housing community or pay for the privilege of a nicer area. Most cost around $300,000. Nicer condominiums go for one million. It is arranged so that people living in the public housing community have huge community schools and walk to work in big factories across the freeway from the public housing. Thus, you can really do without a car (and who could afford one?). People may automatically deduct 20% of their income monthly, which the government then matches, to pay for housing. The government pays the interest on the loan. They want everyone to own a home. Technically, there are no homeless and no drug addicts in Singapore. If you ask an official, they would likely say everyone has their needs met

and the government has stopped the flow of drugs into the country. If you ask a regular person on the street they would likely say they are both here, you just have to look in the right places.

It is no surprise that cars and housing are the most expensive commodities in the country. The nation is broken down into estates, zones or constituencies. Different terms, same meaning. Almost all food is imported because they have essentially no land to farm. Accordingly, it was shocking to learn that there is no recycling. Garbage is sent out to Indonesia. Every inch of the country appears to be occupied. People may only build upward or remodel. It was drastically different from the wide-open spaces (and cooler temperatures) of New Zealand and Australia. In fact, it was the hot temperature that caused our first major loss on the trip. As we left for the airport at 5:30 in the morning no one gave any thought to our Polartec jackets tied around our waists. Michael accidentally left his in the shuttle. The sad thing is that no one in Singapore will have any use for it!

*"Travel is fatal to prejudice, bigotry, and
narrow-mindedness"
Mark Twain, Author*

MALAYSIA   24 July

Malaysia was our first experience with a $2^{nd}/3^{rd}$-world
country and presented thought-provoking and comical
challenges. Immediately upon arrival, we began to drive our
rental car over miles of toll road (it often felt like New Jersey)
from Kuala Lumpur, in the west, to the east coast. As we saw
the first sights of Malaysia, Steve reviewed the Muslim
customs, dos and don'ts from our <u>Lonely Planet</u> guide.
Malaysia is predominantly Muslim.

"In Malaysia it is disrespectful to point and take or receive
something with your left hand." He went on to read a
paragraph of things that might be considered impolite or rude
to Muslims.

The children freaked out. They saw so many women
completely covered except for their eyes and men with
covered heads. This was our first experience in the world that
was noticeably different from what we were used to at home.

Michael cried, "It's too hard! I want to go back to
Singapore!" (and he couldn't wait to leave Singapore, that's
how desperate he felt.)

"What if I point at something? Will they hurt me?"

"What if I forget?" We had to stop our car at a rest stop to
calm their fears.

"No, they won't hurt you. Muslims are just like people
anywhere else. They might have different ways of doing
things, and if we forget, it might hurt their feelings, or they
might think we are a little odd, but nothing bad will happen.
We'll just do our best to remember and respect their customs."

That's at least what we said. What was going on in our
minds was slightly different. Steve and I had plenty of our
own fears. The United States' media can paint a fearsome

picture of Muslims, perpetuating stereotypes of their militant nature and that they are easily offended. We hoped to have that perspective transformed as we traveled. Nervous, we continued on.

It goes without saying that Malays cringed a few times when we forgot cultural protocol. At our first gas stop I made my initial blunder. The young girl attendant (about 13) insisted on filling the tank with super. "Regular," I said. "No, super," **she pointed**. I got out the car manual and started searching, knowing it was supposed to have 92 octane and the "Car Talk" guys say not to give it super if it uses regular unleaded. What I didn't know was that Malaysia is still pumping leaded gas and that "super" **was** the unleaded. I humbly acquiesced then gave and received the credit card and receipt with my right hand. When she asked me to sign I hesitated. She stared then stepped back as I signed with my left hand. What could I do? Are there no southpaws in Malaysia? On the other hand, (no pun intended) it was nice that I made the first breach in respecting their customs and there were no international incidents. I think this eased the kids' concerns a bit. Little did it matter that, as we were driving away, I realized she was Hindu and not Muslim.

The left-hand taboo stems from toileting practices. The toilet is a cubicle with an enamel hole in the ground and a tile on either side for your feet. There is usually a spigot with a short hose and/or a hand bucket to wash afterwards. No toilet paper. You draw your own conclusions and you will see why I got stares eating left-handed. We learned to BYOTP (bring your own toilet paper) at all times.

Malaysia was an interesting country, with a mixture of royal power and government. There are thirteen states with political leaders, but nine sultans rule over nine regions. The nine traditional rulers elect a king every five years from among their ranks. The Prime Minister, however, is the one who really runs the country. He or she must be Malay, have won a seat in the legislature, and then be selected by the legislature's majority party.

Lonely Planet characterized the relationship between the two governing bodies with a story from a Malaysian newspaper. One of the sultans was very charismatic and fond of collecting cars. The law says that the sultan may only have seven cars then must pay significant taxes to the government. This sultan had twenty cars and hadn't paid a dime. One day, he was getting his twenty-first car, and the government decided that twenty-one were definitely more than seven. The sultan needed to pay the tax.

"I don't have the money. May I just get in and feel the car?"

"Okay." Vroom. Off he sped in his new car.

The Portuguese, Dutch, Japanese, and English have all taken turns conquering and ruling Malaysia. Thus, Malaysia is a relatively young country--not having gained her independence until 1957. Seventy percent of the people are Malay or indigenous and thirty percent are Chinese. Just about the opposite of Singapore. It is a curious irony that most of the people live in very poor circumstances while Kuala Lumpur is making a valiant effort to be a modern metropolis. Standing tall on the edge of the city are the Twin Towers, the tallest buildings in the world, looking out over a mixture of new malls and poor housing.

Having just left Singapore we needed a break from traffic, noise and confusion. The weather also came into play: we were still not used to heat and humidity. As in Singapore, the air was so thick it felt as if you were wearing it. Choosing to avoid Kuala Lumpur for the time being we instead risked our lives with the insane drivers on the two-lane highway up the east coast. We thought New Zealand drivers were bad—they are nothing compared to Malay who disregard all passing laws and seem to almost make a game of crossing double lines, passing on curves, blind hills, and coming straight at you only to get back in their lane at the last possible second or just after that second. Don't drive in Malaysia if you can avoid it.

When we weren't trying to avoid a head-on collision we marveled at the landscape, foliage and coastline. Malaysia is a country of extreme contrasts:

1) lush tropical jungle forests vs. miles of stripped, clear-cut mountains

2) gorgeous resort hotels vs. tumble down shacks made of anything people can scrounge together

3) sultan's mansions vs. wide-scale poverty

4) clean efficient city trains vs. rickety three-wheeled bicycles and thousands of smog-producing motor scooters

5) enticing expanses of beaches and clear, warm ocean water strewn with garbage

6) palm trees laden with coconuts swaying in the breeze as the stench of sewers wafts through the air

7) artistically ornate mosques, shrines, and temples badly in need of repair

8) a gently flowing river in KL turns into a rushing frenzy after a bit of rain, carrying raw sewage and immense amounts of garbage

We learned much about the Muslim culture in a short amount of time. As with most religions, there are different degrees of adherence. Many women dressed completely in black with only their eyes showing. Most Muslim women, however, dressed with their heads covered in colorful scarves and long silk dresses. The children found this style very attractive. Perhaps it also helps them to stay cool in the heat and humidity. Thankfully, a bit of our uneasiness was confronted early on when Steve went in to the tourist information office with the kids. Notes from his journal:

• • • • •

We walk inside the tourism office. The usual posters decorate the walls and brochures are assembled in the racks. I fully expect to see men in the tourism office, due to my stereotypes of Muslim women. Based on the little I know about them from the media, I assume that the women basically hide from interaction with outsiders. Needless to say, we are met by a woman extensively covered in colorful, traditional, Muslim attire.

"Can I help you?"

(Okay, don't point. Don't accept anything with your left hand. Is it okay to look in her eyes?) "Uh, sure. We are hoping to go see the turtles."

"Oh, how wonderful. This is the perfect time of year. Let me show you...."

Over the course of the next hour we are fascinated by all the unique things we could see in Malaysia.

"If you have time, you've got to see the cows pulling in the fish nets at the end of the day just a few miles from here."

She laughs and smiles with us and the time flies by. This gracious woman is so pleased that we are in her country. What a fantastic blow to our misconceptions! All of us begin to see that there are good people everywhere, even if they look a bit different and have different customs.

• • • • •

Driving to the east coast, we noticed row upon row of "hawker" shacks where the local people sold anything to survive: food, watches, batik (fabrics decorated by using wax and dyes to color them). Cows, goats, chickens and cats roamed freely. Our first two nights were in a beach hut in Cherating. The tourist lady told us that most people visit the west, but we were in search of the leatherback turtles that lay their eggs at night on beaches in the east. (They have been abused to near extinction. Only 40 are left). The night we arrived, we were exhausted from driving so we passed on the turtle trek, which usually commences around midnight. Of course, that was the only night the turtles showed up for the week that we were on the east coast.

We stayed in a small, one-room structure built on stilts (as are most structures). There were two beds and a small bathroom containing a toilet, sink and showerhead with an all-purpose drain in the floor. To shower you just stood under the spigot next to the toilet while the whole place got wet—no curtain, no door, no stall. Kept the floor very clean! We even had a pot to boil water, which was a daily ritual, as you cannot drink the water in Malaysia. The ocean was 20 yards from our door.

Everyone rode motor scooters. It was not uncommon to see an entire family crammed on a scooter, baby hands and feet sticking out between parents. Clare asked, "Why do they live in shacks if they can afford a motor scooter or motor cycle?" We tried to explain choices people make to survive: the motor scooter is a link to income. Many will set up and sell goods right off their scooters. People are living on the streets. Our children were unable to grasp the widespread level of poverty. Clare said at dinner, "Why don't they just come to the U.S. and get help?" It was great that she continually asked questions about what she saw on this trip and tried to make sense of it all. Experiences in this country were an important part of their education and ours.

Next stop, Rantau Abang. The pleasant manager of the "resort" (that's what it said on the sign) quickly prepared one of the best rooms in the place, which was a hut that was disintegrating at the seams. Instead of just ants we were also living with cockroaches, lizards and two wild kittens in the rafters who played all night. The bathroom was a hole in the floor with two tiles to step on when you squat and a hand bucket and spigot for flushing. We paid RM 50 (fifty Malaysian Ringets—about U.S. $13) for this hut with two double beds sans bedding. The bathroom was truly falling apart and the ants had taken over every inch of it. When I took a shower I was thrilled because the ants changed their route from right under my feet to two columns running up the wall opposite me. "Thanks!" I told them aloud.

It was then that I also tried out a new tactic for washing clothes and trying to stay cool. I just wore my clothes in the shower, soaped up, rinsed off and stepped back out into the heat. My clothes were clean, no need for a bandana to dry off and I felt refreshed until my clothes dried and I started sweating again. With the exchange rate we could have afforded something nicer, more "westernized" as they say, but we thought it was important for the children to "rough it," to see how the locals lived. Actually, we came to realize during our stay in Malaysia, that our hut was much better than the average dwelling, but in our minds, it was a step below backpacking. At least we would never pitch our tents over an anthill!

Our backpacking trip the previous summer turned out to be excellent training for our world adventure. The children already knew how to squat to potty and could brush their teeth with just a Sierra cup full of water. Despite all the dubious character, the hut at Rantau Abang had a million-dollar location with the beach at our door, towering palm trees, and a view of the South China Sea. A brilliant tropical storm that night brought terrific lightening and a power outage. The rain felt so good we just stood out in it with our faces to the sky.

Swimming, walking, and playing in the sand were the high points of the inn. The water was warm and almost clear, the beach not nearly as filthy as it had been further south at Cherating. The inn was used as a private school for about 70 middle ability, local kids to prepare for exams in math, science, and English. They all seemed to be about Clare's age. We met Maas, the inn owner's wife and English teacher who was 34 years old, had three children, and had been married for 21 years. (Yes, she was married at 13!) She was shocked that at 42 I had only three children. She wore a white head covering with a bright, green, yellow, and red flowered dress down to her feet. Her English was excellent and she cheerfully chatted with us about her school. In between classes it was nice to see the Muslim girls in the school, all with covered heads, playing dodge ball on the beach, while the boys played soccer. They were no different from our children, in spite of variation in outward appearance.

That evening, having read about the huge night market in Dungun, about 10 miles away, we thought it would be an important cultural experience. Upon arriving, it was immediately obvious that we were the only foreigners present. It was interesting to be in the minority and stared at all the time. One man tried to overcharge us and give us the tourist price for some crackers. The woman next to him quickly told us a lower price. There was an unspoken tension between being equal to all customers and capitalizing on the tourists.

We were told Americans don't typically come to Malaysia, at least not the east coast. Too poor? Too primitive? We didn't speak Malay and very few people we encountered spoke anything but a few words in English. However, it was very heartening to us, at an early point in our trip, that we could still manage to get there, buy food, and take in the market atmosphere. Like Singapore's street market and many others in later countries, this one was an exercise in claustrophobia management. It was stall-to-stall people, bodies crammed against each other in the evening heat with ear-splitting music competing to destroy our eardrums. The colors, sights and energy of the people were notable nevertheless.

That evening, back at the hut, it was a restless night of sleep, owing to the heat and Clare's bug bites. It was too hot for our 0 degree rated sleeping bags, but there were no linens on the bed so the mosquitoes, flies and moths were dive-bombing us all night. Sweat profusely or be eaten alive? Clare and Bridget shared one bed, with Michael, Steven, and me in the other.

1:15 a.m.

Clare: "AGH! The bugs are eating me!" She was sitting wide-eyed and panic stricken in the bed, tears streaming down her face.

Steve: "It's okay Clare. If you want, we can go sleep in the car."

They went outside to try to find protection in our rental car. Clare slept in the back on a sleeping bag while Steve scrunched in the front seat.

2:15 a.m.

Clare: "Daddy, can we go back inside now?" Sweat was running down her face. The heat in the car was worse than the bugs.

There were definitely times on this trip when we wondered if we would be tried for parental abuse upon our return. Would our children be in therapy the rest of their lives? "Yes, doctor. I am a shattered individual today because of that trip around the world that my parents forced me to go on when I was young." Are these great lessons learned about the rest of the world or simply torture and misery?

We managed to survive the night and woke up the next morning eager to explore new territory. Before we left Rantau Abang, Maas made tea and served it with a fried, fishy, crispy thing for us (too salty but I needed to join Steve in being polite). Visiting with Maas, she shared about her school and her life then we drove all the way to Besut, a small fishing town in the northeast corner of Malaysia. Stopping in a travel office at the pier we made arrangements for a boat trip and lodging at an island off the coast.

"Where can we park our car while we are on the island?"
"We have a high security parking lot."

Steve drove the car over to a lot in the sand with a chain link fence around it and a padlocked entrance. A handful of other cars were there. He paid the RM 20. Needless to say everything we left in the car was stolen when we got back.

An hour boat ride landed us at Palau Perhentian Kecil, the smaller of two tropical islands next to each other. Apparently the mainland office where we had secured a reservation had not communicated effectively with the island office. Instead of a room with two double beds, AC and a bathroom for RM 95 we had a single room with one double bed and a fan. Bridget and I slept on a mat on the floor. Steven, Michael and Clare shared the bed. Thank goodness we brought our sleeping bags. No sink, just a toilet, a hose for showers, big black and red ants, and a gecko! He was so cute. The toilet flowed all over the floor the first time we flushed it because the back pipe wasn't hooked up. Steve and I aren't plumbers but we found ourselves fixing toilets (the ones that flush) all over the world.

We stayed on Kecil Island for three days and two nights in a stilted structure overlooking the water and a gorgeous cove. Astonishing sunsets and tropical storms were the norm. The island had no transportation other than going by foot and boat taxis. Visitors were mostly in their 20's. Steve took the kids snorkeling through the crystal clear water to see rainbow-colored fish swimming around the coral reefs. We ate our dinners right on the sand at night watching the lightening storms out on the water and dodging the bats who kept whizzing about our heads. Our last chance to see the turtles was thwarted by a huge storm.

One day we decided to take the trail that crossed over to the beach on the other side of the island and a komodo dragon rambled across our path. It was about 10 feet long with a two-foot long forked tongue going in and out. With jungle around us, it felt as if we were instantly transported to prehistoric times. I hope these exciting experiences even out the difficult ones over time.

PHILOSOPHY 101: *Doing it 'right'*

In the back of my mind I keep hoping I do this trip "right." Mentally, I know that is a silly concept. However, I am emotionally tied to wanting it to be a powerful experience for my kids, especially. Somehow, I can't escape a sense of responsibility for helping that happen—instead of just letting it happen. What must I do to make it work? How can I help filter their experiences so that they remember what is "important" and not just what I consider silly or insignificant? I find myself saying things like "Boy, isn't this amazing! One of the most beautiful places in the world right where you're standing!" It is a challenge for me to simply let go and let it all transpire. What will they remember about this time together ten years from now? Can I influence that? Should I?

While on Kecil Island, we met a woman from Canada, another from the Netherlands, and a young man from St. Louis (the only American we'd seen in one and a half months). All shared our concerns for the island and Malaysia in general. It is an environmental disaster waiting to happen. Garbage is dumped everywhere. They make pits in the jungle forest and try to burn the abundant plastic water bottles along with cans, tin, and other garbage. Whatever is not burned is just tossed anywhere. It is a sad asterisk to an otherwise heavenly place. How long will it survive?

Early on the 30 th of July, we left the island and drove for eight hours all the way from the northeast corner of Malaysia back to Kuala Lumpur, in the southwest corner. As in New Zealand and Australia the children survived the long hours in the car by singing, sleeping or reading. For some reason the radios rarely, if ever, had reception, so we were very grateful to J.K. Rowling for having put out the fourth Harry Potter book before we left. Steve, Clare and I took turns reading to everyone. Although the drive to Kuala Lumpur was particularly long and hot, the miles flew until we hit the city.

The unlabeled streets of Kuala Lumpur were so confusing. None of the roads were straight so we never knew which direction we were going. Highways and multi-lane streets all mixed into one, with very little opportunities to enter or exit. We invariably found ourselves on a one way, five-lane street, in the furthest left lane needing to turn right. Trying to find the hostel was frustrating beyond belief. Once found, we didn't dare to drive again until it was time to go to the airport.

Our room was up six flights of stairs but it had its own air conditioning! Yeah! The young hostel manager gladly let us choose another room when we found that ours had moldy ceilings and rodent droppings on the beds. We counted our blessings. I found that I could wash clothes fairly efficiently in a sink the size of a dinner plate with a bar of soap and cold water. (I don't know if hot water exists in Malaysia.) We walked the streets of the city, had our evening meal, and mazed our way through the wall-to-wall people of a noisy street market. I had a distinct moment of "What am I doing here? Didn't we wake up on a tropical island this morning?" The extreme contrast made me laugh.

The next day we took the city train to see more of KL. The Twin Towers are an architectural wonder with a westernized mall inside that is spotless, chic and glitzy. Incongruity between that mall and our experiences along the east coast of Malaysia a few days earlier was astounding. Millions of dollars must have gone into making this monument to architecture while the rest of the country struggles to make ends meet. I suppose it's no different in many parts of America; the have-nots living in the shadow of the haves.

Later that night we walked to the underground performing arts center for a fantastic dinner show of Malay dancing and music. Some say that these traditional shows are pure tourism and not always an accurate reflection of the society. While this may be true, it was still a marvelous evening of tasting foods we would probably not have tried otherwise, and seeing colorful and unique dancing. Clare and I accepted an invitation to join the performers on stage to try out traditional dances.

The contrasts of the week caused me to think that impressions of a place depend entirely on what one is exposed to, or not, (by organized tours or personal choices) and one's mode of transportation (walking vs. an AC tour bus). At that point, we had yet to have a guide or tour bus show us anything, for better or worse. We saw the good, the bad and the ugly of Malaysia and Singapore. The poverty, homelessness, and environmental degradation are tragic. Yet, the people we met were convivial and the scenery memorable. Our stay in Malaysia, in particular, went a long way toward helping us see Muslims in a favorable light.

I wonder….can a government's or a country's compassion be measured by the way it cares for its poor, its elderly, its children, or its environment? What will become of this tropical nation? What do tourists see and remember when they come to America from very different countries?

A new feature: FLW (famous last words) from our trip so far…
- "Left, LEFT, STAY LEFT!"
(They drive on the left side of the road. We usually did, too.)
- "I need the itch cream."
(Needless to say we fed a few bugs.)
- "Everyone go potty before we leave."
(5 minutes after we leave . . . "I need to go!")
- "I'm thirsty!"
(Or, insert: hungry, tired, hot, sweaty. . . etc)
- "I don't want to walk anymore!"
(Daddy: "But it's just around the corner!")
- "Is this water safe to drink?"
(No diarrhea! Knock on porcelain.)
- "Mommy, will you please read to us?"
(We just finished Harry Potter #4)
- "Where's the toilet?" "That IS the toilet."
(The ceramic hole in the ground)
- "Sh! We're lost." "Show me the hostel sign!" "Show me the airport sign!"
(We certainly saw many interesting sights unintentionally.)
- "There are ants (cockroaches, spiders, lizards, etc.) in our room!"
- "It's all relative"
- "Just when you think it can't get any worse—it does. Think about how nice the next place will seem!"

*"The more we travel and know one another,
the more we are likely to build a peaceful world"
Margaret Thatcher, former Prime Minister of England*

BAKSHEESH!

A fter the tropics of Malaysia we split the next couple of weeks between two very different countries: Thailand and Egypt. These two poverty-stricken nations furthered our education into ways of living vastly different from ours in the States. Let's compare and contrast.

The Land
Thailand: Lush, green and gorgeous in the countryside. Loud, big, and smoggy in Bangkok.

Egypt: Desert covers 96 percent of the country. The rest of the country lies along the life-giving Nile River. Only one percent of the people live outside the Nile region.

The Treasures
Thailand: Intricately and richly decorated temples, wats (monasteries), and palaces with ceramic tiles, mirrors and gold leaf. The Grand Palace of the King (including King Rama IV, alias the King of Siam from "King and I" fame). Enshrined Buddhas seemingly around every corner: including one 700 years old, made of solid gold, and one 150 foot long gold reclining Buddha.

Egypt: Basically brown with an occasional mosque tower decorated with geometric patterns. Colossal colors inside 3-5,000 year old tombs that were more vibrant than the modern day buildings in Egypt. The Egyptian museum, with King Tut's phenomenal collection of treasures. Karnak's temple, created over the centuries by kings trying to outdo each other in "finishing" the temple. Pyramids and the Sphinx.

Impressive, even without their original limestone and gold leaf covering.

The Environment

Thailand: Tidy. Even obviously poorer areas of Bangkok, Chiang Mai and outlying areas made an attempt to put on a clean face. Buildings in Bangkok rivaled most cities in the world, with lots of hotels and banks. In rural areas, homes are bamboo walls with thatched roofs. Smog so bad in Bangkok you could chew the air. Before we left, a friend who was a native of Thailand told Steve: "If you wear a white t-shirt in Bangkok, it will be brown by the end of the day because of the air pollution."

Egypt: Home to the world's most remarkable, ageless architectural feats. The ironic contrast: Cairo looked like a bomb was dropped and no one had made any attempt to repair the damage. Garbage is dumped so freely it looked as if the city was its own landfill. People readily tossed waste into the street, river, and onto train tracks. As we drove past residential areas, we often saw trash flying out of apartment windows. Buildings throughout the city were made with brown bricks left with rebar (metal poles that reinforce cinderblock construction) sticking up into the sky...waiting for the owner to have enough money to add another story. It was not uncommon to see skeletal buildings of brick with exposed staircases leading to levels without walls, like something out of a Dr. Seuss book or an Escher drawing. Alexandria, the coastal city on the Mediterranean Sea, had a good three feet of garbage instead of sand. Luxor was much cleaner and stood out among the cities we visited in Egypt as a place where people took pride in their surroundings.

The People

Thailand: People kind and hospitable everywhere. The poorest mountain people opened their home to us offering tea and homegrown bananas. Bangkok was busy, noisy, and frenetic while Chiang Mai had a much mellower pace.

Thailand has doubled in population since 1960 to over 60 million people.

Egypt: A distinction must be made between the people around tourist areas and other places . . . hawkers, vendors and would-be "guides" pleaded and connived to deplete our travel budget around the Pyramids and historical sites. Luxor was an exception. Our cab driver, the shop owner, guards at the hotel, restaurant owner, and others were all very gracious.

Egypt has about the same number of people as Thailand in twice the space. Both have roughly equal amounts of people devoted to one religion. Over 90 percent of Thais are dedicated to Theravada Buddhism while most Egyptians are devoted to Sunnite Muslim. A bit over fifty percent of Egypt's people are literate. Despite its poverty, 94 percent of Thailand is literate.

The Transportation

Thailand: Transportation is smog spewing tuk tuks (motorcycle taxis), late trains, and big red pick up trucks for taxis that fit as many people as possible. Tuk tuks in Bangkok provided thrilling/heart-stopping rides (depending on which of us you ask), racing around the city, dodging in between cars, finding space in traffic centimeters away from other vehicles.

Egypt: Taxis and trains piled people not only in them but all around them. Trains sped 100 mph down the track with 100 men or more hanging all around the outside of the engine and cars. Trucks, vans, and any other vehicles often had people hanging on the back end or sitting on top. Both countries' taxi systems had meters in disrepair that facilitated their jacking up prices for unsuspecting tourists.

• • • • •

A little story or two.
THEME: Security.
MEMO TO SELF: Get more organized.
Thailand: Check into the Bangkok train station. Nine bags. "Here is your receipt." "Thank you." Travel about Bangkok.

Steve does a bit of spring-cleaning through his pockets. "We don't need these visa receipts, tickets to temples, etc." Finds a trash can. Two or three blocks later . . .

Steve: "Uh oh!"

Toby: (I hate it when he says that . . .) "What did you do this time?"

Steve: "Uh, you know how we got a receipt for our luggage."

Toby: "Yes"

Steve: "It now has a happy home in the Bangkok waste system."

Toby: "That's not good."

Steve: "Oh, I'm sure it won't be a problem."

Fast forward to our return to the baggage check at the train station, thirty minutes before departure.

Steve: "...but all our luggage has the same tag on it."

Baggage staff: "I'm sorry sir, but you don't have your receipt. (5-10 minutes of pleading) I'm sorry, but you must go to the police station." Quick jog across the station to the police. Not much English there. They basically could care less and send us back. We enlist the nearest tourist office representative. (Keeping track of time? Our train leaves in about 10 minutes.) Finally, the woman says Steve needs to show her his passport and make a copy of it (Read, you need to jump through at least some hoop so I can teach you a lesson, you silly boy.) Make a copy, grab the bags, and run to the train with five minutes to spare!

Egypt: We invested in a nice hotel right across from the pyramids so we could feel somewhat safe. Everywhere we looked in Egypt, there were bored guards toting ouzi machine guns. Towers and barricades with bayoneted guns sticking out created an imposing presence as we drove around. Metal detectors and x-ray machines were in place at the entrance to every hotel and museum.

Time to check out of the hotel.

Steve: "Could you please store our luggage?"

Hotel staff: "No problem sir, right this way."

We load our packs and sleeping bags onto a bellhop's carrier and get the official receipt.

Staff: "Sir, do you have anything of value in your bags, like a camera, wallet, valuables, etc.?"

Steve: "Uh, yeah. I have my computer."

Staff: "You won't be able to store anything of value because we have a big problem with stealing."

Steve: "So, I can't actually store anything in your storeroom because someone might steal it."

Staff: "Yes sir." I snag my laptop and they wheel the bags back to the storeroom. "Sir, you can use our safe deposit box for your computer if you want."

Steve: "Great."

Twenty minutes of waiting, finding the guy with the key, and then finding out the computer won't fit. Back to the bellhop. "I will need to get a backpack so I can carry my computer." He leads Steve back to the storeroom. A large door of the storeroom is wide open to the outside street. Inside the storeroom is a big plywood shed to store luggage. The bellhop reaches to grab a key on a hook about a foot away from the padlock for the door (in plain view of everyone and their mother). Opens the padlock and he gets his bag. No wonder they have a problem with stealing!

• • • • •

Both Egypt and Thailand offered rich architectural histories and works of art. Both main cities were incredibly smoggy. Both had a sense of history much beyond our youthful country. Thailand has had the same king for fifty years. It was hard to grasp the extraordinary extent of Egyptian history. Both had a distinct uniqueness that will be remembered.

PHILOSOPHY 101: *You decide!*

One of the most significant areas of conflict for Toby and me is the need to make decisions. Neither one of us likes to decide things. Inevitably on this trip we are in situations in which we need to make choices regarding what direction to go, what to do, whether to spend money on something, etc. For me, I think it stems from a fear of "getting it wrong" and not wanting to take responsibility for the outcome. Our greatest source of angst is when this is combined with urgency. These are easily our most stressful moments.

Add to that discomfort our unease with making phone calls or asking someone for information and you have a good sense of our greatest challenge in traveling together.

THAILAND   31 July

One of our favorite adventures was a tour Steve booked hesitantly from Oregon on the Internet. It is extraordinary to us that eight months later, with no other communication, someone showed up on our doorstep at the Lai Thai Guesthouse in Chiang Mai promptly at 7 a.m. to take us away. We drove through miles and miles of rice paddies with men and women hunched over all day, knee deep in muddy water. How do they do it? I know how hard it is just to harvest strawberries for 45 minutes. Arriving a couple of hours later at Lisu Lodge, we discovered a peaceful, bamboo, wood, and grass-roofed retreat nestled in the mountains near Lisu Village. The area was breathtakingly beautiful and a complete departure from the city's cement, noise and smells.

Upon arrival we put our gear in our two rooms (mosquito nets on the bed—hmm) with huge windows (no glass, no screens) that opened to the outdoor village. None of the walls actually extended to the ceiling so we could talk to each other right through the walls. The kids were so accustomed to lizards and geckos that they didn't even scream anymore when they saw them. I guess we were accomplishing something on this trip anyway.

After being sized for mountain bikes and helmets we began the first leg of our journey; a 13-kilometer ride into the hills. Workers harvesting rice were the occasional visual diversions from a vast and tropical sea of green jungle. The kids had fun and rode most of the way until we hit some very intense stretches of downhill on uneven road with big rocks. They wisely chose to go in the support truck. Their parents were not as intelligent, but managed to make it to the end unscathed. At our destination, in the jungle next to a river, we feasted on a simple boxed lunch while fending off the numerous stray dogs and chickens.

Following lunch, we climbed aboard elephants for a high adventure that left our bums and backs quite bruised. One does not appreciate the grand height of an elephant until you are sitting atop one. What sounded like a novel and adventurous thing to do in the brochures quickly deteriorated into fear for our lives. The wooden crate upon which we sat was perched just above the elephant's shoulders with a piece of twine (seat belt) stretched across our laps and hooked on a nail. The elephants rambled steadily along the dirt road as we rocked from side to side and held on for dear life, repeatedly shouting new FLW: "No cliff! NO CLIFF!" Our elephant insisted on eating constantly (every ten steps). They eat about 400 pounds of food a day and drink 50 gallons of water. We didn't mind the eating except when our elephants chose to go for the bamboo growing on the side of the road with the cliff that fell 100 feet down to the river. They stood on the very edge and reached as far out as they could. Seeing a few leaves just out of reach that looked especially delicious, they leaned just a bit more . . .

"Agh! STAY AWAY FROM THE EDGE! PLEASE!"

The kids and I frequently screamed and yelled at our elephants (apparently they didn't understand English) much to the amusement of our driver. Sitting right on top of the elephant's head our driver seemed to control the animal using the muscles of his bottom. We laughed heartily when we realized his unique way of driving this huge animal. However, the young lad had the last laugh as he led the elephant down a steep slope and into the rushing river. With our hearts pounding in our chests, we managed to survive the trip back up the vertical cliff to the hut where we would go on our next part of the adventure. It is mind-boggling how sure footed four tons of elephant can be on steep terrain.

In spite of recent rain swelling the river to flood level, our guide Gay persuaded the captain to allow us to go white (actually brown) water rafting. (Thanks Gay!) Hence our second FLW: "DUCK! DUCK!" as we narrowly rafted under low branches, bridges, and through class 4 rapids. Here's how the usual retelling of our exploits went:

•   •   •   •   •

Steve: "We almost lost a kid or two."

Toby: "Not really… Steve is sensationalizing for the general public."

Steve: "I was holding on to them so I was able to whisk them back into the raft after that really big one. I DID consent (reluctantly) to get out before the waterfall."

Toby: "I count my blessings. My husband fantasizes that he is Indiana Jones instead of his mild mannered education professor alter ego. I'm still not sure which of his alter egos wanted to bungee jump in New Zealand. What I do know is that I never heard of Indiana Jones having to get an MRI and Steve has had three due to his ~~mishaps~~ adventures…"

Steve: "It is a good thing I am around to put excitement into your life."

Toby: "I'm not sure whether that word quite captures my sentiments…perhaps fear or foolishness might be closer…"

•   •   •   •   •

The rafting was thrilling, but at the end we had to get out and wade to the shoreline. Walking in the murky mud took some doing, especially when we'd watched the elephants defecate right in the water and I'm pretty certain raw sewage from the scattered homes along the river added to the mix. The mud in the bottom of the river was the consistency of extremely wet dough. Each step clung to our feet and made a sucking noise as we pulled hard to release each foot in succession. From old movies of people in jungles, I had visions of blood sucking leeches clinging to my feet and legs. "Face your fears, face your fears," I whispered under my breath.

Our last leg of the day was a steamy hike through the jungle forest up to the Akha village, one of six communities of mountain people. The Akha are sometimes referred to as the "black dog tribe" because their religion sacrifices and eats black dogs. They also eat snakes, mushrooms, bananas, rice, pineapple, eggs, and chicken. We were invited to green tea and tiny bananas with the locals. They gave us special cups made of bamboo and cut at an angle because "The Farang (foreigners) have big noses." That way we could drink from the tall end and not bang our big noses on the other side. How thoughtful of them. As it was Sunday, we spent some time in the tiny Catholic church on the mountain overlooking the village. It was so strange to hear them singing "Immaculate Mary" in Akha (the mountain people's language) in a Buddhist country. Missionaries sure do get around.

Looking down from the mountain huts or walking through the village I had to keep reminding myself that it was not a movie set. This was their reality; day in, day out, year after year. On the one hand, they endured the heat, humidity, rain, overflowing rivers, and being bent over all day in rice paddies or in the hillside cornfields. On the other hand, they lived in the midst of this peaceful, emerald beauty seemingly untouched by the passage of time.

Along the way, we quizzed Gay about Thailand. The children go to nursery school at 4-6 years of age in the village. From 6-13 they walk two kilometers to primary school and that's about it for education. Most children do not go to secondary school, much less college. Instead they may go to work in the city at a young age. The young women (teens) are encouraged to try to snag a British, American, or European husband.

Thai women are striking so I was shocked to learn that the goal for many young Thai women of the city, such as Gay, is to look more "western." Stores in Chiang Mai carry an array of creams and lotions to whiten your skin. There were many billboards on the roads into Bangkok and ads in magazines that advertised this cream. Gay said she uses it once in a while. Wealthier women have surgery to make their noses bigger and eyes wider. The more extreme will have surgery to extend the femur bone to make them taller. Gay was surprised to hear that in the States there are tanning salons and bronzing creams to make your skin darker and people have nose jobs to make their schnoz smaller. We all had a good laugh at the folly of human beings.

Seeing the women working and selling goods in the street markets, the men (almost all smoking) running tuk tuks or taxis, or the children in the village selling us their handicrafts, I wondered about them all. I grew up with goals and dreams I tried to achieve and still have things I wish to accomplish. My dreams have always kept me going, striving, working very hard, at times having five or six jobs at once. But never have I had to be slumped over all day, barefoot in slimy mud, knee deep in water. Do they have goals, dreams and aspirations or is living as they are enough for the majority of them? Gay trained three months to be a guide. She has been doing it for seven months and hopes to do it the rest of her life. Her one dream in life is to see snow. I wonder how long she will be able to keep up being a guide. It is an exhausting pace but she is in awesome shape. We were not quite sure how she managed to achieve what is considered such a high status for Thai people from her modest beginnings.

Back at the lodge after our all day journey we were treated to another scrumptious Thai meal. The night before, when we arrived in Chiang Mai, we decided to go to the Chiang Mai Cultural Center for dinner, Thai music, and dance. It was an educational overview of the traditions of most of the mountain people in the area. The Lai Thai guesthouse claimed that it was much more authentic and not as touristy as others. This night, at Lisu Lodge, we were treated to not only great local food, but a group from the Lisu Village came in traditional clothing to sing, play instruments, and show us folk dances. After our dinner we joined in folk dancing with them. Our children jumped right in. It was a great night with lightening and thunder occasionally illuminating the pitch-blackness all around us.

The cultural lessons continued in the morning with Gay leading us through Lisu village. It has a population of 550, homes built on stilts, one-room houses with a cooking pit inside and electricity, which is a recent addition. The villagers have no concept of land ownership, or of possessions in general. Everything is shared. The pigs, chickens and dogs roam free. Residents take (and eat) what they need when they need it. This system works for them.

Some of the older Lisu have red teeth from chewing a plant that they say makes their teeth strong. This practice was going on long before toothbrushes and toothpaste were introduced. The elderly still chew the plant and flash a blood red smile. Children brush their teeth at school. We beheld an angelic twenty-four day old baby in a hanging cradle. Her mother was seventeen, her father twenty. Gay said that it is very common for girls to finish primary school at thirteen then look for a husband in the city. Marriages may still be arranged. Some girls end up in brothels in the city trying to survive.

The village tour then continued through the jungle in the pouring rain, atop the bumpy (painful) seats of an ox cart, before returning to the main residential area. There, people were abuzz with preparations for the once a month sacrificial ceremony—a.k.a. a vegetarian's worst nightmare. At the entranceway to the home in which the pigs would be slaughtered, there was a small shrine with sticks, feathers, and blood.

Gay filled us in on some more interesting details about the mountain people and this particular custom here in the north of Chiang Mai:

The Akha and Lisu are animists, meaning their religion believes in the spirit of animals. They sacrifice black dogs, pigs and chickens. Today is the once a month ceremony for the pig slaughtering, so they first sacrifice a chicken. If someone is having bad luck, or has to go into the city, or there is a ceremony of some sort, they will kill a chicken and spread the blood on a bamboo frame with herbs, incense and offerings. The shaman then reads the bones to see if it is a good day for the ceremony, the bad luck has passed, or it is safe to go into the city. If the bones don't reveal a positive answer they sacrifice another chicken and read the bones again.

So, I wondered silently, how many chickens will they go through before the bones give the desired answer? And how does one read bones?

Gay: "The village people have invited you to join them for the celebration. Would you like to go?"

Kids: "What will they do there?"

Gay: "Well, they will kill two pigs and slice them up to share amongst the villagers. Then the men drink the blood of the pig."

Clare: "Yuk! Gross! Disgusting!"

Bridget: "No way!!"

Michael: "I'm not going anywhere near there!!"

Seeing how it was still early in our travels and we are vegetarian, I just wasn't up for pig skewering, so I offered to stay behind with the kids. After all that we have experienced since then we could probably handle it now but at the time only Steven politely (reluctantly) accepted.

After about a half hour waiting outside, with Steve and Gay at the ceremony, curiosity gradually got the best of us. Michael and I were the first to wander back into the ceremonial area. Bridget came shortly after. Clare stayed outside, enjoying a book. Tough choice: a good book or an animal sacrifice. When we entered, Steve and Gay were sitting in chairs along with other villagers in a scene slightly reminiscent of a neighborly gathering watching the Rose Parade, Super Bowl or NBA Finals.

Two very large pigs had been speared and the holes corked with corncobs to keep the blood from spilling out. (After all, they wouldn't want to waste any or Steve might not get his share.) The pigs ran about for a little while, until they bled to death internally. Men carried the pigs to a pile of dried reeds that they proceeded to ignite. Taking turns with handfuls of flaming reeds, they patted all around the pig to burn off the hairs and cook the skin. Close by, in traditionally colored clothing, the women were preparing the herbs for the soup while children played or looked on.

Once charred, the men used machetes to scrape the skin off the pigs. I tried to keep my face neutral. The pigs were then rinsed and laid on banana leaves for the cutting. I couldn't watch. All around us villagers were laughing and chatting away as if they were at a picnic. (Were they laughing about the gringo tourists turning pale?) They were looking forward to a feast but first they would enjoy the blood and raw skin before making the soup. Steve and Gay were offered the blood to drink. This time he politely declined. (I guess the cultural ambassador stuff can only go so far.) Gay sensed our saturation point and led us back to the lodge where it was time to pack before we headed back to Chiang Mai.

At the lodge, the local craftspeople had a display of handicrafts. We selected a few small items. With so many months and countries ahead of us we really limited our purchasing. Suddenly, as a gift to us, the flute maker presented Michael with a circular Thai flute. Michael, Clare and Bridget were so touched that they went through their packs and put together a small bag of toys and coins for his seven year-old son.

In a flurry of hugs and "kap kun ka" (thank you in Thai) we kissed Gay goodbye, invited her to Oregon to see snow, jumped on the truck, and headed back to Chiang Mai. An overnight train ride put us back in Bangkok for one more day of walking before our next flight.

First stop in Bangkok was a visit to the solid gold, 700 year old Buddha. There are so many wats in the city and many of them have priceless representations of the Buddha. From the life sized, solid gold Buddha here, to the 150 foot long

Buddha, or the crystal or emerald Buddhas as small as your hand, they seemingly come in every size and composition. Each one is housed in large, ornate, red and gold shrines. The viewing area was packed with tourists so we paid our respects and found some outdoor tables to eat sandwiches.

As we were on our way out, a darling group of about eight young schoolgirls surrounded us and smiled shyly. They asked where we were from and we told them. (Long anxious pause.) "Did you want something?" I finally asked. Thrilled, they giggled and handed us their homework. Their English class assignment had been to write questions about Mother's Day. One question was "What is Mom?" Challenged by this philosophical question I waxed poetic about motherhood, sacrifices, caring for your children. The blank and confused stares told me I was way off the mark. Then it hit me: " 'mom' is short for 'mommy'. That's another American word for mother." Bingo! That's all they wanted!

There were many times in our trip in which serendipity was the best tour guide of all. Wats seemed to be around every corner. As we walked along the side streets of Bangok, Michael had to go to the bathroom so we turned into another wat, seeking the usual hole in the ground. It was quiet, peaceful, and no one else was there but us--just the opposite of the previous one. No hawkers, no gift shops, just hundreds of different Buddhas lining the walls. The temple was under renovation. We ventured in and sat down for a peaceful moment. As the children were whispering questions about the meaning of all the symbols in the temple, an elderly monk approached us. Without a word, he gave us cold water out of a little fridge. He was quite intrigued with Michael. For some reason, people in Thailand were always staring at Michael, touching his cheek, squeezing him. They also often touched Bridget as if trying to see if she was real. We sat quietly, enjoying each other's presence in silence. This was a very different experience than the usual rush to words when we visit friends in the States.

We were just about to leave our host when another, younger monk came in. He spoke English and was excited to practice it with us. In fact, he would soon be going to Chicago for four years of missionary work. We spent a very long time with him, asking all the questions that had gathered in our minds over the weeks of being in Buddhist countries. A few intriguing pieces of information:

*Buddha's eyes look at a specific angle. Not out at the overwhelming problems of the world. Not down directly at himself but at a distance, just a bit out to find peace.

*Buddha's ears are so long to symbolize the need to really listen carefully and thoughtfully before forming opinions or responding.

*Buddha's numerous curls of hair represent problems he solved for others.

*The serpents over his head really represent just one serpent that protected him when it rained by moving magically and very quickly over his head like an umbrella, so Buddha could focus on meditating.

*The fat Buddha is the Chinese version which they believe represents wealth, prosperity and to want for nothing.

*The skinny Buddha is the Thai version that represents peace and contentment with what you have.

The older monk brought us some longan berry fruit that I really didn't like but ate to be polite. Politeness can get hard on the taste buds and stomach. The younger monk invited us to go to the temple next door where we had a further private audience. He unlocked the huge 200-year-old doors and we went in while he excused himself to go have lunch. After his quick return we barraged him with more questions about everything in the temple. This impromptu afternoon visit in ancient Thailand ended, oddly enough, with an exchange of business cards and we were off.

Overall, this was a fabulous part of our trip. As we walked through the airport on our way out of Thailand Michael said, "Do you know what the hardest part about traveling is?" (I thought . . . carrying your backpack? Filtering water? Missing

71

Oregon?) Michael concluded, "Making friends with wonderful people and then having to leave them. I miss Gay and Ross and Thelma."

EGYPT   8 August

We had so many delayed departures on every mode of transportation, except elephants and rafts that I wish we had a penny for every minute we ended up hanging out in terminals. I'm sure it would all add up to enough to pay for this trip. True to form, we had a five-hour layover in Frankfurt, Germany en route to Egypt.

When we finally arrived, we found Egypt to be hot, but not humid. The airport was unbelievably crowded, like sardines in a can or rush hour on a New York subway. Being somewhat nervous due to the massacre of 72 tourists a few years ago (okay, VERY nervous), we decided to splurge a bit on the hotel for safety reasons. Sometimes spending money has its advantages…we moved through the crowd in line for customs, inching our way toward the Le Meridian Hotel desk at the airport, where we found the aid overly helpful in getting us through the mire of entrance payments and formalities. I was most anxious when he took our passports. They were eventually returned, but warnings from Lonely Planet kept flashing before my eyes: "Never surrender your passport to a stranger." (We didn't mean to! It happened so fast!) This was our first taste of "No, I'm not just being kind, that will be ten pounds please" for non-requested services. Quickly we learned that in this country people offer unsolicited help and then require payment. Relinquishing the appropriate bills to the aid, he hailed a taxi for us and we were on our way.

Driving through Cairo we found worn down, beat up old buildings, poverty, ruins, and nice hotels all mixed together. The air was more polluted than Los Angeles at its worst. People were smoking everywhere, even under "No Smoking" signs (especially under no smoking signs.) Police and big army-looking men with large guns would stand right beneath a huge no smoking sign and blow smoke in our direction. Not the time to say "Um, excuse me, but. . ."

Cars honked incessantly. One of our later taxi drivers explained that Egyptians consider it music. They just keep on honking to make sure other cars know where they are in the stream of traffic and lane changes. Maybe so, but there were certainly a few angry faces or gestures associated with those honks now and then.

The Le Meridian hotel was spectacular with a clear view of the pyramids from our hotel room window and a unique pool with a waterfall for the kids to enjoy. One of its key features was its walking proximity to the pyramids, so we didn't have to bother with transportation issues. Our trek to the pyramids was not without difficulty, however, as we needed to make it past the barrage of cabbies, camel, horse, and donkey drivers all insisting we needed their services.

After paying to get into the pyramid area, we were met by an elderly man who had official tags and the nods of everyone around him assuring us that he was who he said he was—an official guide of the government. He started taking us around, and about a third of the way into the trip, decided it would be a good time to discuss his wages. Lacking a solid grasp of the exchange rate at that moment and not realizing that the tour would be short-lived and information sparse, we lost much more money than we planned.

It seemed like everyone in the area surrounding the sphinx and pyramids had an innocent sounding con.

"What a beautiful family! I'll take a picture for you. You all get together."

"Okay, thanks." How thoughtful of him.

Click

"That will be five pounds."

Yeah, real thoughtful. Later we heard stories of people not getting their camera back until they forked out the money.

However, that incident did prepare me for another one later in the morning. Steve went to get closer to the Sphinx. Having had our fill of history, heat, and hiking the children and I slowly headed toward the exit. A gentleman with a camel came up and insisted we take a picture on his camel.

"No thank you," I said politely.

He kept at us, followed us and finally made the camel kneel.

"Here, just stand next to him for a picture," he implored.

We should have kept walking. Oh well, just standing there couldn't hurt. So Michael, Bridget and I stood next to the camel while Clare tried to take a picture. Suddenly the man put Michael up on the camel. I grabbed him off, having figured out that he was going to make the camel stand, not letting Michael off until we paid his ransom. The children and I started walking away as quickly as possible with the camel man saying, "baksheesh, baksheesh."

"I don't have any money," I told him truthfully while turning my pockets inside out.

We never did get a picture after all. You really need a tough skin to deal with the constant hawkers. It is almost as if they have attended a class because they all use the exact same patter:

Hello   *Hello*

Where you from?   *America*

Ah, America. Egypt and America are friends. First time in Egypt?   *Yes*.

Welcome.   *Thank you*

Then they proceeded to follow us for blocks soliciting while we repeatedly said no.

All that aside, it was astounding to stand near and go into 5,000 year old structures. That amount of time is just incomprehensible for an adult; forget trying to impress children with the significance of antiquity and architectural wonder. The pyramids are the only one of the Seven Wonders of the World still standing.

The irony displayed by the architecture in Cairo was also something to be appreciated. Modern-day structures in the city, just a stone's throw from the pyramids, looked in shambles while these ancient tombs still maintained all their splendor. I suppose that "built-in obsolescence" is a twentieth century invention.

Back at the hotel, swimming was a welcome break from the heat before we met our impromptu cultural escort/taxi driver, Gouda, later in the afternoon. What started as a taxi ride, ended up being a personal tour. He was very boisterous and clearly proud of his country. He picked us up the next two days and took us around the city, showing us many places that would not have been on the normal tourist route. The only problem was trying to negotiate a fair price for him and for us, as we had become all too accustomed to being ripped off.

"This is my city and I will show you all the best places. First we will visit this, and then this, and then this."

"Uh, okay. And what is this going to cost us?"

"Don't worry about that. After we go, you decide how much you want to pay me."

I guess that sounded fine, but made me rightly nervous because at the end of the day, what we offered to pay him was never enough, and we are not so great at negotiating. It was so difficult to weigh the standards of the United States versus Egypt for the fair value of things. In the end, I think both parties felt cheated. The next day we got a bit smarter and set a price beforehand.

However, Gouda's excursions did reveal some fascinating places. First stop was the oldest Christian church in Cairo, known as Al-Muallaqa (the suspended) or the "Hanging Church." It was built on top of a water gate, the southern tower of the old Roman Babylon fortress. Described by Lonely Planet as "the most beautiful" place of Christian worship in Cairo, it was established in the fourth century. It was a little unnerving looking through the floorboards down thirty feet or so to the ground below.

Second on Gouda's agenda were the churches of St. George and St. Sergius. The latter was built over the place where it is said the Holy Family lived while hiding from King Herod. Parts of Egypt look as if they haven't changed since Christ was here. Feeling as if we were traveling through a time warp we walked the streets with odd sensations about the reality of the area's historical and biblical significance. The bible story of Mary and Joseph coming here from Israel with a newborn baby suddenly took on life as we became aware of the heat of the desert and barren terrain they had traveled for days.

Balancing out world religions, our third stop was the oldest mosque on the African continent. Never having been in a Muslim mosque before, we felt very uneasy about trespassing into the sacred space of another religion. However, at Gouda's encouragement, we entered the door and left our shoes with an attendant. We were quickly met by a sociable gentleman who put us at ease and spent the next hour explaining all about the architecture, the religious practices, and answering all our questions about the Muslim practice of faith. As we sat, fascinated by this holy place in the Muslim religion, a shrouded body was brought in on a stretcher, just yards from us. It was a dead man being spiritually prepared for burial. The men who brought him in stood around the body and prayed. There were no other women in the mosque. A dividing wall separated the spaces where the men and women prayed, but no one seemed to mind that I was on the wrong side.

Our guide finished his explanations by telling us all about his wife dying and leaving him with four children who are now in their teens and twenties "and anything you wish to contribute. . ." For once, I didn't mind the twenty pound donation to him after his gracious welcome, fascinating information, and touching story. However, having to pay to get our shoes back was truly annoying.

Last stop for the day was the Papyrus Institute where we were very impressed at the ancient fine art of paper making from the papyrus plant. The demonstration was educational but the hard sell that followed, to buy painted papyrus paper pictures, (try saying that three times!) caused me to finally go out into the heat where Gouda was smoking. I was growing weary of Cairo as it began to feel like one long con. "Ah, an

American tourist. Baksheesh, baksheesh!" I didn't want to buy anything and I was sick of cigarette smoke blowing in our faces. Clare, on the other hand, had been studying Egyptian history at school and had spending money from her godmother. The combination was just right to spend sixty pounds on two pieces of art.

En route back to the hotel we beheld the gorgeous Nile River looking like a lively green serpent snaking through a desert valley. Along the way Gouda pointed out the island where papyrus is grown because it requires so much water. The golden sunset shining off the river illuminated the pyramids for our return. For a moment, Cairo looked serene.

At the Egyptian Museum the next day it was interesting to see a separate entrance for residents and tourists. Charging tourists extra makes complete sense but we wondered why the locals were so heavily searched and padded down. We only had to walk past heavily armed guards, through metal detectors, and pass our packs through the x-ray machine. It was one of those moments where we were not quite sure whether to feel safe and protected or terrified.

Heat and the absence of air conditioning, fans, or any form of circulation made it challenging to be amazed at the 5,000 year old relics, art works, mummies, carvings and jewelry. The museum is massive in size, but the desire to stroll in wonderment became overpowered by the urge to seek air and coolness. Any single piece from this museum would probably be the pride and joy of a museum in the United States, but there was so much on the premises it was difficult to appreciate it all.

King Tut's room was extremely popular for the pieces on display, but even more so because it was dark, cool, and the only room in the entire museum with air conditioning. People were crammed in there. The golden jewelry, funeral mask, and sarcophagi were intricately carved. Hundreds of spectacular gold artifacts, a golden chariot, animals, servants, and food were buried with the boy king to help him on his journey to the afterlife. How unbelievable it was for them to have created these magnificent treasures with such rudimentary tools. All this for an eighteen-year-old boy.

While Steve was determined to soak in every artifact in the museum, the rest of us found a place to relax near some huge sarcophagi. Clare and Bridget had brought their little paper fans from Thailand with them. They were a hit with some of the good-natured guards and policemen who were also miserably hot. More than one offered to trade their uniform hat for a fan. Bridget lent hers to one guard while we went to the bathroom. He was extremely grateful and returned it with sincere appreciation.

That evening we began our trek to Luxor. Once again, Steven wisely invested in a more expensive venue of transport to insure our safety. The cheaper, local trains were so run down in appearance that they resembled the old cattle cars used to transport unsuspecting prisoners to the Nazi concentration camps in the forties. The Cairo trains at least had windows, but they seemed to be just as packed with people as the old cattle cars. Passengers hung from every possible space on, above, to the sides, and in back of the trains. Our overnight train to Luxor cost significantly more, but it was worth every pound for the air conditioning, excellent vegetarian meal, and the tiny shelf-like bunks. In a four-bunk compartment, I doubled with Michael. Fortunately we are both fairly small, as the bunk was about the width of a diving board.

Our four a.m. wake-up call on the train came all too soon after going to bed at ten p.m. The cool of the early morning greeted us as we arrived to behold Luxor; such a departure from Cairo both in cleanliness and serenity. A much smaller city, Luxor is truly charming and the people kind, gentle and pleasant. The hotel staff where we stayed was exceptionally amiable and the guards frequently enjoyed joking around with our children.

Luxor's primary attraction is the Valley of the Kings and Queens. We had been advised to go as early in the morning as possible to beat the unbearable, inevitable heat. As it was 5:30

78

a.m. upon our arrival, the hotel bank office was not yet open to change money so we had to wait until 8 a.m. This proved to be a set back. As the clock ticks the temperature rises. Still, we were glad to take a nap. Steve returned at eight. The staff could not open the safe, but told him to go to town to an ATM that was open 24 hours. We could have left early after all!

Our taxi driver that day was a sweet, gracious, and easy-going young man who did **not** lay on the horn like a percussionist in a rock band. He drove us to the West Bank of the Nile where we explored the tombs of ancient royalty. Hieroglyphics artistically carved and painted into the walls led to the underground tombs. They contained the spells from ancient theological compositions that would assist the king or queen's course through the underworld and into the afterlife. In many places the colors were so vibrant, it was hard to believe that they were 3000 years old.

Most tombs were robbed of their riches centuries ago, which is what made the discovery of King Tut's tomb so spectacular. The longer a king reigned, the more elaborate the treasures in the tomb because of their amassed wealth. Workers took years to dig the tunnels, carve the chambers, and paint the incantations. "The Boy King" was only in power for nine years, yet the gold that was discovered in his tomb was very impressive. Tour guides around us kept saying things like "Imagine how fabulous a tomb such as Ramses' must have been."

The children had a good economics lesson in supply and demand out in the heat of the valley. Being indescribably hot, vendors can charge whatever they please for bottles of water. Even though we had brought our own with us we quickly sweated out every ounce we drank. We had long since realized why it was cheaper and less crowded to visit Egypt in August—only fools and those of us on tight budgets venture into the fray in the height of an Egyptian summer. Thus, we eventually fell prey to the water vendors, paying anywhere from one to five pounds for a bottle of the precious liquid.

I can't say which was more fascinating; the fact that the ancient Egyptians constructed these tombs hewn from the earth without any machinery or that the people today survive out in that same desert living in mud brick or thatched homes. The small square shacks have one window and no door, just an opening. Barefoot children roam the streets or ride on donkeys. Some homes appear to be as worn down as the centuries old ruins still dotting the desert valley floor or hills.

How do they live out there? Void of water and wells they must take drums on donkey carts to the canal, a green, filthy offshoot of the Nile. There, they fill the water drum and haul it back on donkeys or the women will walk for miles carrying water jugs on their heads. I wondered if they think about the grand hotels with electricity, running water, air conditioning, and clean swimming pools just across the Nile? And if they do, how do they feel about it? What is the division of economic levels there? Has it changed much in 5000 years from the laborers building grand temples and tombs for dead kings and queens to the people of today working in the fields to feed Egypt or the hotels to take care of the tourists? With so much curiosity there was no one to ask politically sensitive questions.

After our exploration we returned to the East Bank, the hotel, and our air-conditioned room with renewed respect and awe for the people who live in that heat and relentless sunshine. Dinner at a local restaurant was interrupted when both Bridget and Michael came down with diarrhea. It was the first slight indication of anything in two months of traveling. Not that anyone cares about our children's intestinal health, I only mention this because throughout our entire trip we were all healthier than we have ever been at home. This came as a total surprise because we truly anticipated much more illness traveling around the world, especially spending so much time in third world countries and on long flights in packed airplanes with little sleep and poor air circulation.

It was also, however, another opportunity to experience the kindness of strangers. The owner noticed the children weren't feeling well and brought them hot lemon water, an Egyptian cure for diarrhea. He was so loving and gentle toward the children who appreciated some hopeful remedy for their ailment.

Michael and Bridget were feeling well enough the next day for us to explore the massive Karnak Temple on the East Bank. Over hundreds of years, each king or queen would add some monument to their regalness and say "There, the Karnak Temple is at last complete!" The next reigning monarch would follow the same routine. As a result, the vast grounds devoted to the gods are filled with one grandiose structure after another. Most mind-boggling is the "forest" of 134 thirty-foot tall pillars representing closed and open lotus flowers, each exquisitely painted and carved. The hall is over 6,000 square meters, enough to hold both St. Paul's Cathedral in London and St. Peter's Basilica in Rome. The entire temple is an incredible example of one-upmanship throughout the centuries as each succeeding leader tried to leave his/her mark bigger and better than the last.

Under the archways of these ancient temples Steve and I had philosophical discussions about the recurring themes of the Egyptians: patriarchal societies, ousting of one race and culture for another, non-rightful ownership of another's land, and man's need to keep outdoing the other guy. Quickly coming to mind were parallels from United States history past and present. For instance, Las Vegas, Nevada, (another desert area) with its collection of gargantuan, high tech, flashy, water-wasting, energy-sapping hotels and casinos is a fine example of a modern-day version of old Egypt. "My temple to mammon will be bigger, better, have more gold . . . "

We bid farewell to Luxor, trained back to Cairo, and took a day trip to Alexandria before our three a.m. flight to London. Clare read in school that they were excavating Cleopatra's palace there. When we arrived, we couldn't find any sign of Cleopatra and there was not much else to see. However, the ocean breeze was a welcome break from the southern heat. Finding public toilets (always a challenge) presented another problem and became a walking quest. We have seen a great deal more of cities, villages, and towns while always in the proverbial search to relieve someone's bladder.

Waiting at Cairo International Airport from 5:30 p.m. until 3:00 a.m. gave us our first real insight into these marvelous children we had with us. Most international airports allow people to enter the interior terminals to mill about, shop, eat, and even sleep on uncomfortable chairs while waiting for flights. This, we ignorantly assumed, would also be the case at the airport in Cairo. Wrong again. Not only were we not permitted past the entrance lobby, there was no place to wait for eleven and a half hours until our flight. No chairs. No restaurant. No gift shop. The airport is located in the middle of nowhere and every last Egyptian pound we had had been spent to pay the driver from the Alexandria fiasco. (The previously agreed fare somehow nearly doubled by the time we reached our destination.) Thus, returning to the city was not an option.

Parking ourselves at some tables in a downstairs "deli" (cigarettes, soda and cheese sandwiches), we began our vigil. Hours passed by writing, playing cards, sleeping sitting up, and walking laps up and down the corridor and stairs. The children invented a game that kept the guards in stitches. Both shifts. Michael sat on Clare's lap with his arms behind him and she put her arms through to function as his own. Then Bridget sat across from them and they played hand song games with Clare being Michael's arms. This was to become a useful and very popular "show" the children enjoyed putting on for each other, for us, and anyone nearby. Never were we so relieved to get on a plane! On to England!

"To travel is to live"
Hans Christian Andersen, Danish author

ROYAL SERENDIPITY

After Egypt, arriving in England was a feast for the eyes and refreshing to the soul. England was bursting with color and a hint of autumn was in the air. Actually, just breathing air without smoke and smog was fully appreciated as we healed our lungs. We relished in cool breezes, amazing sunsets, wind blowing through the trees, quaint villages, acres of farmland, rolling hills, and a loving reunion with long time friends, the Fife family. Mary Kate (my college roommate and long-time friend) is Michael's godmother and her son, Brogan, is my godson. Being with them was like a homecoming to me. Our children were thrilled to play with theirs, stay in one place for a moment, and not be tugged to the next spectacular site. Steve and I reveled in the opportunity to have late night conversations with Bill and Mary Kate.

Alton, Mary Kate and Bill's town, is quintessentially British. Picture postcard perfect, Alton boasts Tudor architecture, pleasant parks, cobblestone streets, kind people and everything in walking distance. Bill is a farmer and was harvesting wheat. We each took turns riding in the huge combine and learning about the trade. The kids enjoyed playing with baby animals and swimming in the pool next door. Godparents got to re-bond with godchildren. We just had to stay beyond our intended two days. Michael's highlight was Mary Kate's treat to visit the real Thomas the Tank Engine. He marveled at the life-sized versions of his favorite trains along with Sir Topham Hat. Alton would prove to be our recuperation and rejuvenation base over the course of our trip. We all looked forward to our return trips to England in

October and November, but for now, we were off to Scandinavia.

<u>NETHERLANDS</u>   17 August

Crossing the English Channel by ferry brought us to our first train in mainland Europe. Activating our Eurail passes, we headed for the Netherlands. Over 90% of its people live in urban settings, making it one of Europe's most densely populated countries. I never have understood why it is called Holland and Netherlands until now. Similar to Great Britain and England, Netherlands refers to the whole of the country, while Holland refers to the dominant part. The Rhine River crosses through the Netherlands and empties into the North Sea here, after it has traveled all the way from Switzerland and Germany. Since prehistoric times there has been a battle against nature to transform the large marshy area along the coast into usable land. The infamous dikes of Holland hold the North Sea back so that they can farm land that is 23 feet below sea level.

Amsterdam, its capital, was full of energy, activity, street performers, restaurants, canals, bikes, trams, busses, and very tall people. It is a splendid city. The youth hostel was right in Vondelpark; acres and acres of trees, paths, playgrounds, cafés and open spaces where we were witness to the ancient Brazilian fighting dance, Capoeira. In Capoeira people young or old (although typically college age), male or female, gather in a circle playing drums, rattles, and bells and "fight" by swinging legs and arms without ever touching each other. They are drenched in sweat after 10 minutes. Its origin is the black slavery days of 18th Century Brazil. The deadly martial art Queimado that the blacks were learning was outlawed, so they disguised it as a folk dance with music, singing, and acrobatic maneuvers.

Highlights of Amsterdam were walking the canals, Anne Frank Haus, and a bike trip to the countryside. The visit to the Secret Annex (the Frank family's hiding place in the attic during the Nazi invasion) is something one must experience in

84

person and, preferably, without young, hungry children. Standing in line for over an hour just to enter the museum already put a dent in Michael's interest level. Clare was fascinated and Bridget full of questions. Although we spent hours there, my first thought upon leaving was, "I've got to come back here again. Alone." It is a place that deserves unspeakable reverence and unhurried time to fully digest.

We purchased Anne's full, unedited diary to read on our travels. It was such an interesting description of relationships and adolescence amidst the hovering tragedy of the Holocaust. To think that two entire families and an extra guest remained within the confines of that attic for years, never setting foot outside, is beyond my comprehension. I had not known that they were very well off prior to the war, so it was also a compelling tale of how these occupants experienced a gradual decline into poverty. No telling, yet, what impact this special museum had on the children. Our greatest task was trying to explain the big "Why?" of the Holocaust and impressing upon them the overall theme of anti-discrimination. It was a moving trip through that time period.

• • • • •

THEME: Just missed it
MORAL: Don't sweat it
STORY: Thursday, our last day in Amsterdam, we thought that we would invest in a guided bicycle tour of the countryside before taking the 7 p.m. train to Copenhagen. The night before we called and left a message on a machine that we would join the tour.

PLAN: Store gear at the hostel. Stroll through town to the bike meeting place. Meet the guide at 9 a.m. Have a leisurely ride and relaxing day seeing the countryside, visiting a cheese factory in Edam, and seeing the dikes.

REALITY: Late start out of the hostel. Cram all our stuff in hostel lockers. Race out of the hostel to the meeting place. After a few blocks, it's getting too late! Get a taxi! Make it to the meeting place at 8:55. Relief! 9:15 . . . . 9:30 . . . . no guide. Read small print on the brochure: "Tours only on

85

Wednesday and Saturday." Oops! *Steve eyes a bike store across the street.* "Let's just do it ourselves without the guide!" *Walk to the bike store to rent bikes for the day.*

"We don't have kids' bikes, but Fred's store does."

Steve calls ahead.

"Yes, we have kids' bikes, but we can't reserve them."

"Okay, we'll be there in 5 minutes."

2 km walk... 15 minutes. As we approach we watch the family in front getting the last kids' bikes. Bummer.

"There is another bike store down the street."

Seven bike stores and one hour later, we finally get bikes for everyone. Off we go. Stop at the tourist info place.

"You can take a free ferry to the other side of the river and ride in the countryside, but we don't have a bike map."

"No problem!" *Toby winces with nervousness regarding Steve's navigational confidence in an area he has never been to in his life.*

Ferry across the Amstel River to the countryside. Bike through pastoral farmland, viewing windmills, dikes, and sheep. After 3 hours of not necessarily direct travel, the kids are exhausted, but surprisingly resilient with minimal whining. Finally, we discover civilization in the form of the oceanside village of Mondickedam, which is still 2 hours away from Edam, our intended destination. Skip Edam. Have a nice lunch in a cute town instead. As we begin our ride back to Amsterdam the rain comes pouring down. Soggy, but in good spirits, we make it back to Amsterdam at 5 p.m. as it starts to dry out.

Clare: "Let's ride our bikes to the hostel, grab our stuff, and ride back so we don't have to pay for the tram."

"Great idea!"

We race to the hostel, grab our stuff, load up the bikes, and ride to the rental place through a maze of streets, and hundreds of people. Toby is very impressed by Steve's phenomenal navigational skills. We walk the next 1.5 km to the station to catch the train with perfect timing! We even have time for Toby to run out and get pizza. Whew! What a day.

• • • • •

The overnight train took us to Odense, Denmark, birthplace of Hans Christian Andersen. Denmark was bikes, buses, blondes, blue eyes, bakeries, big baby carriages, and more tall people. The country consists of a large land mass and about 500 small islands. Odense was a storybook town with a sense of humor. As we walked to the HCA house, we saw a statue from one of his fairy tales: the one-legged soldier. Down a bit further, was his missing leg, standing as a parking pole. His boots were around the corner in front of a house. We have certainly read many of HCA's tales, but did not know much about the man.

His is a bittersweet story of a rise from poverty, of love lost, and ultimately of recognition for his works in his old age. The stories of The Little Match Girl, The Little Mermaid, and The Tin Soldier are somber, heart wrenching stories that parallel his own life and his sometimes-pessimistic perspective. He also had an unusual talent for paper cutting. As he told his tales to children he would often use his ever-present scissors to cut paper. When the tale was complete, he revealed his creation, typically a scene from the story. The Hans Christian Andersen Museum was located in his childhood home. A fascinating display included his original writings, paper cuttings, many of his belongings, and pictures of people and experiences in his life.

Andersen traveled extensively, but he often said that his favorite city was Copenhagen. Although Copenhagen is the largest city in Denmark (about 500,000 people) and holds over one fourth of the total population in the country, it was a relaxed, spacious place and we spent a glorious day walking every inch. It was much less dense than Amsterdam and her canal waters were clean and clear. The palace grounds, parks, and gardens were very accessible. A marionette show, the famous Little Mermaid statue, a star shaped moat, and Rosenberg Castle filled the morning. We were astonished that the inside of the castle appeared untouched since it was first occupied in the 16th Century. The glittering gold crown jewels in the treasury looked as if they came directly from a fairy tale.

Our 12 hour day on foot was rounded out with a trip to Tivoli Park, which is Copenhagen's Disneyland, but smaller and a fraction of the price. It was very inexpensive to get in the door, so it was packed with people. We saw a comical ballet with excellent dancers and a high wire act.

A brief aside...Michael was such a kick to watch "walking" down the streets. In between whining about walking too much, he often pretended to be a car, train, or plane. He made all the right sound effects for whatever vehicle he was at the moment, weaving in and out of people traffic, revving up and racing forward, dodging obstacles like light poles at the last moment (Michael! Watch out for that. . !). He ran up and then back to us, typically going twice as far as any of us. I guess he had a legitimate gripe about walking too much.

PHILOSOPHY 101: *An Example?*

Toby and I often talk about how people represent their countries. We have met so many people from many different nations. Each time we encounter someone on a slightly deeper level than just passing on the street, our image of the person and, to some extent, his or her country is formed. As the kids and I sat in the visitor center of the Malaysian Tourism Office and talked of sights to see with the veiled Muslim woman, our impressions of Muslims were shaped. While we sat in a youth hostel listening as an amiable Australian man described how he enjoyed his travel to a particular place, our perceptions of Australians were forged.

Of course, it is dangerous to create stereotypes with limited samples of people, but it certainly is a natural tendency. It heightens our sense of how people perceive Americans based on their encounters with us. Are Americans loud, obnoxious, and pushy? I have unfortunately witnessed our compatriots adding to that stereotype during my travels.

What do people think of us? I feel tremendous responsibility for the image of Americans my family and I provide others.

In this regard, I am often very grateful for Toby. She is truly our family ambassador as she cheerfully engages with people around us. At home I often kid her about making phone calls to buy airline tickets or get something on mail order and I overhear her talking about the attendant's divorce, politics, or their sick dog. I call and I get airline tickets. She calls and gets someone's life story in five minutes. Yet, in our current travel situations, this is surely an asset. I hope to say that people who encounter us will form images of Americans as friendly, caring people and not simply consumers of their country and wares.

On the other hand, it is not so easy as we travel for hours on trains and the kids get restless and start being silly or loud. Trains are generally pretty quiet places, so I am always thinking we are invading their space with our noise. I can't blame the kids for wanting to play around, but Toby and I seem to constantly be shushing them. Well, I am sure that people will be forming the image that Americans do not have perfect families anyway...

SWEDEN   23 August

Next stop, Sweden. Ah, Sweden! If you've ever been fortunate enough to visit Vermont, you have seen Sweden. Behold her attractive, cozy and scenic, towns, farms, lakes, forests, and rivers. More than half of the country is covered by forest. Over the course of the last 100 years, there has been a mass exodus to the cities (21% lived in urban areas in 1900, 85% today), leaving the rural ways of life behind.

As fate would have it, Sweden rail was repairing several sections of track throughout the areas we traveled. Whether this is a regular feature of Sweden, or a special event just for us was unknown. One thing is sure, however, little things like this cause one to pause and consider whether life is preordained or happenstance. On our trip to Goteberg we were placed on a bus for a segment of the journey. On that bus from Halmstad to Varberg, we met a wonderful woman named Anna who gave us her card and invited us to call her if we couldn't find a hostel in Goteberg (or even if we could). Steve left his good REI parka on that bus. We spent the next week trying to retrieve it through phone calls and visits to every possible office. As it would turn out—we lost a jacket, but gained a friend.

We did not want to immediately burden Anna and her family with our presence, so we decided to press on to Amal, Sweden, a gentle lakeside town of 10,000. Our intent was to get to at least one small town in each country as well as visit the big cities. Amal was a nice respite from the hustle and bustle of Copenhagen and Amsterdam. We didn't get there until after ten at night and had a 1.5 km walk to the hostel.

Throughout our trip the kindness we received from total strangers was remarkable. They seemed to appear, as angels, anytime we needed a bit of help. A case in point... as we wandered through peaceful, empty streets in search of our lodging, we encountered a sweet gentleman. He was out walking his dog and led us to the hostel, which was in a quaint old train station. We thanked him and he left, but he returned two more times to make sure we got in, got a room, and were all settled. What a generous gift of his time he gave us. The next two days in Amal were spent with relaxing strolls through town, a picnic next to the marina, and the mandatory sandcastle making at the edge of the lake.

NORWAY   25 August

Oslo, Norway was bursting with excitement when we arrived on the train. Thousands of people were pouring into the festively decorated city. People on the train were abuzz with talk of the day.

"Oh, you must be here for the Royal Wedding!"
"The what?"

Serendipity struck again for we had arrived just two hours before the royal wedding between Crown Prince Haakon and his wife to be Mette-Marit. We quickly checked into our hostel and headed downtown to stand with the throngs along the parade route. Our vantage point was three to four people deep, right next to where the TV cameramen had a platform monitor and across from a youth band. Two kilometers away, at one end of the street, was the royal palace. A block from where we stood was the church. Clare and Bridget climbed a pillar to see above the crowd while Michael and I watched the monitor to view what passed before us a few feet away. Steve peered through cracks in the crowd. After an hour, the prince, princess, and entourage drove by to the cheers of their sea of admirers.

The crowd thinned out during the wedding as people raced home to watch on television. We crept to the front to see the parade up close for the prince and princess' return trip to the palace. It was quite impressive to watch from our front row view as kings and queens from Sweden, Norway, Denmark, Spain, and many other royalty rode past thousands of people and uniformed guards. The prince and princess looked splendid as they drove by in a convertible.

The next day we visited the palace and wedding church. Everything about the wedding and church decorations reflected the simple beauty and earthiness of Norway. Huge baskets made of twigs, vines, moss, and roses adorned the church inside and out. The cool fall weather, together with the décor was reminiscent of a country wedding.

Norway is about as long as California with hundreds of islands dotting its coastline. It has a peculiar shape, as it wraps up and over Sweden and Finland, reaching around to Russia and taking with it all the coastline along the North and Norwegian Seas. I'm sure at some point in history the Swedes and Fins were not especially happy about that land ownership. Much of Norway's history is colored by the infamous, violent Vikings who pillaged and plundered so many other countries from 800-1100 AD. The Viking Ship Museum in Oslo was a fascinating place dedicated to this era, complete with a few authentic ships taking up most of the interior space.

These days Norway's riches lie in the continental shelf in the North and Norwegian seas that are rich in oil and gas. Consequently, territorial disputes frequently arise between Norway and its neighbors, Iceland and Russia. The country is home to four and a half million people, while a Norwegian population equal to more than half the population of Norway (2.5 million) lives in the United States. Liberal attitudes in the country regarding relationships contribute to the statistic that half of the babies born in Norway are to non-married couples. It was not so surprising, then, that the future queen, princess Mette-Marit, was a commoner with a child born out of wedlock.

Our next adventure was a trip to the Fjords. We got up at 5:00 a.m. to catch the 6:30 train out of Oslo because the 8:30 trip was full. According to the staff, we could catch the tram to the train station "just around the corner." (We should have learned to be wary of that phrase.) A few blocks later, we got to the tram station. That tram didn't run until after 6:30. Lugging our gear, we walked to a busier street to catch another tram. By that time we had walked over two kilometers. The tram ride saved us a couple of blocks more walking . . . just in time to catch our ill-fated train.

Twenty minutes out of the Oslo train station our engine died. An hour and a half later a new engine arrived. On the way, we made friends with Ann Marie from Illinois and Jenny from Australia who were both a great deal of fun for passing the time away. Our new engine lasted about an hour before smoke started pouring down the tracks. It had caught fire. All passengers were emptied out at the next train station and we ended up standing in the stairwell on the next train through, which was the 8:30 trip we couldn't get on in the first place.

Finally, we got to the Flam railway, a tiny train that took us down a steep mountain to our boat for the fjord trip. There was a mad dash for seats because there were now two tours trying to get on instead of just one. The interesting thing about the train seats was that they popped up when you stood. Steve had gotten us all waffles with raspberry jam at the train station

92

to eat on the train. As we grabbed our seats he put his backpack down on one bench along with Clare's waffle. Needless to say, in an absent minded moment (not his first, and not likely his last), he grabbed his pack to stow it above and Clare's waffle went flying; jam distributed equitably. We were very popular on that train.

It was well worth the hassles, however, as the fjords offer some of the most breathtaking scenery in the world including colorful, tiny towns at the base of majestic mountains and clear blue waters. An adventurous beginning turned into a magnificent day to be awe inspired by nature. The fjord trip ended in Bergen, on the southwestern edge of Norway, where we spent a few days exploring this cute wharf town with old-world charm and lots of character.

Our last morning in Bergen was spent on a great mountain climb exploring Norwegian troll homes and taking in the view from the top of the mountain overlooking the city. In the late afternoon we decided to visit a small town outside of Bergen because our train back to Oslo was not until 11 p.m. Needed to make the most of those Eurail tickets!

$\bullet$ $\bullet$ $\bullet$ $\bullet$ $\bullet$

THE TALE:

We head for the train station. The next train is in 10 minutes! Stuff our luggage in the lockers quick!! Head for the train. Oops, locked the tickets in Steve's pack in the locker! Steve runs back, opens the locker, and gets the tickets. No money to lock the locker back up. Run up to the cashier to get change for the locker. Dash back to lock the locker. We manage to jump on the train as it pulls out of the station. Never a dull moment. Dale, Norway is a cute town. Problem is, by the time we got there, everything was closed.

$\bullet$ $\bullet$ $\bullet$ $\bullet$ $\bullet$

Our last stop in Scandinavia was with Anna and her family in Varberg, Sweden. I had learned so much about her and her work while we rode the bus the previous week. One story she shared stands out and warrants repeating. While she was living and volunteering in India she met a mother traveling alone with her fifteen-year old daughter. As it turns out, the daughter was a drug addict and in desperation this single mother quit her good job and said, "It's time for you to see the real world." She gave up everything to take her daughter traveling. They were poor and lived on beans and rice, but by the time Anna met them the daughter had been sober for three months. The drastic efforts of the mother had turned the daughter's life around. I made a mental note to share that with parents I counsel back in the States. Not that everyone can drop everything and travel the world, but traveling does make one step back--far back--and see a broader perspective of life.

It was wonderful to experience a simple Swedish home and their generosity to strangers from a foreign land. Their English was more than sufficient for the adults to have great philosophical conversations about the state of the world while our kids and theirs (three great kids ranging from 10-15 years) enjoyed entertaining each other. It was a weekend filled with games, chats, singing, Swedish church, and cultural exchange.

The Holmdahls live in a modest condominium with just enough space for our children to crash on their floor in sleeping bags while their oldest sacrificed his small room for Steven and me. One of the highlights of our time with them was a trip out to the Holmdahl family home on a nearby lake. This thirteen -bedroom house had been in Anna's family for 300 years. As long as there was room, any relative who wanted to be there could stay. The acres of land around it were undeveloped, natural, forested beauty by the water. Around every corner of the house, as we took our tour, was an old picture of some ancestor of the family. This impressed me the most because I am from a large, spread out family. Beyond my immediate family, I barely know any of our numerous relatives. Yet, Anna could name all the faces in the old tintypes and recite stories of long ago. Is it because Americans tend to move around so much or is Anna's family unique in being rooted in one area? In U.S. schools, we are usually accustomed to learning about kings and wars rather than the experience of the people. Swedish history of a different sort came to life that day. After the tour, we rowed boats on the lake, were treated to a tasty lunch, and played a delightful Swedish game of "Kub" on the front lawn. It was marvelous how close people could become with each other in such a short period of time.

However, more incredible still was the way God brought people into our lives and we into theirs, just when we, or they needed it most. We learned and shared a great deal with each other. Their oldest was just becoming sober after a battle with alcoholism and shoplifting. He and I spent long stretches of time talking about life, its complexities and struggles. A budding songwriter, he even shared two of his recent works. I was touched and honored to be welcomed into his adolescent world of joy and pain. Zach told me that his greatest desire was to visit Ireland, a dream he felt was completely out of his reach. Before we left, Zach and I made a pact: he would continue to strive for a life of faith, hope, and sobriety and I would send him a Celtic cross from Ireland. It was a promise that I would find much more challenging to fulfill than I anticipated.

When it was time for us to move on once again, Anna dropped us at the train station. Through hugs, kisses, and tears we said good-bye. At the last moment, she whispered to me her husband was leaving her. Stunned, we talked about it as much as we could before the train pulled up. I told her we would pray for all of them. "Maybe that's why we met," I said. She was sure of it.

*"We think of travel as a matter of place,
when in fact, place is a matter of people"*
Sonny Landreth, Guitarist, Songwriter, Singer

NOT ONE MORE STOP!

<u>GERMANY</u>   3 September

W ith heavy hearts we pulled ourselves away from our Swedish friends and headed to Germany. Despite our efforts to obtain reservations for the overnight train, we couldn't get them. Having been instructed to "just take your chances," we hung out in the Copenhagen train station with hundreds of others. As each train arrived and large groups filtered out, we gained hope. Once again, our prayers were answered: five seats in a smoking section cabin, but there was a door to close us off and we could open the window for air. Thank God for small blessings!

Sleeping on trains can be a fine art and like all good artists we experimented with different methods until it evolved into a somewhat workable system. Clare and Bridget fit on the floor on sleeping bags. I tried sitting up and bear hugging a sleeping bag. Steve stretched out with Michael on his lap. Remarkably, we were all asleep when the train arrived in Cologne (early). There was a riotous scramble to wake the kids, stuff the sleeping bags, and then find and put on shoes and backpacks. Needless to say, we didn't make it. The train pulled out. No worries! We just jumped off the train at the next station. As it turned out, there are two train stations in Cologne, and we wanted the second one anyway! Good thing we didn't have our act together on the train . . . God was looking out for us and maybe had a good chuckle as we ran to catch our next train going south alongside the Rhine River.

96

That train delivered us to St. Goarhausen, a lovely town on the Rhine River, but on the wrong side! Consequently, we took a ferry across the river to St. Goar. A hike up the mountain brought us to the youth hostel, situated just below the local castle. Spectacular views from our attic bedroom revealed the castle out one window and a view up and down the Rhine from the other. St. Goar is a tiny old village seemingly untouched by time. The likes of Geppetto's Tudor streets in Pinocchio awaited us.

Steve is a mutt. His ancestry is German, French, Scottish, Irish, and English. Our European travels would connect us with his roots. My ancestry is Lebanese and Lithuanian, two countries not particularly safe to visit at that point in time, so we missed out on my family's history. Germany's Rhine River was a bit of a pilgrimage for Steve and it was always entertaining when he was asked his last name for reservations. The good citizens of Germany always beamed when he responded, "Rhine." (Our line in the States, when trying to give our name, is: "Rhine, like the river." It's startling how many people are unaware of this famous, historically rich body of water.)

The next day we embarked on the classic trip down the historical waterway. The wide, dark green river is dotted with numerous castles all along the mountainous shores. Miles and miles of rushing river, vertically tiered wine vineyards, and small towns and farms met our eyes as we spent hours on the riverboats. The area is rich with folklore and history that Steve read to us as we weathered the wind and rain of the top deck (best viewing with the least amount of cigarette smoke). Most of the history of the area consists of archbishops and kings who got rich taxing riverboats while the French repeatedly abused the castles when they came through. The kids became experts about castles and some Rhine family history . . . they always knew the last line . . .

Steve: "And on your left, a castle showing a fine example of medieval architecture where tolls for the river made some archbishop rich and in 1676 . . . "

Kids: "The French blew it up."

Is it possible to visit too many castles? We certainly saw our share of them throughout our travels, but two stood out.

1) Burg Eltz

GUIDEBOOK: "... a lovely 40 minute stroll gently meandering through the forest up to a stunning medieval castle in Moselkern, Germany."

Us: a two-hour struggle with grumpy kids through quiet, unappreciated forest because it was late and everyone was hungry. By the time we got there, it was 5:45 p.m. and we assumed we would only be able to see the outside. Thankfully, we caught the last tour. The castle was well worth it and it became one of our favorites. When I imagine a castle, this is it. Berg Eltz has enchanting towers, spiral staircases, and ingenious technology for heating and fireplaces (40 in the castle), potties (20), and stately rooms and furniture.

The tour had been advertised as English speaking. After her first long speech in German, our guide smiled and said in English, "Any questions?" I was tempted to say, "Yes, what did you just say?" but I only asked what was the room we were standing in called. When the tour ended we were not looking forward to the walk back, as it was about 7 p.m. We had enjoyed the company of a man from Iowa who lived in Thailand and worked for foreign intelligence. He kindly brought the five of us and his girlfriend all the way back to Koblenz in a tiny Mercedes the size of a shopping cart (all the rage in Germany).

2) Neuschwanstein

This is the castle of King Max Von Ludwig II that was inspiration for Sleeping Beauty's castle in Disneyland. Located in Fussen, Germany, the natural setting for this exquisite castle has got to be the most striking in the world with lakes, mountains, and waterfalls surrounding it. King Max was a lover of art and opera. Both are reflected in the castle décor. The Neuschwanstein took over 17 years to build, but unfortunately for Max, he had only lived in it for 172 days when he mysteriously drowned in a lake.

One of the most important experiences we wanted our children to have was to be with the people of different countries and not just see the sights. To this end, we spent six delightful days with our friend Juliane in Munich. We met on our cross-country train trip in the United States a few years ago. It was great to get her perspective of living in Germany. She is a physical therapist who was born in East Germany. Although Germans are glad to be united again, she told of the continuing animosity from some West Germans to East Germans because west sees east as depleting their resources. Then again, the north and south are basically divided along religious lines. The north is primarily Protestant and the south mostly Catholic.

We often subtly slip in alongside tours in different places to learn a few things, and in a church in Munich we learned that ten percent of Germans' income tax is devoted to the churches. In many countries that we have been, the church buildings are often falling apart. Not so in Germany.

Highlights of our time with Juliane: Wandering through old Munich, seeing the Glockenspiel, and hearing Bavarian music as we walked through the famous Hofbrau house. Also, the lightening demonstration at the German National Museum was fascinating. Streaks of lightening were generated and shot down to a model house, displaying the value of lightening rods. We had long, silly evenings of laughter and games in her apartment, and the kids played with all the equipment in Juliane's physical therapy clinic. It was great to renew our friendship and play in her part of the world this time.

Our most moving experience of the trip was a visit to Dachau, the German concentration camp. Much has changed since Steve and I were each there separately 20 years ago. As we entered the visitor center, a movie about the camp in English was about to play, so we rushed into the theater, having little time to really consider whether the film would be appropriate for the kids. Signs on the wall advised not to bring in young children, but we decided to give it a try. "If you feel uncomfortable, Daddy or I will go outside with you, so just let us know." They were intrigued by the horror of the old black and white pictures flickering by.

The experience seeing the film was certainly gruesome, and a powerful reminder of the evil amassed at this sight to carry out the atrocities. Clare, Bridget, and Michael were silent as we left the theater. Should we try to help them sort through their feelings right then and there? We opted to allow the somber atmosphere to continue as we began a look around the camp. After a few minutes, we talked about how sad it was that the Holocaust happened to all those people and how important it is to counteract racism today so it can never happen again. They were amazed that my father had been in the war and involved with the post-liberation efforts. I don't think it scared them, but made them really think about some of the realities of World War II. They didn't have any nightmares afterwards, anyway.

People in Germany and at home asked us why we would want to take our children to such an awful place, especially since we don't allow them to see violence in any other form of media. We certainly don't want our children to grow up in fear. And we don't want them to be numb to violence. We want them to recognize evil in the world in all its forms and be willing to fight it rather than be passive and build fortresses around themselves. Such a fine line we walk as parents in choosing the experiences we allow our children to have. Which will harm them emotionally? Which will make them stronger? Wiser? There were true horrors at Dachau. Should we ignore them, simply acknowledge them, or face the horrors? It is such a powerful story of man's inhumanity to humanity. I guess our hope is that this visit will cause them to speak out against equal crimes against humanity as in Rwanda and Yugoslavia, and our own treatment of the poor at home.

We decided to invest in the official tour in order to learn more about what went on in Dachau. Sometimes increasing knowledge is the best approach to addressing fears. A very thoughtful German man in his 30's was our guide. He told us that his doctoral dissertation was on issues related to the camp so he enjoyed volunteering to provide the tours. His dedication

100

to telling the story of Dachau was clearly evident from the first moment he spoke. While the three-hour tour ultimately turned into more than four hours (the kids were burnt out after four hours, so we excused ourselves), the information was fascinating and moving. One of the men in our group told us that his father was in Dachau during World War II, so he had to come see it. What a profound feeling to realize that this man would not be alive if his father had not escaped.

At one end of the compound is the prison. Visitors may now enter where "special" prisoners were held. It was chilling to walk the halls and rooms where nothing had changed in 60 years. In the center of the camp two barracks were reproduced to resemble the original thirty. Each section of the barrack showed a different phase of the living accommodations. As the war grew long, the Nazis were less inclined to provide space for the prisoners. The accommodations at Dachau began with individual bunk beds but ended with the final living space filled with three-tiered structures where large groups of people would sleep.

Perhaps the most emotional part of the tour was a walk through the "garden" next to the crematorium. Birds were singing, tall trees shaded the shrubs below, flowers grew, and signs along the way marked the history: "Pistol execution range", "1000 people's ashes buried here", etc. It is all so horrible. The mind and heart simply don't want to believe this massive cruelty was possible. You would hope we would learn to prevent such atrocities but recent events, indeed even the rarely acknowledged genocide of our own Native Americans, prove otherwise.

As we stood in the peace plaza before leaving the compound, Clare said to me, "Mommy, we've got to do a show about this when we get home." I began to write "Never Again" almost immediately, putting the pieces together as soon as we got home. The show opened in May 2003 and toured the city.

The children's perspective as we walked out the gates: "It was scary, sad, and depressing to be in a place where 1000's of people were killed. Like a Hollywood set or a bad dream but real. It was hard but it was important for us to go see what Hitler was really like." It was such an emotionally heavy day. That night Juliane's flat seemed even more filled with love, laughter and hugs as if trying to counteract the historical tragedy.

AUSTRIA   10 September

Off to Austria and Bavaria. Austria, although a small country, has had an influential, imperialist past. Getting the award for longevity, the Hapsburg family ruled or was influential in Austria from the 10th to the 20th century. Everywhere we traveled in Europe, and even in places abroad, their names seemed to keep popping up. In New Zealand, for instance, the glacier we explored was named after Franz Josef, ruler of Austria in 1848. The Austrian Empire once included parts of Italy, Belgium, Germany, Spain, Switzerland, Turkey, former Yugoslavia, and Hungary until its loss with Germany in World War I relegated it to a fourth of its original size.

At this point in history, tourism seems to have the greatest influence in the country. The population has been gradually shifting west towards the Alps since World War II. We can certainly appreciate why. Bavaria is such an enchanting place. Architecture takes its cue from the natural surroundings. Mountains, forests, lakes and pastures convey peacefulness. Wood carved balconies and hanging flower baskets adorn homes and buildings.

Our first day in Salzburg was spent with Juliane and her friend Katja. It is a day trip from Munich to Salzburg, so they decided to join us. We entertained ourselves on the train trip out by playing "Go Fish!" in English, German, and Spanish. Neither of the women had ever heard of "The Sound of Music." They made the pilgrimage to visit Mozart's birthplace rather than pay homage to Julie Andrews and cast so we put off the Sound of Music sights until the next day.

Some of our most enjoyable experiences on this trip were unplanned. We split up from Juliane and Katja in the afternoon, each pursuing our own interests. They took the

Mozart tour while we walked aimlessly through the streets of Salzburg. Peeking in the door of Dom Cathedral, we ended up spending the next hour listening to a rehearsal with a small orchestra and soprano. With no amplification, the acoustics of the cathedral dome were celestial. Unexpected moments of beauty are the little treasures that are perhaps the most appreciated. The rest of the day we enjoyed meandering throughout picturesque Salzburg with Juliane and Katja. Through tearful goodbyes we saw Juliane and Katja off at the train.

We thought that we might take a brief aside here to give you a typical morning on our travels:

• • • • •

"Wake up, get out of bed, drag a comb across my head." *Toby does the smell test to determine if you need to take a shower and dry off with a bandanna. Hunger pangs strike, so we race off to get in line for a sumptuous hostel breakfast consisting of two rolls, a pat of butter, and lukewarm tea (included in the price. What a deal!) After that filling treat we notify the kids of our plan for the day.*

Steve: "Today we get to go to a cool castle hundreds of years old. We will have a nice walk through a king's garden and see the gazebo from the Sound of Music movie. We can picnic along the lake and see the lights of the city on our way back."

Kids: "No way! We don't want to go anywhere! Why can't we just stay in our room all day? We're tired of walking! We are bored of castles!!"

We then manage to drag the kids out of the door and after the first hour of whining, they have a great time seeing the Hellbrun Castle, built by an archbishop with a silly sense of humor and an obsession for water. Throughout the castle gardens are fountains, statues, running water and themed caves and grottos. All of them have hidden waterspouts, which the archbishop used to his folly on his guests. As there was no electricity hundreds of years ago, he ingeniously did

*all his tricks with only water pressure. Today it still functions
in the same way and the water tricks are played on the guests.*

*After the tour we spend two hours at a great playground in
the castle gardens. The evening ends with tasty apple strudel
in town as the lights of the historical buildings reflect on the
river. The kids have a great time.*

• • • • •

Rarely, if ever, were our kids all grumpy together. They
each had moments of wanting to just stop and times when they
were ready for adventure. We asked ourselves: Why did they
put us all through that initial grumpiness? Why couldn't we
save time and gray hairs and just get up and go? Granted it
was tough to be together 24 hours a day, 7 days a week, for 8
months, but why couldn't they just appreciate this
"opportunity of a lifetime" and be profoundly grateful to their
parents? Stay tuned for answers to these important questions .
. . . .we hope!

Then again, we could understand why they might get a bit
frustrated with their frugal parents. Needless to say, we kept
the big picture in mind (in spite of our savings, we would be
paying off loans for this trip for quite some time when we got
home). Steve and I wanted to get the maximum experience for
the least money. They wanted to get the maximum experience
period. At some point, I guess we balanced each other out a
bit. They pushed us to do things we might not ordinarily do,
while we (hopefully) taught them a few things about delayed
gratification, and/or alternatives to spending lots of money. A
case in point was our decision about whether to take the Sound
of Music Tour.

• • • • •

*In Salzburg, the Sound of Music Tour costs 400 shillings
per person (about $30 each). A guide-equipped van takes you
around the city and countryside to see the sites from the movie
while sharing details about where it was filmed. Interesting
trivia is thrown in for good measure. (Austrians question why*

people want to visit the set for an American movie when this is the birthplace of Mozart, but oh well . . .).

Steve: "Let's just buy this nifty tourist book and do it ourselves!"

Kids: "But we want to go on the tour!"

Steve: "With the $100 we save we can do something else fun!"

He invests in a $12 book, a 24-hour bus pass and off we go walking around the city and taking buses to visit the sights. A few hours into the adventure, Steve loses the book. As a result, we miss out on the stimulating trivia, but still manage to see most of the locations we remember fondly from the movie. One of the sights is the church they used to film the wedding scene that is outside of Salzburg.

Steve & Toby: "Let's take a train out to Mondsee to see the church! It is supposed to be lovely out there." We take the bus to the train station. Toby's turn to go get info upstairs at the tourist desk.

"We don't have train info." She runs downstairs to the train desk.

"Trains don't go to Mondsee. You'll have to take a bus." Back upstairs to the tourist desk.

"Here's the timetable, but you can't use your bus pass." Downstairs to the bus info. (Who needs a Stair Master?)

"It costs 63 shillings for adults and 32 for children." Upstairs again to report findings and discuss options. Should we go anyway?

After much deliberation, we decide to go for it. We get to the bus stop just in time to see the exhaust of the last bus for the day driving away. We walk to the Marionette Theater instead. $30 per person and it is "Don Giovanni" in German. Too expensive and probably too confusing for the kids. We walk to a quaint little toy store to look at trains for Michael. Upon hearing us speak English, the owner uses her broken English to inquire if we are from New York.

"No, Oregon."

"The World Trade Center has been destroyed. My son lives in New York."

It is 3 p.m., September 11th, which is 10 a.m. New York time. All of our frustrations that day are suddenly put into a new perspective. Stunned, we wander aimlessly and end up in a tiny deli watching an Austrian newscast on a 4-inch screen with the Austrians and a family from Portland, Oregon (one hour north of our home—small world).

Bridget asks, "What's happening, Mommy?"

What do you say when you want to protect your kids from the evils of the world as you are trying to show them the beauty of the world? How do we balance calming their fears versus understanding reality?

"We don't know yet Bridget. Let's say prayers for everyone back home."

We live the next few days in a dual existence; that of tourists trying to experience the world and of Americans far from home trying to find out what is going on.

• • • • •

Overall, we had a delightful time getting to know Salzburg. Yet, it will be forever in our memories as the place in which we first heard about the tragedies in the United States on September 11th. As people recall where they were when John F. Kennedy was killed, so will we have etched in our minds the tiny toy store in Salzburg where the lady informed us of the news in her broken English. Confusion reined in the city as rumors spread that many more planes hit many more targets, including the White House. Walking back to the hostel that night we stopped outside a hotel where an open window three floors up had an English-speaking channel on. We stood in the dark street below straining to listen to the news. In each hostel that we stayed over the course of the next few weeks, we picked up bits and pieces of the story as it unfolded.

It is so odd to be in a foreign country when something so catastrophic happens. How does one respond to a national tragedy when you are thousands of miles from home? I suppose the same way as if you were there: pray. Are we a part of the experience of the U.S. or isolated? Did we know anyone involved? How safe are our families and friends?

How safe are **we** now? Should we end the trip and return home? In the next weeks we went on with our adventures, but continually reflected back on the situation at home. I can't describe how it felt to be traveling, seeing the world, trying to educate and enlighten our children while so many lives had just been destroyed. Everything else seemed trivial compared to that.

It all struck me as a strange parallel to the people of Germany, more specifically the city of Dachau, during the Holocaust. While thousands of innocent men, women and children were tortured, starved, raped, and murdered on a daily basis life went on as usual outside the camp. People sang, danced, laughed, worked, ate and slept, went to school, married, gave birth and died while from 1933-1945 human suffering inside Dachau knew no limits. Twenty years ago, when I visited, I took a bus far out to the isolated camp. Today the town of Dachau reaches right up to the camp's borders. People pass it daily as part of their lives. What must they think to pass this horrific episode in history every single day? How do the people of New York feel now, walking in Manhattan and seeing the sun shine through where the Trade Center Towers once stood? We dealt with the news in the best way we could at the time by praying, visiting cathedrals and lighting candles for the victims and for peace.

As we trained out of Austria winter was steadily approaching, bringing wind, rain, and clouds. I didn't mind the weather one bit. It seemed to match the mood the world was in at the time.

HUNGARY   12 September

Our next stop was Budapest, Hungary. We decided to head there in spite of not knowing the language and not having any guidebooks about the area because the hostels in Vienna were all full. On the evening train close to Budapest, a young man identified himself as a tourist office representative. He reserved us a spot in a pensione and led us to a waiting van that drove us to the pensione. Egypt had ruined me: the entire time this service was being rendered I had two thoughts: "How much is this going to cost?" and "We are being kidnapped." Much to our pleasant surprise, everyone was genuine and the assistance didn't cost us anything. The pensione was very nice. Steve reasoned that they were trying to boost tourism.

Budapest is really two cities, Buda and Pest, which are separated by the Danube River. Combined, the cities hold about two million people, which is twenty percent of the total population. Until the end of World War I, Hungary was three times the size it is now—combining Austria, and parts of Romania, Croatia, Slovakia, and Ukraine. It was communist from the end of World War II until 1989, when it adopted democracy. There were no easily identifiable signs of communism during our stay. On the contrary, capitalism seemed alive and well with the usual street vendors everywhere, as we had seen in the rest of Europe.

Over a couple of delightful, sunny days we observed the old buildings, churches, statues, fountains, and Eddie Murphy filming his next movie. Budapest is a poor city. Still, despite the prevalence of graffiti and homeless people begging on the streets, it is clean and the residents very good-natured. The sight of Eddie Murphy seated at a café with multiple cameramen and the flash of the usual Hollywood entourage hovering around him appeared very incongruous with the rest of the city. Directly across the street from this crazy scene was the Cave Church, one of the highlights of our excursion through Hungary. Carved into a mountainside, the original worshippers used it during the communist years when religion was illegal. Decades later when it was discovered, it had been sealed with a cement wall 2.5 meters thick. It was reopened and restored in 1992.

• • • • •

OUT OF MOUTHS OF BABES, OFT TIMES COME GEMS
or
A CLASSIC STORY OF FOOLISHNESS

We look out the window of our pensione in Budapest before heading to the train station to return to Austria.

Bridget: "Daddy, the train station is across the street."

Steve: (In his infinite wisdom from traveling many countries) "What usually happens in big cities is that they have a few different stations that service different parts of the country. This east station in Budapest probably has trains going to Russia, while the west one, we came in on, goes to Austria. We have to go back to the west station."

Bridget: "Shouldn't we just check?"

Steve asks the lady at the reception which station has trains to Vienna. She has no idea. He decides to go to the west station, since we arrived there from Austria, and asks for the shuttle van to pick us up at 12:15 (a 10 minute ride) to get to our 12:40 train. The van gets us at 12:45. So much for that train. We will take the next one. A few blocks into the trip the driver says, "This trip will be 3000 forint (about $15)." We don't have 3000 forint, because we were leaving the country and had rid ourselves of as much forint as we could. Furthermore, we didn't know the trip back to the station cost money because the trip to the pensione was free. A bit miffed, we ask the driver to drop us off at the corner and he tells us which bus and tram to take. We drag our gear along and get the bus and then the tram and reach the west train station.

Steve goes to train information. "When is the next train to Vienna?"

"In an hour, but it goes from a different station." He tells Steve directions for the subway. We get on the subway, changing trains twice. As we walk out of the last station Steve says, "I have a funny feeling about this . . . " After two hours of making use of the city's transportation system, we climb the stairs back into the sunlight, and see our pensione on the left and the "east" train station in front of us . . .

• • • • •

To add insult to injury, I was fighting a cold that day so I decided to drink an entire bottle of water just before we left on the shuttle from the pensione to the train. This may sound foolhardy, but I reasoned that I would have access to a bathroom on the train by 12:45 p.m. By our 3 p.m. arrival at the train station, the children and I were ready to burst. However, throughout Europe, you need to pay for bathrooms. What few coins we had left were spent on the Budapest transportation system taking us in a circle back to our point of departure. Needless to say, the station facilities charged more than we had in our pockets for the whole family to relieve themselves (and they don't take Visa). It was time to take stock of our wants and needs. I had to go the worst, but Michael had the least ability to hold it. Not wanting to deal with soiled pants, Michael won the potty lottery.

When our 5 p.m. departure time rolled around a change of tracks was announced. I had to waddle in excruciating pain carrying backpacks clear across the train station. You know the sign in a train bathroom that says "Don't use these facilities until the train has left the station"? There is a point at which the rules need to be bent and I was doubled in half and filled to the brim, so . . . But for the record, for those of you sticklers for rules, I was committed to not flush until the train started moving. As a last straw, the train was late leaving, so I stayed in the bathroom for a half hour until I could flush. I laughed so hard as I finally sat down in my seat. What a day! Off to Vienna, the cultural Mecca of Austria.

AUSTRIA   14 September

After our train station fiasco in Hungary we landed in Vienna, Austria just after 7 p.m. To me, Vienna had a certain aura around it as Europe's capital for the arts. Haydn, Beethoven, Mozart, Strauss, Schubert, Brahms, Schoenberg, and other famous composers all spent a large part of their lives performing here. A pilgrimage to Vienna would not be complete unless time was spent dedicated to experiencing the artistic talents of the locals. In the main squares, people were dressed up as Mozart and other celebrities of that age, imploring you to purchase tickets for a symphony. You couldn't help but feel a bit guilty for not taking them up on their offers and honoring the great composers, but we opted for a few of the other artistic experiences instead.

We learned to always ask about family rates and 24 hour passes on public transport. There were pros and cons to this approach. They were the most economical way to go. Yet, once purchased, we certainly felt like we needed to use the pass as much as possible. Steven secured a transportation pass for this city of the arts. It freed us up to go everywhere and anywhere, but also pushed us to keep moving. Those days found us up and out of hostels early then staying out late.

First stop, the Imperial Palace, with the intention of watching the famed dancing Spanish Horses in their training session. An error on posted schedules had put everything one day off. Before we knew what was happening, we had paid to join the masses to see the formal dressage, standing two floors above the show ground of what appeared to be a former palace ballroom. It was difficult to see around the huge pillars, but when I finally found a spot three people deep looking down onto the show floor, the dressage set to Mozart was impressive. The horses danced, did intricate steps, and leapt into the air. I just kept wondering if the horses enjoyed what they were doing. We had managed to squeeze in a bit of Mozart after all.

We jumped on the underground metro train and landed at a huge park in the throes of early autumn. The children spent three hours playing. All of us tried out the zip line, a long wire hanging between two posts. A rope is attached to a pulley on the wire. Jumping off one post while hanging on the rope for dear life sends you through the air to the other post. It is a highlight of any playground for the young and the young at heart!

While some may tour the world to view the unique architecture, sample exotic cuisine, and take in philharmonics, our kids will be connoisseurs of the playgrounds of the world.

There was the pirate ship in New Zealand, a trampoline in Singapore, the driftwood swing in Malaysia, rope tree swings in Norway, spinning merry go rounds in France, and zip lines in numerous countries. Steve and I surrendered hours of sightseeing to simply play with our children and chat on park benches. Add to that all the time they enjoyed building sandcastles on beaches and fairy houses in forests, and you get an idea of how we spent our spare time.

Vienna's main square is home to St. Stephen's Cathedral with an interior that combines art with architecture. Yet, Viennese street performers just outside the church were much more intriguing to our children. Mimes stood as statues or acted out scenes when coins found their hat. We had a great dinner at the youth hostel and then Steve took the girls to stand in the back of the State Opera House for a Peter Pan opera in German. On our budget, standing room tickets were a great way to squeeze in some activities that we would not have been able to afford otherwise. Sunday morning we got in the SRO line for mass at the Imperial Chapel to hear the Vienna Boys Choir. It certainly was an appropriate place to hear them sing, as they sounded like angels from above. In fact, that was where they were...high up on the top balcony, where nobody could actually see them.

PHILOSOPHY 101: *Intimacy*

I hadn't expected much of a relationship with my wife on this trip. It was one of those things that I was resigned to sacrifice for the greater good of the overall experience. Not that I wouldn't make an effort to find moments of tenderness, but with all of us in close quarters for 8 months I figured that we wouldn't get many opportunities for dates.

About four months have passed and that was a pretty accurate assessment I'm afraid. There have been stolen moments of peaceful togetherness as the kids play at a park or when friends, new or old, watch the kids for an hour so we can go on a short hike alone. Those are cherished moments! We get an opportunity to talk and be romantic for a brief space in time.

In the first decade of our marriage together, we would go out on "dates" and Toby would often say "let's pretend that we are going out for the first time" and try to renew the excitement of little things like holding hands and a kiss on the cheek. We don't have to pretend much these days! Those simple acts of intimacy are highly valued when everyday is filled with traveling, learning, and playing with the kids. We are very much focused on being a family rather than trying to lead two parallel lives of parents and a couple in love, as we attempt to do at home. Parenting is the overriding theme right now, for better or worse.

One of the things I miss the most is the opportunity to simply sleep next to my wife. At the end of a long day at home, I always could count on the refuge of the brief time before sleep to catch up on the day and cuddle next to each other. Hostels are not very conducive to that time alone—bunk beds are not exactly made for marriages. Once in a while, however, we do manage to stay in a pensione or hotel with a double bed and renew our connection.

Our next stop was Innsbruck. The hostel was situated at the foot of gorgeous, snow-sprinkled, Austrian Alps. It was cold and raining when we arrived. We thought we might have snow in town by morning. Instead, it was another fun, easy day of hiking and playing in parks.

We took a bus up into the mountains to the village of Igls. After a picnic lunch, we spent time in a tiny church that was intricately painted with cornices, pillars, and moldings. The artists took flat walls and made them appear to be three-dimensional, ornately decorated scenes. A tram took us through the forest back down the mountain to Innsbruck where we hiked to the Olympic ski jumping stadium. A wrong turn brought us to a hidden park just as the clouds cleared, the sun shone, and the children played and built fairy houses in the forest for over an hour. Back on the correct trail we reached the Olympic site and had an eagle's eye view of the city and mountains.

A great day of hiking means sweaty laundry. The Innsbruck Hostel apparently took cost cutting and money saving very seriously. They had not replaced any burnt out bulbs, there was no heat in the rooms, no hot water in the kitchen, and guests pay to use the stovetops. The clothes washer did not work and posted signs forbid washing in the sink. Bridget and I had but one option left. We washed clothes out in the shower, hung them to dry on the cold radiators and prayed they would be dry by morning. I felt it a silly prayer but I said it nonetheless. Despite freezing temperatures the clothes were dry by morning.

The next morning we had a crisp, pre-winter walk through the quiet streets to the train station. Not a word of complaint or a bit of whining from the kids as the scenery that surrounded us was unbelievable. The Austrian Alps were covered in snow. Some peaks, encircled in clouds, appeared like islands in the sky. Brilliant shafts of sunlight would cut through dark clouds while sudden breaks revealed sections of mountain looking like windows to heaven.

SWITZERLAND   18 September

The journey continued to Switzerland with some of the most awe-inspiring mountain scenery yet. Over sixty percent of Switzerland is the majestic Alps, but only ten percent of the population lives there. Our trip through them continued to be breathtaking. Fortunately, we were about the only ones in the train car. The "oohs", "ahs", and "wows" emanating from the family were accompanied by jumping up to plaster our faces against the windows to look down at the rivers and stare up at peaks or waterfalls. We were just thrilled at our children's wonderment of nature. Thomas Gray, an American Poet, saw the Alps for the first time in 1739 and reflected: "There are certain scenes that would awe an atheist into belief, without the help of other argument." Rolling past these inspiring mountains, we would have to agree. It is difficult not to

114

believe in God after visiting heaven. An odd contrast were the locals who sat reading papers or looking disinterested as we rode along, a bit amused by our excitement.

A few interesting tidbits about Switzerland, which is isolated not only geographically but in the Swiss people's political perspective as well: the country remained neutral in both World Wars, is not a member of the European Union and has refused to join the United Nations. On the other hand, it has been the headquarters of the International Red Cross for over 100 years and is the home of the World Health Organization; painting a confusing picture regarding their beliefs about globalization. Further, many Swiss have been influential in world philosophy, including Jean Piaget, Carl Jung, Jean Jacques Rousseau, and John Calvin, many of whom Steve is intimately familiar with in his Educational Psychology course at Willamette University. Recently, the famed, secretive Swiss banking industry reluctantly agreed to pay Holocaust survivors $1.2 billion in reparation for riches acquired during World War II.

We visited the tiny nation of Liechtenstein along the way (blink and you miss it) and then headed on to Zurich. That leg of the journey passed quickly as we enjoyed the company of a Miami Herald journalist, Robert. He did his best to update us on the situation in the States. The children inundated him with stories from their journeys. It was heartening to see them excited to tell about their adventures, particularly our mishaps. At some point, hopefully they will be willing and interested to tell stories of more significance, such as how a scene touched their hearts or influenced their perspective of people.

For some reason, Steve's camera was not taking daytime pictures well so he tried to find a way to get it fixed in Zurich. It turns out that they don't honor an American warranty and it would take 3 weeks to fix. So, we were not able to take daytime pictures. We opted to try to fix it in England, where we would be a bit more stationary. Not being able to photograph Switzerland, however, was like being dehydrated on the ocean; surrounded by water with an unquenched thirst.

Our destination was "Our Chalet" in Adelboden, Switzerland. This seventy-year old chalet is one of the four international Girl Scout/Guide houses in the world. It was the vision of an American woman named Helen Storrow. It had been a dream of mine all my life to visit it, which I did in college. What a thrill it was to stay there with my family 21 years later.

We had the most unforgettable, peaceful time there and a great deal of exercise on our hikes in the Alps. Two Scout moms from Wisconsin and Michigan were traveling Europe with four of their teenage Scout daughters and a friend. They became great companions to all of us. The kids did the "Our Chalet Challenge" with the older girls, some of which involved orienteering (finding directions with a compass), submerging up to their necks in a snow melt river, putting on a campfire program, and hiking a mountain before dawn to watch the sunrise. The campfire program was shared by all at the chalet, including a robust group of elderly Girl Guides from England and staff from Poland and Honduras. Steve and I accompanied the hike, but passed on the river dunk. All the girls were awarded a patch on our last night. The staff said no one had ever achieved it in three days before so the girls were understandably proud of their accomplishment.

The night hikes were spectacular, as there was no moon and the stars appeared close enough to grab. The constant ringing of cowbells was music to our ears and the fresh mountain air intoxicating. We had an eerie feeling of not being in reality, but in some set of postcards or a coffee table book as we walked amongst the majestic mountains. No one wanted to leave Our Chalet. Who would? Some places and experiences become written on your soul and stamped "must return." Such was the case with Our Chalet and our next destination, Taize, France.

FRANCE   21 September

Two buses and two trains landed us in central France, the middle of wine country, in Taize. In the summer, 6000 people

116

a day, young and old, from countries throughout the world, make their pilgrimage to Taize for a week or weekend of "simplicity and kindheartedness." For 60 years, they have come to hear Brother Roger's message of reconciliation among people. Brother Roger began by providing refuge to Jews and others during World War II and then by taking care of German soldiers after the war. This was quite controversial in his community, of course, but over the years, served to establish him as a leader in bringing peace in the world. You may be familiar with Taize songs, used all over the world for church services.

We were fortunate to be there in the off-season with only 500 guests. On the bus trip in we met Wilma, a friendly South African Anglican priest. She had been going to Taize for years and was a wealth of information and a grand companion for the weekend. During a stay at Taize, the day revolves around contemplative prayer and music three times a day. Individuals choose to attend the prayer service in the main chapel, play at the playground, sit around and chat with young and old from around the world, or walk to the lake. We did all of these.

Meals were very simple, but delicious. A permanent tent was erected on the grounds where everyone stood in lines to be served soup in a small plastic bowl. If one desired a drink of tea, coffee or warm milk the same bowl served as a cup. Why waste the water to wash extra dishes? Serving and cleanup was performed by volunteers and visitors alike.

There were also large group lessons led by the brothers and small group discussions led by volunteers that centered around the theme of reconciliation and bringing peace to your community. The events of September 11th put a fresh perspective on biblical verses and the discussion of reconciliation.

The biggest highlight was Saturday's international celebration. The young volunteer staff (who spent two weeks to three months working there) presented a fantastic show of song and dance from Africa, Philippines, Argentina, Chile, El Salvador, and India. The heart-rending song and dance finale united 100 young people in native dress from more countries

117

than we could count. It nearly brought me to tears as an example of hope for peace. I have to believe that if it could be so there, on that micro scale, it was a start that could spread outside the Taize community.

The weekend passed all too quickly. On Sunday, we took a long walk with Wilma through the neighboring villages. Nothing has changed with time. Stone and brick buildings with slate tile roofs looked to be centuries old. The kids loved Taize and want to return because they met so many wonderful people. It is hard to explain to them that the same volunteer staff will not be there, but the feeling of quiet serenity, fun, and kindness will.

It was a very different experience to go from the peaceful closeness of rural Taize to the "official" holy place of Lourdes. This is the town in southern France where Mary appeared to young Bernadette. In one of Bernadette's visions, Mary pointed to a spot on the ground and told Bernadette to dig. A miracle spring emerged there that still flows today and draws pilgrims from all over the world seeking healing. When Steve was there twenty years ago, about thirty crutches hung from a line above the spring, implying the many healings that had taken place there. For some reason, when we visited, there was only one hanging there.

Clare and I braved the cold waters of "the baths" which have been constructed to help people make use of Bernadette's spring for healing. It was a very quick and abrupt process of stepping into a small room, stripping down to your birthday suit, being wrapped in a freezing wet cloth to save some shred of modesty and then getting dunked by two women. Hundreds of people come to do this every day of the year. The entire experience was disappointing, devoid of any feeling of warmth, caring or spirituality. If there is a fast food of religious experiences, that was it.

I've never seen so many wheelchairs, gurneys, nuns, and nurses in one place. Hundreds of people with practically every disability seemed to be there. The daily procession of the sick is a solemn and emotional occasion. The nightly candlelight procession gathered thousands of people for prayers that were led in many different languages. Those moments were very inspirational. Still, the seemingly wall-to-wall glitzy souvenir shops detracted from the sacredness of the town. You can buy everything from Virgin Mary golf balls to ashtrays. With the massive crowds and tacky religious items, it was difficult to find the same spiritual serenity there that we found in Taize. Nevertheless, it is a nice small town and a fascinating place to witness the daily gathering of people longing for healing.

SPAIN   26 September

Barcelona, Spain is fairly close to Lourdes and became our next stop. It is the second largest city in Spain, behind Madrid, with 1.5 million people. Spain's history is an interesting one of vast imperialism similar to other European nations, as is evident in most of the America's using the Spanish language. For those of you in the states who have visited Mexico, Spain has an extremely different feel to it. Barcelona is a very European city with similar architecture and grandeur. The Catalan Spanish spoken in Barcelona, requires people to speak with a slight lisp. Rumor has it that a king many years ago had a lisp, so he made all his subjects pronounce "s" sounds with "th." Accordingly, people will tell you they are from "Barthelona."

It was a glorious sunny afternoon when we arrived and began walking in search of the tourist information office. We walked a good distance only to find that it had been relocated to a place we had passed nearly an hour previous. After taking two metros the children and I parked on a bench in the underground with our gear while Steven went above for a map and directions. Watching the trains come and go and the people getting off and on passed the time easily until a gentleman came up to us and motioned for me to scoot our packs so he could sit down. Not that we were taking up all the available bench space, there was a good forty feet of it, he just seemed to want to sit in that particular spot.

I noticed his long pants were soaked as if he had either spilled something all over him or had not made it to a toilet in

119

time. The smell suggested the latter to be true. He began blabbering incoherently so that I couldn't figure out what language he was speaking. I couldn't tell if he was talking to me so I kept watching the children and the trains. The children were visibly nervous about his presence, as was I. Finally, he threw his coke bottle on the floor at my feet spraying three of our sleeping bags. I looked at him and he kept talking. "I'm sorry, I don't understand," I said in vain. He went through what sounded like a list, "Espanol? Frances? Ingles?"

"English," I said. That seemed to calm him down a bit as if to realize that I wasn't ignoring him, just couldn't understand. Which was half true: I couldn't understand but I wasn't giving him attention because he was scary, not in his right mind, I had the children, and we were alone on that platform. The entire time I kept praying and hoping that with the constant coming and going of the metro someone would see him and help him who spoke his language. Not knowing what else to do I offered him an apple. He showed me that he had no teeth. "I'm sorry," I said in English.

He went on about I know not what then picked up the bottle he had thrown, drank from it then hurled it across the floor. As he stood there in front of me he offered his hand. I took it to shake a good-bye. He then kissed my hand and started to walk away. I silently prayed for him and for our safety. Turning again he offered me a cigarette. "I don't smoke," I said in English. He returned a smirk that said, "Of course you don't," then settled himself further down from us. Trains came and went. He didn't get on. When he was finally out of sight I cleaned up his mess and we moved to a different bench and prayed that Steven would return soon. Once we felt safe again and the adrenaline stopped pumping through my veins I recalled the many parables about Jesus appearing in the form of a child, a homeless person, an addict in need—all in answer to the question "Who is my neighbor?" If that man had been Christ, had I done right by him? Is the same behavior expected of us if we are scared to death by this person's presence and don't speak his language? There is nothing like traveling to constantly humble a person and challenge your resolve to put your faith in action.

While Vienna is a city devoted to the performing arts, Barcelona is a city devoted to the visual arts. Picasso began studying art here when he was 14 years old, and they have a museum dedicated to his works. We spent three days on our feet combing the city and marveling at the original genius of the architect and artist Gaudi. His work is very striking, eccentric, unique, and surreal and has left an imprint on many buildings in Barcelona. You should look on the Internet for a picture of Casa Milá, built from 1905-1910, or Casa Batló when you get a chance. One of his most interesting buildings is the unfinished "Templo de la Sagrada Familia" which our family dubbed the "sand castle church" because that is exactly what it looks like—drips of wet sand piled high to create multiple spires. Gaudi began building it in 1884 and was only one fourth of the way through it when he died in 1926. It continues to be built today.

It was nice being able to speak a bit of Spanish. Traveling in foreign countries and being ignorant of the language certainly created a distance between the locals and us. So here in Spain, we were able to bridge that gap somewhat with our feeble Spanish. I think people anywhere appreciate it when you at least try to speak their language.

Barcelona is a grand city with regal arches and fountains. One of my favorite memories in Barcelona was the kids' new games they made up to make the miles pass by quickly as we walked. In one game, they ran ahead of us to a bench or wall. Then they proceeded to sit down, pose and wait for Steve and me to catch up to them. All of them had one leg crossed over the other in the same direction, chins resting on hands with an elbow on one knee, and a foot bouncing impatiently. They counted and then all switched in unison as we approached and then they ran ahead and did it again. Another game they played was to run ahead and hide somewhere. Steve and I tried to sneak up to them, but they would see us and run ahead a bit more and hide again. Each one of them contributed to the craziness. They are so creative. Next destination, Italy.

121

"It is impossible to travel faster than light,
and certainly not desirable,
as one's hat keeps blowing off."
Woody Allen, Actor and Director

PHILOSOPHY 101: *The Wall*

Three months, 12 days, 9 hours and 38 minutes into our trip and we have hit the proverbial "wall." As we finish our time in Barcelona, we are totally burned out. Tired of running from bus to train, hostel to hotel, church to big famous building full of important history. To think we have four months or so left. I expected this moment would come. I had just hoped that it would be later, when the end was in sight, not in the middle. Then again, I also knew that these two months through Europe would be our most hectic, with lots of changes in where we are staying, different languages, and hours on trains, buses, and subways.

Now what? Can we climb over this hurdle and regain our enthusiasm? There is just too much to take in and a finite amount of energy to delegate to moving our legs and filling our memory banks with the sights and sounds. Before the trip we often discussed whether it would be better to go to one country and stay for six months to a year or visit as much of the world as we could. Variety obviously won out. The price we pay now is schizophrenia and the "If it's Tuesday, it must be Belgium" mindset. What city are we in again? "I'm sorry, I didn't mean to give you French Francs for that Italian pizza." "Is this Déjà vu? That castle sure looks like one we have seen before."

We need to make a conscious effort to spend more time playing in parks, not filling each day from morning to night, and staying a day or two longer in one place. It is not such an evil to stay in our hostel/hotel until 10 a.m. now and then. We decide to eliminate a few days of our European expedition and head for our "home" in England early. It will be nice to stay at Mary Kate and Bill's house for a few days to rejuvenate before our trek to Africa.

ITALY   29 September

The terrorist attacks on the United States and subsequent war in Afghanistan clearly had reverberations throughout the world. Just two days before we arrived in Rome the State Department issued a warning to Americans not to visit Italy. Oh well ... we hoped they were being overcautious. As we traveled throughout Europe, the security at train stations steadily increased. National Guard type people with machine guns wandered about, occasionally stopping Arab-looking people for questioning. As Steve sported his new beard and regularly looked disheveled, he certainly qualified for suspicious looking, but seemed to escape scrutiny.

The disparity between news coverage was interesting. USA Today sold in Europe seemed to focus on healing and patriotic types of things, impact on the U.S. economy, etc. Meanwhile, European cities' newspapers talked in great detail about the bombing that was taking place, how many soldiers were being deployed where and when, and highlighted points such as a Red Cross building being bombed twice in the last couple of weeks or how the war was pushing terrorism into Africa. Most Europeans we talked to were very skeptical about the war. Yet, nobody had any better ideas of how to respond to such a brutal attack. Many were very empathetic, coming from countries where terrorism and war has been an on-going, tragic reality. As one young man whispered softly, "I'm so sorry for your country. We have dealt with terrorism for decades." Some spoke of our country's need to maintain "respect", others of a need for reconciliation. As a counselor, my gut reaction was that the U.S. government should sit down with the opposing parties and talk it out. I think we were all confused about what is the right thing to do to stop terrorism, but were not confident that all the deaths in Afghanistan would accomplish its purpose. I believe war is not the answer. War begets war.

I have always thought of Italy as one of the great cultural places in the world. They have such a rich history of sculptors, musicians, painters, and architects. The names of Michelangelo, da Vinci, Raphael, and so many others beckoned us to see their works. What they lack in natural resources, they make up for in talent, I guess. Two-thirds of Italy is mountainous and it generally doesn't have the best climate, so agriculture has a difficult time of it. The exception seems to be wine making, as Italy, the world leader, produces about 1.5 billion gallons of wine each year--slightly more than France. The land is also rich in building stone, most notably with marble, which perhaps accounts for the many priceless works of art sculpted by its native sons. We looked forward to exploring all that Italy had to offer.

Our expedition to Italy began on an overnight train with four changes. We had to choose between a 10 a.m. or 7 p.m. departure from Barcelona. Due to recent bomb threats and heightened security throughout Europe, rental lockers were no longer an option in train stations and airports, which certainly put a damper on our traveling. Rather than hang out all day in Spain with our gear, we decided to jump on the morning train. En route to Padua, Italy, we arrived at Cerbere, on the coast of France, just missing the next train. It was 12:30 in the afternoon and the next connection was at 11:50 p.m. Time to be optimistic!

We took our gear down to the tiny beach town to spend the rest of the day and evening. The children had a fantastic time simply playing in the sand and water while collecting polished rocks and sea glass. With free toilets and water nearby, our happiness was complete. Steve and I took turns watching the children and gear so the other could take a long walk. The town was windy, cold, empty, and just what we needed to rejuvenate our energy level: a nothing day.

After tasty Chinese food (in France, no less) for dinner, we were back at the train station. While we waited, the girls got some schoolwork done and Michael slept in my lap. It was a definite challenge trying to stay awake until the train arrived and there were no guarantees of finding seats. We got lucky again, however, and slept until our connection in Ventimiglia, Italy at 8:36 a.m., just in time to jump on the next train to Milan. There was no time to call the next youth hostel to see if they had space. Ironically, after rushing for that train it then sat in the station for an hour. Officials never gave any explanations. Italians have great patience, I guess. The train finally headed out, but stopped in the middle of nowhere for two hours getting us in to Milan extremely late. The next train to Padua was very full, so we had to separate in different cabins. The kids had a joyful time with a family from California while Steve and I were on our own in cabins near by. As we traveled we could hear their voices and laughter echoing down the halls of the train. It was very encouraging to hear them talk of our adventures with enthusiasm. The train left Milan an hour late.

Padua station appeared at 7:45 p.m. By that time, there were no hostel openings. After wasting coins calling hotels (that no longer exist) from our five-year old, Lonely Planet guide, we decided to go on to Verona, where they had room for us. We reached Verona at 10:20 p.m. and waited for the bus to the hostel. Angel #1 of this trip appeared out of nowhere, (speaking English!).

"Are you going to the youth hostel?"

"Yes."

"Then you are at the wrong bus stop. You should be at the one across the street."

Thanking him, we crossed the street, looked back, and he was gone. At the bus stop we met a very sweet couple from São Paulo, Brazil (Angels #2-3) who led us to the hostel through many winding streets and turns. I doubt we would have ever found it without them. Bedtime came near midnight in a gorgeous old Italian villa. So much for decreasing our running around!

Up at 8 a.m. for the hostel breakfast of 2 rolls (included in the price). Not being coffee or tea drinkers or into hot whole milk (served in a bowl and eaten like soup)—we did not have anything to drink. Grumbling tummies aside, we were out of the hostel by 9 a.m. to explore Verona—a place full of surprises. An ancient neighborhood church was close by, so we attended mass in Italian before strolling the cobblestone streets. There is something comforting about mass being the same everywhere in the world. Even when you don't know the language, it is fairly easy to follow along, although the kids did get bored easily (then again they get bored when it's in English, too).

Did you know that Romeo and Juliet was a true story? Juliet's two-story house sits shoulder to shoulder with other villas in downtown Verona. Passing through an archway you enter the Capulet's courtyard and stand under the famous balcony. It is sad to report that the place is nearly covered with "lovers' graffiti" which Verona has apparently permitted. It detracts from the antiquity and special aura of the place.

After a full day of walking all over Verona we jumped on a train back to Padua. With hostel reservations secured, we felt safe, even if the train was late. We got to Padua in the early afternoon, and after a bit of wandering about, asking directions every 100 feet or so (mixing Spanish and English we seemed to get by), we finally arrived at our hostel. We unloaded our gear and decided to take the short train ride to Venice for dinner at a sidewalk pizzeria. Traveling five on a budget we made constant decisions about experiences to invest in, or not, and compromises that could help to stretch our lire while still affording memories. After dinner we opted for a one-way taxi boat ride on the Grand Canal and a nice (long) walk back to the station. The only way to see Venice is to walk her cobblestone streets. The city was enchanting at night and the weather balmy.

The walk back was a bit further than we expected, and, in spite of running the last few blocks, we still missed the train to Padua. No problem: another train left in half an hour. Problem: that train didn't get in to Padua until 11:10 and the hostel is locked at 11 p.m. Steve called the hostel manager. The same exhausted chap had been on duty for two days straight. He told us he would wait for us as long as we skipped the bus and took a taxi as soon as our train got in because he wanted to lock up and get some rest. It was a more expensive option, but natural consequences for our bad behavior and timing.

The next day the same man told us that we could easily walk the 2 km back to the train station. He must not have gotten the rest he so needed because his calculations were a bit off. Two hours and about 10 km later we had had a great walk through the city, seeing the sights of Padua and caught the 11 a.m. train to Venice to see it in a different light, literally. Venice is such a unique city with only walking streets and boat canals. There are no cars anywhere, just numerous interesting shops and colorful buildings. However, I am probably the only person in the world who has gone to Venice and not felt comfortable about being surrounded by water. It just looks so unnatural to me to have front doors right at the water's edge, as if the entire town is flooded. We made the afternoon train back to Padua, had dinner at a great pizza place near our hostel and looked forward to Assisi.

Before leaving early the next morning we visited the Cathedral of St. Anthony (patron saint of lost people or things--I invoke his name frequently on Steve's behalf). Besides being an impressive structure and burial place of the saint it has become a pilgrimage site for people all over the world. His tomb is nearly covered with photos. Whether they are dead, kidnapped or missing there are prayers to St. Anthony for lost loved ones as well as prayers of thanksgiving for those found. It was intensely sobering to see so many pictures of children and babies. One woman was missing her five children. I couldn't help but wonder what had happened in the lives of all those people--the lost, the found, the searching--and praying for their wishes to be fulfilled.

Throughout our travels we were very flexible about changing plans, trains, hostels, cities or even countries at the last minute. Sometimes it was something as simple as there not being any rooms available in one place that would force us to a new location we'd never even heard of; like Lucca. Florence was full so we landed in this small medieval town that quickly became one of our favorites. After walking the quiet streets of Lucca to our hostel, we decided to race back to the train station so we could see nearby Pisa at night. Jumping on the train as it rolled away, we realized our Eurail pass had been left back at the hostel. Hoping the conductor would be kind, believe us, and let us stay, we sat anxiously in our seats. An angel appeared in the form of a very good-natured conductor who understood enough English to get the gist of our story. Now we just had to get back from Pisa. The famous leaning tower looked surreal with the rose-colored lights illuminating it against the dark night. It is so hard to comprehend its tilt even when you stand next to it—buildings are just not supposed to look like that!

The following day we were finally on our way to Assisi. The Italian trains are second only to the Egyptian trains in being the worst in the world; run down, dirty, graffitied, and consistently late. Many of the trains have toilet doors with very questionable locks. You often have to choose between risking being locked in for good or being walked in on by a stranger. We had to switch trains in Florence to get to Assisi. Some of the trains only stop for a matter of seconds so you need to be at the door ready to jump out when it reaches the platform. Two minutes before we got in to the Assisi station we grabbed our bags and headed for the door. I looked around and we seemed to be missing something...

"Where's Michael?" I ask Bridget and Clare.

"He's in the bathroom."

"But he left five minutes ago!" I rush down the aisle to the bathroom. "Michael, we've got to go!"

With a combination of anger and terror he calls out, "I'm locked in!"

I knew his frustration because earlier I had had difficulty with the lock. Frantically pushing and pulling from both sides, we tried to set him free. Fortunately, the train stopped a few blocks from the platform for a few minutes (for some unknown reason, Angel #?), giving him time to escape before we had to jump off. I held him close to calm him down and we got off the train. Just one more for the list of close calls.

It is so funny to get an image of a place in your head from an old movie ("Brother Sun, Sister Moon") and then finally go there. Maybe because Salzburg has still maintained its charm or because Adelboden is as quaint as it was 21 years ago, I expected Assisi to be a lovely mountain village surrounded by spacious rolling hills. Well, it was still lovely and a medieval wonder, but what a shock to my romantic system to get off the train and be assaulted with the sight of a huge McDonald's next to the train station.

Unexpectedly, we were just in time for the feast of St. Francis. Oct. 3rd was the 775th anniversary of St. Francis' death. Pilgrims and tourists like us were pouring in from all corners of the globe. We took a bus up to the ancient stone and brick city and got off at the main exterior gate. The hostel was down the hill outside the city.

Steve: "Let's check in at the hostel and then explore the city."

Toby: "Fine."

After a bit of misdirection, we finally arrive at the hostel.

Steve: "We'd like to get a room for five."

Staff: "Could I see your passport please?"

Steve explores pockets in his pants, jacket, and backpack. "Uh, Toby, I don't suppose you have my passport…"

Toby: "No."

Steve: "Then it is hopefully waiting patiently for me on my nightstand in Lucca."

Lucca was a five-hour train ride away. Thankfully, the hostel manager allowed us to stay and we made plans for Steve to spend the day riding trains back and forth to Lucca to retrieve his passport. A quick phone call back to the Lucca hostel staff resulted in them finding his passport and leaving it at the desk to be rescued.

In spite of that setback, our first night in Assisi was memorable with a picnic on the fountain steps near San Rufino, the church in which Francis and Clare were baptized as children. Unexpectedly, a crowd began to gather and we were treated to a thrilling display of flag throwing and choreography done to drum and herald trumpets. The highlight was one member jumping over the other eleven while spinning his large flag below him before landing.

The children and I spent the next day walking around the city and visiting the various sights from the lives of the two saints while Steve journeyed all the way back to Lucca. An extremely knowledgeable Franciscan invited us to tour the artwork of San Francesco. The city was still recovering from the big earthquake four years ago but San Francesco (St. Francis) and San Ciara (St. Clare) cathedrals were repaired. His art lesson was enlightening: the general public of the age was illiterate so the artists used eyes, hands, specific colors and the settings to tell the story without words. Hand gestures depicted rage, blessing or acceptance. Eyes on one panel looked to another panel foretelling the future. The children were most impressed that Giotto (the fresco artist) kept the location of Francis' burial a secret by depicting all the right people in the wrong place. Steven rejoined us by 5 p.m. and we went back up to the city again for an evening walk. The view of the valley from up there was probably just as picturesque as it was 800 years ago.

Assisi was fascinating, peaceful, and a good place to recharge before heading to Rome: the New York City of Italy. Rome is noisy. People walked very quickly on the crowded sidewalks and took their lives in their hands crossing the streets where the cars all seem to be in a huge hurry to get somewhere. It was very clean for a big city and lacked the huge skyscrapers of New York, so you didn't feel so hemmed in. On a city bus we witnessed our first real pickpocket attempt. It was very unnerving to watch darling little girls, younger than ours, work in a group to rob passengers. One attempt was thwarted when the young woman caught them in the act and yelled at them until they returned her Italian translation guide. An odd thing to steal, but I guess they want just about anything.

Naturally, we were there to take in the historical sights and saturate our brains with history. The catacombs are fascinating, the Colosseum gruesome and sad. It was such a huge, elaborate, ingenious feat of architecture--all for the purpose of killing people and animals for entertainment. The Vatican and museum are enormous. The Sistine Chapel is impressive, although the crowds made it a bit of work to see. It was unreal to see how much wealth the Catholic Church had used over the centuries for artistic purposes. Catholicism was the official national religion in Italy until 1984, so the Catholic Church has had much support over the centuries to build ornate churches and amass artistic riches. On the one hand, you could admire the collection and appreciate the church supporting the arts. On the other, they acquired all that wealth from the people and squandered it on frills instead of meeting the people's needs. This fact left us with mixed emotions as we walked for hours through exquisite artistic pieces. So many impressive works of art were gathered in Rome that it felt incredibly liberating when, as we walked back to the pensione, Steve suggested a walk to one more, big famous fountain and we all said, "Forget it!" We really didn't have to see everything in every place, even if we never intended to revisit.

PHILOSOPHY 101: *email*

Communication during travel has certainly been revolutionized with email. One dollar a minute phone calls are now unnecessary to keep in touch with loved ones. The Internet is available to us in even the remotest parts of the world, such as on an island off the coast of Malaysia. It is great for us to be able to maintain contact with our friends and family cheaply (ranging from $0.75-$6.00 an hour). I'm sure that we would not have nearly the amount of contact we would have otherwise. Our twice-monthly newsletters can instantly go out to one hundred people to let them know how things are going. Instead of only being able to stay in touch with a handful of people, just about everyone we know is able to get some word about our adventures and tribulations.

On the other hand, it seems to be a much less personal way of communication. We have only sent a few postcards, whereas we might have sent quite a few without electronic access to people. Someone's voice is certainly much more intimate than typing on the screen. Every keyboard in the world has been different, with unique characters and placement of letters in different places. Messages to people are often agonizingly slow to type out. Then there is the inevitable computer crash to add to the fun.

Communication with people during this time of uneasiness in the United States, due to the September tragedy, has been particularly unsettling at times. Paul, one of my closest friends, wrote me about our newsletter being insensitive to the events in the United States. His words truly struck me regarding our inability to really comprehend the atmosphere in the states and deep fears people harbor due to terrorism. To Paul, it appeared that we were off having adventures while people at home struggle to make sense of an historic catastrophe. People have died, terrorism is on the mind of every American and we are telling stories of fun and frolic. The country is in mourning and we aren't wearing black.

What he didn't know was that our newsletter had been written well before 11 September when the world as we knew it was still "normal." We wrote a brief paragraph at the beginning about the tragic attacks then the pre-written letter followed. Clearly that did not capture the immensity of the moment. While safety has constantly been in our minds on this trip, a whole different perspective of safety in the United States is being formed in our absence. Email messages from Paul and others about people's state of mind in the country are often difficult to read and respond to, as emotions cannot adequately be conveyed or be interpreted from the screen. In the days to come, our challenge is to understand two perspectives of the tragedy simultaneously.

There certainly is an email culture that exists with people who are traveling. As we enter an Internet café, we typically enter into a community of travelers with the common bond of missing friends and family. At the same time, as silly as it may sound, we try not to look like tourists as we travel about. We are particularly aware of the label "Americans" in a world where some now look upon us with empathetic sadness while others look at us as targets. Walking into an Internet café seems to reveal our secret identity.

Significantly unnerving for me was a time when I sat in a café in Italy emailing people at home next to a youth who was reading his email and the news in Arabic. As I occasionally glanced over at his screen, Arabic writing and images of the war in Afghanistan flashed by as well as cartoons and doctored photographs of the Statue of Liberty and President Bush that implied his anti-American perspective. Was he a person to fear or have an interesting conversation with? I decided to err on the side of safety and slipped out as soon as I could.

In the end, I'm unsure whether email and the influence of technology has been a good resource or an impersonal mode of communication that has not done justice to the depth and intensity of emotions we or our friends and family have experienced this year. It will be interesting to have face-to-face discussions with people when we return.

FRANCE   9 October

After four days in Rome it was another overnight train, this time to Paris. We shared a sleeper coachette (6 bunks in one room—3 on each side) with a sweet Italian woman. Clare entertained Michael and Bridget from across the bunks by doing hand puppet shows. Based on stereotypes, we braced ourselves for obnoxious people and a busy city. Both presumptions proved false. The people we met were very friendly and Paris was filled with trees and wide, spacious streets.

The weather in Paris was a breath of cool, fresh air after Italy. I don't know how our bodies coped with the constant change of weather. After nearly 4 months of travel, we had been blessed with great health. We watched an afternoon storm then headed out to walk the city for the evening. The Eiffel Tower at night was more striking than during the day.

Brilliant lights bathed it in a way that gave the dark steel a peculiar glow that seemed supernatural. We walked a good five hours, mostly in search of toilets or a place to buy food, then went to bed. The next day was filled with the famous Louvre Museum and the Tin Tin Exhibit at the small Maritime Museum. Tin Tin is a comic strip by Herge that Michael loves. Herge, the French author, was a humorous man who loved the sea. His humor was very evident in the exhibition. Tin Tin, a young journalist, is the hero of his adventures.

Our tight budget made us keep an eye peeled for "deals" whenever possible. After standing in the very long line to enter the Louvre, we encountered the museum billboard announcing a reduced entrance rate after 3:00. Okay then, off to Tin Tin first. By the time we arrived back at the Louvre the museum employees had gone on strike so entrance to the world famous establishment was free! Wow! Four hours later, as we approached the exit the strike was called off and it again cost a pretty penny to enjoy the museum. Things seemed to balance out in that way throughout the trip.

During our travels through the city we also came upon the tunnel where Princess Diana was killed. There are still memorials and fresh flowers put there by admirers. The overpass was covered with messages from people all over the world who never met her in person but felt a connection all the same. How profound for one person to have a universal effect on so many. The world does not seem so large sometimes.

I have no idea how many foot miles we logged over this European segment. At this point in Paris, we all counted the hours until our return to England. We were ready to just be in one place with Mary Kate, Bill, and the kids for a few days before heading to Africa. We were at the halfway point on this odyssey and quite concerned about the state of the world. Being out in the world, ironically, often isolated us from news of what was going on in the U.S. and the Middle East. That was both a relief and frightening at the same time. Sentiments toward Americans were fluctuating. We tried to keep a low profile, prayed constantly for peace and that we would make it home safely.

"The journey is difficult, immense.
We will travel as far as we can,
but we cannot in one lifetime
see all that we would like to see
or to learn all that we hunger to know."
Loren Eiseley, Writer and Anthropologist

I'LL BE FINE
UNDER THE TREE...

<u>KENYA</u>   16 October

Jambo! (Greetings! In Swahili) Our African adventure began with an overnight flight from London to Nairobi, Kenya. The British Airways terminal was hauntingly quiet in London and, as this was our first flight since 11 September, we were very anxious. Inside the terminal seats were empty, shops were empty, and there were no long lines for the women's bathroom so we were shocked to find the plane full. I could not help glancing at our fellow passengers and wondering... We landed safely, without incident, and thanked God. After $100 for transit visas into Kenya and a taxi ride to the Norfolk Hotel it was time to enjoy the people and landscape of East Africa. October is springtime and the jacaranda trees were brilliant purple, the acacia were crowned with leaves, and flowers bloomed everywhere. It was quite a contrast to the otherwise brown earth. The Tudor style Norfolk Hotel is the oldest in Nairobi. It was a calm place to wait the four hours for our shuttle to Tanzania.

Once again, a trip we booked six months earlier had materialized. While our inclination is to do everything ourselves, Steve's research into safaris revealed that families with kids under 8 years old could not go into the national parks without guides. Pair that with the uncertainties of Africa and we opted to find a company to help with the details. There are 115 safari companies in Tanzania and Thomson Family Adventures is the only one we encountered who was willing to take young children. It would be our most expensive part of the trip, but would prove to be well worth the assistance.

Our first challenge was catching the right shuttle. Instructions were that we would meet our 2 p.m. shuttle to Arusha at the hotel and "the driver will have your names upon boarding." Unfortunately, there were a few shuttles that came by and each driver seemed to think that we might be on his shuttle. We passed the first one by, but opted for the second because we didn't want to be stranded. The driver let us on in good faith that Thomson would pay him, as we had paid them in advance for the ride to Arusha, Tanzania. That choice turned out to be fortuitous because on that shuttle was a young man named Michael who was on his way to climb Kilimanjaro.

•   •   •   •   •

A few hours of traveling through the desolate countryside and we arrive at the border between Kenya and Tanzania. Steve goes in to pay the $50 per person visa fees.

"I'm sorry sir, but we don't take credit cards or traveler's cheques."

"Is there anywhere near here I can get cash?"

"Not that I know of."

The nearest bank is over one hundred miles away.

Steve comes back to the shuttle.

"I don't suppose anyone on here would have $250 in cash that we could borrow?"

Silence.

Steve searches the eyes of everyone on board for any vulnerability. It's like a teacher asking that difficult question in class nobody wants to answer. People are looking out the window, looking at the floor, etc. Needless to say, they are a bit annoyed with us, as everyone wants to get going. One *young man looks up briefly and meets Steve's eyes. Like a deer in the headlights, he is caught. Steve looks desperate enough for him to act. Michael just happens to have $255 in cash on him for us to borrow all but $5. Our trip angels are working overtime here. He nervously, but generously consents and as soon as we get into Arusha we head for a bank. Oddly, they only have $5 bills, so we repay Michael's faithful generosity with fifty $5 bills and repeated thanks.*

Note to future travelers: carry green backs to the borders! And forget about American Express. We temporarily invested in it just for the trip and it carried no privileges whatsoever. Thank goodness for Visa.

• • • • •

The five-hour trip from Nairobi to Arusha was on a bumpy road in a vehicle with little or no shocks. We passed dry, brushy ground with tabletop acacia trees, palms, cactus, and gum trees. Some areas looked desolate while others looked almost forested, with hundreds of trees, but spaced out enough to remind you it was a desert. There was a lonely beauty to East Africa. Viewed from a window, it was hard not to feel like we were watching it all on National Geographic. Herds of cows, goats, camels, and gazelles completed the picture. The bouncy shuttle trip prepared us for a true game drive. We had no idea what was in store for our bums.

TANZANIA   17 October

In 1964 a rebellion on the island of Zanzibar, off the eastern coast of Africa, threatened to destabilize the region. The governments of Zanzibar and Tanganyika (the mainland) decided to join the countries to form Tanzania in order to quell the Zanzibar revolution. Tanzania is one country in name only, as they remain essentially separate, with different judicial and political systems. The people, however, are very proud of their country and over the course of our time here we learned many songs proclaiming that pride. Since 1964, Tanzania has moved to the forefront of African liberation movements with such

137

actions as helping to overthrow Idi Amin and ending white rule in Zimbabwe. Arusha, our first stop in Tanzania, was chosen as the site for the United Nations tribunal to examine war crimes during the genocide in Rwanda.

The Great Rift Valley in Africa is the largest visible valley on earth, formed by a geological fault. It extends 4,000 miles from the Dead Sea in the north to Mozambique in the south. The rift ranges from 20-50 miles wide and is still slowly widening, causing scientists to believe that Africa may split into two continents within a few million years. The walls of the valley average about 2,500 feet but rise to as much as 9,000 feet. The wildlife in this valley is unmatched anywhere else in the world, which is what brought us to this wondrous place.

The first two nights of the expedition were spent at the Impala Hotel in Arusha. Far too nice for our standards, especially after seeing how the real residents live on our travel here: homes as small as the bathroom of our hotel room. Tanzania is one of the world's least developed countries. A typical Tanzanian home is built from whatever people can afford: sticks and mud, mud bricks, or cement bricks with thatching or corrugated tin for rooftops with no electricity or running water. In some homes, the family cow and goats have their own room to insure against theft or being killed by wild animals. This is the way the majority of people in Tanzania live, particularly in the rural areas, but often in the cities as well.

Our Thomson guide, William, met us the first night in Arusha and became our constant companion, teacher, camp counselor, naturalist, big brother, and historian for the duration of our trip. A native Tanzanian with 21 years experience as a guide, there wasn't a question he could not answer. We met our driver, Richard, the next morning as we climbed into the huge old British Bedford army truck. It was designed to seat eighteen, but with our timing during the low season and cancellations due to the attack on the United States, we had William, Richard, and John (our cook) all to ourselves. The open-sided truck became our daytime roving classroom, playground, and observation deck for 12 days. The crew quickly became like family.

First stop, Sakila village and Sakila Primary School. Here we had the first indication that we had chosen a quality company with a conscience. With each passing day we saw examples of Thomson's compassion for the people and wildlife of Tanzania. Sakila School serves three villages and 900 children, kindergarten to seventh grade. We often fight for small class sizes in Oregon schools. In Sakila, they had 60 students in a first grade classroom, while 112 were in the seventh grade classroom. These are typical class sizes even though only fifty percent of eligible children in Tanzania are enrolled in school.

Former Thomson Safari goers initiated an organization called "Friends of Tanzania" to support Tanzanian schools through Thomson. With their support, Thomson built seven new, sturdy, brick and cement schoolrooms for Sakila. It was clear from our later travels through Tanzania and Kenya that this school was pretty unique, and fortunate to be getting the help.

I wish I could capture in words the reception we found as we climbed out of the truck. Children came running from all over the school grounds. They all wanted to touch us and shake our hands. It was as if we were celebrities of some kind. Was it our funny pale skin? Were they accustomed to Thomson Safaris, and knew this was where the new school came from? Were they just thrilled to have visitors? With their words coming to us in Swahili, answers to those questions remained a mystery.

Sakila was a peasant village. The children were all so thin. They walk from 1 to 6 miles to get to the school by 7 a.m. Most don't have lunch there, but play soccer instead. They walk back home at 2:30. The young girls will leave large empty buckets on the way to school then fill them with water and carry them home on their heads. The principal, Mr. Andrew, explained that teachers can't give homework because children have no time to do it. As soon as they get home they must tend to animals, work in the fields, and take care of

139

younger siblings. Great facts to use on our kids when they don't want to do their chores at home! Were they attentive to how kids their age lived very different lives here? Michael remembers, "They didn't have very good bathrooms."

We were ushered to the new computer center, an empty room consisting of a cement floor, cinder block walls and a few benches. No electricity, no computers. Because of Thomson's outside support they were expecting it to be filled and working soon. In the meantime, it became a concert hall where we were sung to by the school's a cappella choir. A student led them in great harmony and an African beat. After the concert we had a chance to speak with the children through a translator. Each of our kids had established pen pals with the help of Thomson. In a small ceremony, their pen pals came up and shook hands to introduce themselves. Connecting a face to the letters from previous months was very touching.

With William translating I asked the children of the school about their future dreams. They didn't understand my question so I asked if any of them knew what they'd like to be when they got older. Long pause. These were peasant children living in a rural village. Finally one raised her hand and said in English, "a doctor." Several said "a teacher" and one "a police." Thinking back on those moments and our whole trip to that point, I realized that if life is about being the best person you possibly can be, these children were already doing it. They worked hard in a school that didn't come close to standards in the United States. In spite of the challenges that were obviously before them, many had ambitions of helping other people.

After visiting two other classrooms, our children joined in a soccer game (about 30 kids to a side on a dirt field). It was a great icebreaker. The Sakila kids made a special effort to pass the ball to ours and include them in the game, especially cheering Michael on when he kicked a ball. A kindergartner latched on to me and wouldn't let go of my hand the entire time we were visiting. How I longed to take her home.

Particularly as we spent time in impoverished areas such as the Sakila School, Clare was constantly on the lookout for

140

new ideas and projects. Her mind seemed to be continually abuzz with creative perspectives. Much of her talk after visiting the school concerned ways her school at home might raise money to help them out. She would offer a new fundraising plan every day for about a week. It was fun to hear her excited and wanting to take leadership, particularly for an important and valuable cause like supporting a school with a fraction of the resources that she enjoys at home. These were moments to be proud parents and a rekindled hope that this trip would indeed promote our children's sensitivity to needs of those around them.

Mr. Andrew drove with us into the hills for a delicious lunch with a local family. Thomson Safaris not only supports schools, it pays a number of different families to provide lunch to their clients, which "spreads the wealth" as our guide put it. We enjoyed a post-lunch walk into the Arusha National Park forest where we saw Colobus and Blue Monkeys. Colobus monkeys are gorgeous with a white stripe going down a body of long black hair to very fluffy white tails. The older ones have white fringes coming off their shoulders like a cape. What I remember most about that walk was watching Clare and Bridget hand in hand with two little children from our host's family.

The next day, we stopped at the Arusha Cultural Heritage Center, a place to see a Maasai and Warusha village without intruding the tribes themselves. Swahili is the common language although each of the 120 separate tribes in Tanzania also has their own language. English and Swahili are the official languages of the nation, but many in the rural areas do not know English beyond a few words. One third of the people practice traditional religions, particularly in the rural areas. About one third of the population is Muslim. There are also many Jehovah's Witnesses. Christianity is popular, mostly Catholicism, and other denominations are present.

In our Bedford truck we left Arusha and headed for Tarangire National Park and the wildlife. On the way we saw many Maasai and Warusha villages. William filled us in on the Maasai culture. The Maasai are the largest and oldest tribe around Arusha who have resisted modernization. For the past 700 years, the Maasai have held fast to their culture in dress, male rite of passage, marriage rites, and medicine. There are about 740,000 Maasai living in either Kenya or Tanzania today. It is impossible to have anything but intense admiration for these people who survive in the hot, dry conditions. We certainly don't agree with their extremely sexist way of life, (women do all the work and must marry whomever chooses them) but respect their fascinating culture.

It is easy to spot the Maasai on the roads. All the young men are referred to as warriors, dress in a bright red cloak, and can usually be seen with a shepherd's stick and a herd of cows or goats. At the age of 7, the elders cut or pierce the earlobes of both boys and girls and place a small stick in the hole. Gradually, they increase the size of the stick and hang many earrings so the hole gets bigger and bigger. The women wear vibrant, bright colored clothing with very short hair and multicolored earrings all about their ears. All of the people go barefoot or wear sandals made from old tires.

The Maasai don't keep track of their ages. Important events in a person's life, such as the time for male initiation, are judged by the height of the child. The ceremonial circumcision is usually performed around 13 years of age without anesthesia. If a boy cries the other boys and girls make fun of him and the family is shamed, so there is pressure to not react to the pain. Following the ceremony, the boys wear black, paint their faces white, and often wear ostrich feathers in their hair. For the next 6 months they must stay in the bush all day long, must not have any contact with water, and only come home at night. They can only drink cow's milk and cow's blood during that time.

We saw a number of these boys on the side of the road. On one occasion, William carried on a brief conversation in Swahili as we passed them. Afterwards, he laughed as he told us that they were begging him for water. He whispered, "Sometimes they cheat!" So with hundreds of tourists passing by on the road, they are not always true to their ritual. After the six months they may finally bathe and are given the red cloak of a warrior.

While most Tanzanian women in the urban areas don't marry until their 20's, Maasai girls marry at 15 and start having children. The boy's parents who are responsible for a dowry arrange the first marriage. It is common for a man to have three or more wives, but he must pay for any dowry after his first wife. Just the women and children live in the house, unless the man comes home to that house for the night. In a family, there are typically up to 10 children in a home. They sleep on banana leaf mats with a cowhide blanket. Each wife builds her own house, often with the help of the other wives. The women build the houses in 5 days and they last about 5 years.

In order for a man to own land, all he needs to do is to claim it, clear it, and plant a farm. It is first come, first served with an abundance of available land to be had—reminiscent of the homesteading of Oregon and the West. Each man essentially creates his own village with his wives.

If a Maasai or his cows get sick, some go to the local witch doctor for advice. According to William, the doctor dispenses wisdom such as "move your house 500 yards north . . . that will be two cows please." We passed the home of a witch doctor who has 32 wives, 200 children, and a huge herd of cows and goats.

Toward the end of our trip in Africa, we had a guided hike with a Maasai warrior named Mengoriki who wore the traditional Maasai cloak along with Nike's (no socks) and a nice looking gold watch. He was such an odd sight mixing signs of western affluence with Tanzanian poverty. On our walk he taught us about traditional tribal plant remedies (i.e. the gum tree root is good for diarrhea) and toothbrushes (they take a branch of a bush cut it, chew the end to make it a brush, and then brush their teeth). In exchange, we taught him how to play "Go fish" with a deck of cards we had handy. Awkwardly, he managed to learn how to hold his cards and ask Michael if he had any two's. What a great sight it was to see him laughing with the kids as he won.

AFRICA—THE WILDLIFE

"Happiness is not a station you arrive at,
but a manner of traveling."
Margaret Lee Runbeck, American Author

We constantly tell the children that the purpose of our travel is not simply getting to a place and seeing something, but learning from the journey as well. Perhaps this was especially true in Africa, simply trying to take as much in as we could while driving. There was so much wildlife to enjoy as we rode along in the old Bedford.

It was difficult to know what to expect beyond our knowledge of seeing animals in zoos and the few animals we have seen in national parks in the states. People we know who have gone on safaris talked of bone jarring jeep rides, heat, dust, and "lots of animals." In anticipation of the mosquitoes, we had begun our course of malaria medicine and were wary of the promised bug bites. Would the kids quickly tire of the bouncing and baking in the plains or get bored of seeing the animals after the first day?

Once again we were pleasantly surprised. The weather was perfect with cool nights, comfortable days, and essentially no mosquitoes to be found anywhere. Unlike the many jeeps bustling around us, we were in the ancient Bedford truck, high above all the other cars, in bouncy bench seats, with plentiful space for the kids to walk around while we sought the national parks' finest. William, our guide, appeared to be significantly different from most safari operators. While we certainly covered significant ground on our drives, we also stopped frequently for long periods of time to watch nature unfold in front of us. Other jeeps would come and go hastily in search of the "Big 5" (lions, rhinos, water buffalo, elephants, and hippopotami)—spotting an animal, taking a few pictures, saying oohs and aahs, and leaving in 10 minutes. Thankfully, we would wait patiently for stories to develop before our eyes.

It paid off as we saw dramatic scenes of every animal imaginable in our ten days of adventure.

With apologies to my dedicated zoo educator sister-in-law, Linda, it will be difficult to set foot in a zoo again. Seeing animals in the wild alters your perspective of seeing wild animals. As time passed, it was interesting how our expectations of seeing animals rapidly escalated. We entered Tarangire National Park, the first of three national parks on our safari, including Ngorongoro Crater Conservation Area and the Serengeti Plains, not really knowing what we would encounter. Immediately, we were in awe of a few giraffes, zebras, and wildebeest. Quickly this viewpoint changed until we had high expectations for seeing a "kill." While this may sound gruesome, witnessing the dance between hunter and hunted was simply fascinating. Our concept of "driving around looking at animals" radically changed. It was phenomenal to witness the gradual stalking, hiding, the chase, kill, and meal. It was much more than looking . . . it was watching nature's saga evolve.

Our second day in Tarangire, we sat spellbound as we saw two cheetahs gradually move through the brush closer and closer to a herd of impalas. Watching their intent stares while simultaneously seeing the unsuspecting gazelles was suspenseful. Suddenly, one of the cheetahs sprung toward the impalas and the chase was on. She set her sights on one in particular and at an incredible speed crossed the plain to close within a few feet of the impala. Miraculously, the impala leaped away from the cheetah just in the nick of time and ran. The cheetah zigged and zagged with every leap and turn of the impala, but this day, the impala was to be the victor as the cheetah soon tired.

We were fortunate to see three more cheetah chases over the course of the next week and a half, with the cheetahs more than evening the score and getting their meal of a Thomson gazelle each time. In one case, a mother cheetah left her two cubs for the kill and then called them over for the meal. Another time, four adolescent cheetahs in training chased a baby gazelle with their mother showing the way. One would

145

catch it, let it run away, and then another would chase it down again, until the gazelle had no more energy and it became lunch. (Talk about playing with your food.)

Our introduction to African wildlife up close at Tarangire was quite impressive. In Tarangire, our campsite was right next to a water hole where different animals appeared each day. One of our favorite afternoons was spent sitting by the hole watching a herd of elephants ramble in and give themselves drinks and baths. It was especially fun to see baby elephants joining in alongside their mothers. The next day, a huge herd of elephants surrounded us and crossed right in front of our truck as we watched them grazing in the grasses. Another morning we laughed and delighted in the antics of a baboon family of 30 playing in the trees and grass. The babies are so tiny and the dominant males so fierce and proud. Along the way each day we loved to see graceful giraffes walking along or nibbling between thorns on leaves of very prickly trees. What an opportunity to witness the wild. However, sometimes, the wild was a bit too close as the following story from Steve's journal on October 21st will attest:

• • • • •

"Hyenas have incredibly strong jaws. An old Maasai man got drunk one time, wandered into the national park, and fell asleep in the grass. A hyena came by and bit off his arm, crushing right through the bone. That is why the hyena poop you see is white, because they eat bones of other animals. They are scavengers."

I look around the old Bedford safari truck. Our three children, Clare, Bridget, and Michael, are listening very intently. William is a knowledgeable guide for our travels through the national wildlife parks of Tanzania, but in this case, he may have stepped over the line a bit. We are heading back to camp for dinner as dusk arrives. Looking to stretch every penny, we are on the budget safari, which means we are staying in tents at the public campsites in the game reserves. The kids play soccer with Richard while John prepares our dinner and I look on.

146

"Wah-woooo."

"What's that sound?" Michael asks.

Richard responds, "Oh, that is just hyenas." It sounds like they are about 50 yards away.

After dinner, Bridget sits in my lap. "Daddy, are the hyenas going to eat us?" I figured that was coming.

"No, Bridget, we are very safe. We wouldn't put you in a dangerous situation."

"I'm scared."

"That's okay. Remember that William has been doing safaris for 20 years and he has been just fine."

"Yes, Bridget" William chimes in, "the mosquito netting on your tent protects you. The hyenas are afraid of it." Bridget looks skeptical. "A couple of years ago, I woke up at night and looked out my mosquito net and a hyena was looking right back at me. I smiled, she smiled, and then walked off."

Thanks William. I'm sure that calmed her fears. Needless to say, Bridget and Michael are very worried. Toby and I try our best to reassure them: "You're safe."

Bedtime. It is a moonless night and pitch black outside. I take the kids to brush their teeth and go potty. In each public campground there is one bathroom with a guy's side and a girl's side, each with a sink and a single toilet. It is about 50 yards away from our tents. We pass by some trees and brush along the way.

"Daddy. Look in the bushes."

"It's okay, Bridget." I quickly shine my flashlight along the bushes.

"No, Daddy, you have to go slowly to be sure you don't see any eyes. William says you don't have to be afraid unless you see their eyes."

More points for William. I slowly pan my flashlight through the bush. No eyes. We get the bathroom thing done and head for bed. A quick goodnight to Toby and the girls in their tent then I crash with Michael in my tent. Thankfully, the kids fall asleep pretty quickly after a long day.

Two a.m. rolls around and all that water I drank at dinner kicks in. Time for a bathroom run. All the stories about hyenas

147

instantly come to mind. I am a bit nervous as I look for the flashlight in the tent. Should I just go in the bushes next to the tent and save the walk? I step outside the tent and flash the light into the bushes. I see eyes gleaming back. Okay. Change in plans. I'm going to explode, so there is no alternative but to go somewhere; I opt for the bathroom instead. As I walk over there I very carefully shine the flashlight into every nook and cranny of the bush next to the bathroom. No eyes, thank God.

I make it to there without jaws clamping on my arm and tearing it off. Phew! I am halfway done peeing when I hear rustling in the bushes outside. The noise grows louder. My heart beats faster. Somehow I have to get back to the tent. The noise grows louder still, as if someone is felling a tree about 30 feet away from me. Then it occurs to me...more noise is actually a good thing here—it must be an elephant, although with no moon, I can't make him out and decide not to annoy him or her with my flashlight beam. My adrenaline is high, but no danger from the elephant.

I slowly make my way back to the tent, cautiously scanning the territory around me and glancing backward now and then. As I approach, there is a hyena standing right in front of my tent door. Now what? Thoughts of valiantly saving my family from the gruesome jaws of death battle with thoughts of running like hell for a tree. The gods of heroism (or stupidity) call my name and I decide to take the hyena head on. Recalling from my childhood a National Geographic special about the skittishness of hyenas, I summon all my strength and whip out my trusty pencil flashlight. With one eye carefully scanning for the location of the nearest tree, I flash a tiny beam of light back and forth at his eyes. Its magical powers have the desired effect and the hyena quickly scurries away. I jump in the tent next to Michael who is peacefully sleeping the night away, ignorant of my courageous efforts to save his life. Thank goodness for that 1-millimeter thick nylon mesh, I think, as I zip up the tent.

Mental note to self: drink less fluid before bed.

• • • • •

148

On one safari drive, we watched three male lions stride imperiously past a herd of impalas and down to a water hole. One lion walked right next to our jeep and brushed against it. Wow! Cool!! Steve leaned over to take a picture. The lion looked up and let out a furious roar, inches from him. With a frenetically beating heart, he jerked back into the jeep, with significant energy focused on not dampening his underwear. He didn't get the picture. It was the first of many occasions in which we increased our comprehension of the word "wild." In spite of their appearance, these animals were not exactly soft and cuddly. William, on the other hand, was very amused as he sat safely on the other side of the jeep.

PHILOSOPHY 101: *Wealth*

I have waved and smiled at every person in Tanzania. Those I didn't get on the way in, I got on the way out. Okay, so I exaggerate a bit, but not too much. People have been so open here. I know I've waved to just about every kid and 90% have either waved first or enthusiastically responded. Many women and some men as well. Are we celebrities, oddities, or simply someone to be friendly with?

There are those times that kids come running and waving at us and come with hands indicating a desire for food or money. "Now don't make me feel uncomfortable" is my quick reaction. "Sure, I am spending thousands of dollars to be here and you live in a mud hut, but I'd appreciate you not making an issue out of my vast wealth compared to your poverty." When those moments come there is certainly emotional turmoil. I don't really know what to think, feel, or do when confronted with the disparity in our situations. I am not prepared to respond in an adequate way that might just address a bit of the gap.

At home, when confronted with open hats or hands I sometimes toss a few coins in, but more often rationalize that we support many social service organizations. When we get home I know we will support organizations that address needs in Africa, but their individual need is not so easily dismissed.

Encountering the face of poverty I instantly feel pangs of guilt about my reaction here and at home. These are individuals in need and organizations may or may not be available to comfort them. One on one is such a challenge...particularly as I sit here writing this in a "luxury tent cabin" overlooking the Great Rift Valley and Lake Manyara. The gap feels even wider. I have a bed that is clean and comfortable, a warm shower and a filling meal, which is drastically different than the experience that the faces I passed on the way here will have tonight. Music rises into my consciousness. John Lennon whispers to me, "Imagine . . . No need for greed or hunger . . ." No world shattering answers seem to be coming to me though...

Our next stop, the Ngorongoro Conservation Area, was very unique. It was a crater caused by a great volcanic mountain collapsing. The only way in was to take a jeep down a steep road into the crater. It has one of the greatest concentrations of wildlife in Africa. Here we saw lions, warthogs, zebras, wildebeest, a few endangered black rhinos, thousands of pink flamingos fishing at the edge of the crater's lake, and black kites. A story from Steve's journal October 22nd...

• • • • •

William must be psychic or something. While we drove towards our campsite in Ngorongoro Crater he told us of the evil black kite, which is a large bird that has grown accustomed to feeding off of people's food at the campsite. He relayed the story of a woman who was eating her sandwich on the lawn and as she lifted it to her mouth, a black kite flew down and plucked her eye out as it reached for the sandwich. Well, thanks again William for terrifying the kids.

We arrive at Ngorongoro Crater just in time for lunch after a bumpy ride from Tarangire. The one huge tree in the middle of the grassy area is filled with black kites.

William: "You can eat in the car or under the tree—just don't sit in the sun because the kites will bother you."

Everyone but me opts for the car. I am eager to take my bottom anywhere but the car.

"It's a beautiful day, I'm going outside for lunch."

Bridget: "But Daddy, what about the black kite?"

"I'll just sit under the tree. I'll be fine."

I merrily walk up to the tree and sit down under its shade, enjoying the view of the awesome crater below, and eating my lunch. Ten minutes and a kite or two fly closely by.

"Good thing I'm under this tree so they can't get me," I say to myself.

Well, they must have been doing reconnaissance on the first fly by because ten minutes later three fly right by my head. I feel the wind as the first two fly by. The last one bangs a wing into my head, knocking my sunglasses off, and pecking the hardboiled egg out of my hand as I raise it to my mouth. With my eyes intact, I pick up the rest of my lunch and head back to the safety of the car. My kids are laughing hysterically as I approach.

• • • • •

The Serengeti Plains are barren and filled simultaneously. William described the sparse trees around our campsite as the woodland. Not exactly a forest in Oregon terms, but a forest for the Serengeti, nevertheless. Here we were treated to tremendous numbers of wildlife. We were in the Serengeti as the summer was ending and the short rains were beginning. With the short rains, the dry, brown land we saw before us would be transformed into lush green land. A herd of 1.5 million wildebeest, 500,000 zebra, and thousands of gazelle would migrate from the Maasai Mara in Kenya to the Serengeti. As the rains were just beginning, we could see the early signs of this massive movement.

We drove to a waterhole where thousands of wildebeest and zebra stretched all around us. It was difficult to see the end of the herd. Sitting in our truck for a couple of hours, we were treated to a hundred nervous zebras slowly walking into the water to get a drink and within a few seconds stampeding out of the water in a rush of sound as one of the zebras got spooked. Shortly thereafter we could appreciate their timidity. Driving away we encountered a dead zebra on the side of the road near another water hole. Its stomach was torn open and its insides were spread on the ground. Driving on, we noticed a few feet away from our truck, a lioness lying on her front paws, panting heavily, with blood on her mouth. A few feet more on the other side of the road, another lioness hovered over her zebra catch in the brush.

Over the course of the week and a half of camping in our tents we quickly realized that we were not just watching the wildlife… notes from Steve's journal, October 25th…

• • • • •

As I sit here in our camp on the Serengeti plains and reflect on the week, it has become obvious that we are intimately part of the wild as we pitch our tents each night. In Tarangire National Park hyenas walked through our camp nightly. In the Ngorongoro Conservation area a black vervet monkey stole a banana peel out of our car. A black kite soared down from the sky whacked me in the head and stole my lunch. About ten zebra grazed next to our tents one night. I awoke in the middle of the next night to the sound of a huge bush pig that ripped open our tent, dragged Michael's backpack outside, and then stole his underwear. The next morning, Michael giggled loudly when I suggested that we should go looking for the pig wearing them. Here in our camp in the Serengeti a baboon family surrounded our camp and stole some food. Huge cape buffalo drank water from our camp faucet making bathroom runs dicey. Elephants trumpeted and crashed through trees 50 feet away from our tents, and each night we are serenaded by lions roaring 100 yards away.

How close are we to becoming somebody's next meal? William has a lot of confidence in those tents at night. Unlike our comfortable home in Oregon, we are in a relationship with the wild here in Africa. As I enjoy the sun setting over a nearby baobab tree, I feel excited and unnerved, strangely harmonious and totally out of my element at the same time. I really have no idea what it is like to accept these dangers as part of life, yet tribes like the Maasai have lived with this for centuries.

• • • • •

INTERESTING TIDBITS YOU CAN USE FOR "Who Wants To Be A Millionaire":
Facts about the wildebeest migration from Maasai Mara, Kenya to Serengeti, Tanzania which begin with the short rains in November:
- During three weeks in February 8,000 wildebeest babies are born each day. They can stand immediately and can run at full speed within an hour. In total, about 500,000 wildebeest are born, but 250,000 perish during the migration.
- The wildebeest herd expels 125 tanker trucks worth of pee PER DAY, and 400 dump trucks of poop (our kids like this fact in particular).
- The wildebeest are really dumb and can hardly see. The zebras are their eyes and ears on the trail. The zebras, on the other hand, like hanging out with the wildebeest because they can run faster--so the lions usually get a wildebeest instead of them.

Tips from the Maasai Warrior:
- A type of apple tree out in the bush has many uses. Its fruit looks like a yellow cherry tomato and is good for stomachaches. The roots are boiled to cure diarrhea. The branches can be cut and used as toothbrushes: one end is sharpened for dental floss and the other is chewed and mashed up to be used as a brush for cleaning teeth.
- The gum tree's sap is used for gum and the roots can be squeezed to get water to drink. You can cut a branch and stick it in the ground and it will grow into a tree. It has thorns, so the Maasai plant them in a perimeter to protect their homes and make pens for their animals.

Rules for visiting gorillas in Uganda (courtesy of William):

153

- Only 6 people per day can spend 2 hours with the gorillas. (Get your reservations early!) That is all the human contact they allow.
- When you visit, you must stay 20 feet away from the gorillas and allow them to come to you. When they are within 10 feet, you must kneel. When they are within 5 feet you must sit down cross-legged.
- If one comes up to you, you must not look at it. You must sit still and let the gorilla check you out. After a while you can look it in the eyes and allow it to play with you.

Some other useful facts:
- A giraffes' tongue is so long it can wrap around your head. They have the same number of vertebrae as humans. They have a special joint in their head that allows them to tip their head very far back to get to the leaves they want.
- Rock Hyrax poop pellets are used for treating people with epilepsy. While it looks like a large mouse (the animal, not the poop), its closest relative is the elephant.
- The Serengeti Park is 14, 763 square kilometers and was founded by Germans, Michael and Bernhard Grzinek in 1951. He and his father wrote the famous book The Serengeti Shall Not Die.
- The leaves of the sandpaper tree are so rough that craftsmen use them to sand their carvings.

In Steve's journals, he highlighted the animal antics we were privileged to witness. I might add for concerned grandparents, aunts and uncles, that I never once felt we were in danger. Even when I was taking a cold shower in the dark before dinner and heard an incredible noise just outside I was not worried. Knowing that hyenas have a penchant for shoes, I simply grabbed my boots, brought them in and closed the door. Minutes later Steve and the kids came running up to inform me that an elephant had just rearranged a tree behind the shower stall.

No matter where we were camped, our days fell into a routine. I was up every morning about 5:30 to watch the sun rise. The staggering array of purples, oranges and reds presented a dramatic backdrop for the dark silhouettes of the baobab, tabletop acacia, and gum trees. We had breakfast by 6:30 and then jumped in the Bedford for a game drive until 12:30 or 1:00. After a break until 3:30, we took off again until dinner at 7:30 p.m. At dinner we typically talked about the day, shared jokes with our guys, and sang for each other. Every night we liked to thank John and Richard for dinner by singing them different songs. One of my special memories was sitting outside the truck with John as he patiently taught me "Tanzania, Tanzania" a melodic, favorite folk song of the people here.

The hardest adjustment for me was being in national parks where your movement was restricted to within 100 yards of camp (for obvious reasons—our fellow campers had big teeth and horns). It felt so strange to not be hiking all over the place and experiencing the landscape on foot. The only part of our bodies getting exercise was our arms trying to keep our bums on the seats of the truck. In desperation I started walking and running circles around the camp.

Another oddity for all of us was being cooked for, cleaned up after, and all our needs met by Richard, John and William. We are just not used to this kind of camping. It certainly went against my Scouting grain. However, with each passing day we tried to help all we could and became closer to our crew. It was very gratifying near the end as we broke camp at the Serengeti and the men comfortably let us strike the mess canopy tent. We had become friends, not just clients.

It was a very emotional good-bye on our last day as hugs and kisses were shared all around. Richard and John went on their way, but William, ever the thoughtful leader, had lunch with us and discussed our time with the kids. Then he graciously stayed with us a good portion of the afternoon seeing us safely through Arusha to the open food market where we bought food for our remaining meals. We would not have accomplished that without his help, protection, and Swahili.

After two weeks it was so strange to be on our own again. Walking back to the hotel the kids said, "Well, it's just us now. I really miss them." Our last day was a Sunday. We walked back to the church William had shown us the day before and went to the most joyous, uplifting mass we'd attended in years. The singing was incredible, the priest energetic and humorous, and even if we didn't understand a single Swahili word, it was moving. We ran into our Tanzania border angel, Michael, in town on the way to church. He had successfully climbed Kilimanjaro. It was a nice way to end the whole adventure, seeing again the stranger who was kind enough to lend us the $250 to get into the country. He headed out at the same time and we kept waving at him in his shuttle bus and chatting with him at each border stop. But this time we had the cash . . . and scores of memories to take with us.

Not a single McDonald's, no cell phones, no smoking, no strip joints. Guns extremely rare. Welcoming, warm, smiling faces quick to say "Jambo!" and "Hakuna matata" and fantastic animals in wide open spaces. What a marvelous place. A nation of people who seemingly have nothing . . . and everything.

"May the road rise to meet you.
May the wind be ever at your back.
May the sun shine warm upon your face,
and the rains fall soft upon your fields."
An Irish Blessing

MY FAVORITE COUNTRY IS

IRELAND   1 November

The journey out of Africa began with a seven-hour bus ride from Tanzania to the Kenyan International Airport. Our overnight flight left at 11p.m. and arrived the next day at 4:30 a.m. in London. All concept of time, days and sleep was nonexistent. A few trains later we were walking the streets of Alton. We are quite certain that none of us would have survived this sojourn without the Fife's oasis of love, friendship and familiarity to return to every few weeks, months or countries.

The days that followed were again filled with laughter, stories, playing and planning of the Fife's first-ever Halloween party. The English don't generally celebrate Halloween (an American export), although many stores in Alton were decorated for Halloween, causing a bit of controversy with the locals. Mary Kate is American, Bill is Canadian and before we left for Africa, our children had asked if they could plan a party for them. In Africa, whenever there was down time, the kids would brainstorm the whole event. The Halloween party ultimately hosted eleven children and eleven adults, most of whom came in costume and enjoyed an array of desserts and games we have learned from around the world.

Here's a thought. In the United States if you asked ten different families how they celebrate Halloween you would likely get ten different answers with a few similarities in games or food. As we observed other cultures, their celebrations and traditions, I wondered what was truly "traditional" and rooted in history and what was unique to the people with whom we spent that time? We were often asked if we were a "typical American family." Hm. Define "typical American." How have we interpreted "typical England" or "typical Thailand" based on our experiences?

We constantly found ourselves at a loss for words just trying to explain our adventures to family and friends. Our Native Alaskans have thirty different words to describe snow. I thought about that numerous times throughout the trip especially in the more dramatic mountainous countries like Norway, Austria, Switzerland, and New Zealand. The English language just does not seem to contain enough words to do justice to nature at her best. This challenge repeated itself in trying to convey the peaceful loveliness of Ireland, England, Scotland and Wales. Like Netherlands, Scandinavia and Europe, the British Isles possess picture-perfect regions of rocky coastline, gentle mountains, placid valleys, wandering rivers and waterfalls.

The Welsh countryside shimmered in brilliant greens under sunny skies on our morning train ride west across England. Arriving in Fishguard, Wales we caught the ferry to Ireland. The three-hour crossing provided the perfect opportunity to catch up on some much needed schoolwork. Our arrival in Rosslare, Ireland was just before the village grocery store closed, so we stocked up for a homemade dinner in the youth hostel. The Rosslare Youth Hostel sits on a hill just above the harbor and has a very good-natured hostel manager.

As has grown readily apparent, there is the usual way of doing things and our way. Most people, we were to learn, travel from Dublin, in the north, south to Glendalough, our intended destination for the weekend. We traveled from Rosslare, in the south because that port was closest to London.

An early morning walk back to the port brought us to a bus that took us to Arklow, which was about half way to Glendalough. In Arklow we wandered aimlessly, asking people on the street about the bus to Glendalough.

"I think it departs near the park."

"You might try over by the library."

"It could be the bus that picks up at the top of the street over there."

People were so willing to be helpful. Trouble is, we could never find the bus. Steven ultimately found a tourist office agent...

"Actually, there is no bus to Glendalough, but you can get to Rathdrum. Once you are there you'll have to ask around. I'm pretty sure the bus leaves by the post office."

An hour later we finally figured out that the bus office was cleverly disguised as a tiny grocery shop. The woman at the cash register told us that the next bus to Rathdrum left in an hour. In Rathdrum, we were forced to take a taxi the last ten miles to our hostel in Glendalough. However, the one taxi in town was gone for a couple of hours. Time to explore the local park. It was a lovely day, so the kids enjoyed a running stream and grassy hills. They each turned a tree into a bed and breakfast that we were invited to tour.

Glendalough is infamous for being one of the main stops on the "Wicklow Way", which is a 120 km walk through some of the most incredible terrain in Ireland. For me it shall remain the place where a miracle occurred. Recall the promise I had made to Zach back in Sweden? How hard could it be to find a silver Celtic cross for him? Walking the streets of Glendalough I searched all the village shops until I found exactly what I was looking for—a handsome silver cross and chain priced at 50 pounds. Given the exchange rate and the months of travel still ahead of us it was far beyond our budget. I vowed to keep searching.

Although we had reserved the "family room" in advance, when we arrived at the hostel the manager had no record of it. The hostel was booked solid but she was able to find us another room that had been recently vacated. After our long journey we were thrilled to have anything at all. The room was clean and empty. We put away our gear then went on a walk.

Later that afternoon, Steve and the children were playing a game in the common area and I was collecting laundry when I noticed hanging on one of the bunk beds was a silver chain and an intricately designed Celtic cross. It was the exact one I had seen in one of the shops. I turned it in to the manager. Surely someone would be calling for it. The manager said that, it was the strangest thing, but she had found our reservation and would we like to change to our original room? "No thanks," I assured her, "we were really meant to be where we are now." She smiled in agreement. Throughout our stay I continued to check with her to see if someone had called after the cross.

Three days later, no one had phoned to say the necklace had been left behind. The manager said that, due to its high value, it would need to remain available for three more months, in case someone called, before I could claim it. I told her all about Zach, the present struggles in his life, his parents' separation, his dream to visit Ireland and my promise. "No one will call," I said, "that cross was meant for him. It's a miracle." I gave her an envelope addressed to Zach in Sweden. Inside I had written him a letter with the Irish Blessing. The manager was thrilled and said she would be happy to send it to him in February if no one claimed it.

Glendalough boasts of two picturesque lakes at the base of rugged mountains, an old mining town, and the 10th century monastic home of St. Kevin. The forest was bursting with fall colors as we walked Wicklow National Park. Through a biting wind and gathering mist we hiked to the top of a waterfall. It had a classic Irish moor feel to it, peaceful but mysterious. Wild mountain goats accompanied us for a brief spell and we expected a leprechaun to jump out from behind a bush at any moment. The day had started out with clear blue skies so we had neglected to bring our windbreakers. Now, ice was beginning to flow through our veins.

Hiking back down we found the rocky ruins of an old mining town at the edge of the upper lake to take refuge. The three walls of an old roofless church served as our haven for oranges and crackers. The children each took possession of one of the old stone houses and played merrily in spite of the cold. Another trip that began with whining had ended with adventure.

Acquiring food was also an adventure in Glendalough. Early on in our travels we learned to pack ahead, purchasing food whenever we could. Part of the charm of these quaint little villages is the lack of amenities such as grocery stores. Thus, we never knew when or where we would be able to purchase food. It was not unheard of to carry a jar of spaghetti sauce and a bag of pasta for days "just in case."

The nearest "store" to the youth hostel was a good 45-minute hike along a thin, winding road which the locals navigated like the Indy 500. On our first trek we set out early enough to reach the tiny store just before sundown. It took the children so long to agree on an item, by the time we headed out the autumn sky had turned black. As there were no sidewalks, with each approaching vehicle someone yelled "CAR!" and we dove into the hedges, tall grasses or jumped the rock walls.

Still, Ireland is enchanting and homey. It's everything I had hoped it would be and the people are gracious. Our driver, Joe, who took us from Glendalough to Dublin, seemed to know everyone on the bus and everyone outside as well. People would walk up and say something like "Hey, Joe. Could you please drop this little package off to the Clanahan's on your way?" Joe would dutifully take the package and drop it off on someone's doorstep as we rode along.

We fully expected rolling green and rocky hills peering out from under heavy mists that blanketed the landscape. We were not disappointed. However, as we walked the hills we were surprised that there were so few trees. Ireland has the dubious distinction of having the least amount of trees in Europe (with the exception of Iceland). Only 7% of its land is forested, while it has the fourth greatest percentage of bog land in the world (17%). In spite of its inhospitable weather and land, the English have made claims on all or part of Ireland since the 12th century, so any mention of the British seems to be a sore point. It became apparent as we traveled about that the people of Ireland are certainly proud of their country and especially their famous writers such as Oscar Wilde, Thomas Moore, Jonathan Swift, William Butler Yeats, Samuel Beckett, and James Joyce.

Our ride through the Irish countryside led me to believe that all of Ireland is a series of quaint, spread out villages similar to those in Vermont. Then we hit the outskirts of Dublin. The suburbs could be any nice suburb of California or Oregon, but the city is distinctly Irish. New structures and development have been kept to a minimum, so that it still feels traditional. Huge trees, old churches, pubs, Trinity College, and old buildings like the hostel we stayed in made it very appealing. The abundantly flowing river Liffey runs through the middle of the city and is impressively free of garbage. The name Dublin comes from the Gaelic *Dubh Linn*, which means "black pool" because of the dark waters of the Liffey.

Dublin takes special pride in her native son, James Joyce. As we walked through the streets of Dublin there were brass plaques inset into the sidewalks marking scenes depicted in the famous novel Ulysses. The ferry we took from Dublin to England is the largest ferry in the world and was named the Ulysses, in honor of James Joyce. The entire ship was designed with his book in mind. Restaurants were named after places and characters in his book, a walking tour was designed around quotes from his book, and paintings throughout documented moments in his life and literature. The ship was quite a shrine to the novelist.

However, we are getting a bit ahead of ourselves. The morning we left Dublin we asked the hostel manager how to get to the port to catch the ferry. He said that we could just follow the river. Needless to say, the following events are another example of our family curse. We never seem to take the easy way.

• • • • •

Steve: "Can we walk it or should we take a bus?"

Hostel manager: "Well, I guess it is about a half hour's walk from here."

Steve: "Gee, the ferry doesn't leave for another two hours, why don't we go ahead and walk?" (More famous last words...)

At 8 a.m. we embark on a nice walk along the river, with our packs and sleeping bags in hand, for about 2 miles. We turn at the beginning of the port and see a ferry ship parked at the dock. Another half mile down the road we find the Stela ferry ship, which is the British company that crosses the English Channel.

"Sorry, this ship is not going anywhere. You want the Irish Ferry which is further down."

"Thank you."

It's about 8:45 as we begin walking what turns out to be another two miles. We finally see the Irish Ferry in the distance around 9:15. By now, the kids, who have been great up to this point, have reached their limit. Justifiably, the whining starts.

"Hang on! We are almost there!"

Fifteen minutes, another mile, and we haven't made enough progress. It still looks like a long walk. Steve decides to run ahead and buy tickets. Toby is now carrying her pack, Michael's pack (he gave up), Steve's pack, and two sleeping bags. Steve runs for about 100 yards and decides he is not going to make it. It is 9:30 and the ship doors close at 9:45 for the 10 o'clock sailing. Steve runs across the street to flag down a car. As it turns out, a small car is already waiting on the side of the road. Not enough for the whole family and luggage, but it is a start.

"Looked like you and your family could use a bit of help."

"You are an angel!"

Behind this car another pulls up. The driver is a friend of the guy in the first car.

"Half of you can get in his car."

"Great!" (Miracles come in all sizes.)

163

He drives us the rest of the way, and, as usual, we make it with that familiar five minutes to spare. We are off to Holyhead, England on our way to the Lake District.

• • • • •

LAKE DISTRICT, ENGLAND   5 November

From Holyhead we had to change in Chester on our way to Ambleside. We missed our next train by four minutes (okay, so we don't always have five minutes to spare), so we had the opportunity to enjoy a bit of Chester. Michael and I sat with the gear while Steve and the girls played hunter/gatherer and went in search of food. An hour and a half later, walking in a chilly fall night, they had enjoyed a very cute Tudor village and returned with the evening's provisions. As they arrived at the station, they saw the sign for the free shuttle into town. Oh, well.

Three trains later, we arrived at 8 p.m. in Windermere with a driving rain against the train windows. In our pattern for the day, we missed the bus to Ambleside by a few minutes. We had a choice between a two-hour wait for the next one or a taxi.

"How much to the hostel?" I inquired of the youthful looking taxi driver.

"Eight pounds. But I can't legally take five people."

"That's okay. We'll wait for the bus."

As I was walking away, an older taxi driver behind him said: "Wait a minute. Look here. These two count as one (pointing at Michael and Bridget)."

The young taxi driver, having received the elder's suggestive permission, gave in.

"Okay, get in."

Eight pounds and 10 minutes later we were standing in a large, comfortable hostel right on Lake Windermere. Our room looked out on the water, trees, and mountains. Traveling on the trains that evening we had seen fireworks in the distance. While settling into our room they began over the lake

164

right below us. "It's Guy Fawkes night!" a fellow hosteller informed us, adding the English ditty:

Please to remember / The 5th November:
Gunpowder, Treason and Plot.
We know no reason / Why Gunpowder Treason
Should ever be forgot.

History and legend have it that Guy Fawkes was a traitor against England who got caught just before he lit the fuse to about 40 barrels of gunpowder under the Parliament building in 1605. The tradition is to hang him in effigy while celebrating with small explosions and fireworks. An awesome display of lights flashed in the sky as we ended a long day.

For the next two days we enjoyed Ambleside even though it was dark, cloudy, cold, and windy most of the time. Fabulous fall colors surrounded this amiable village as we hiked to the town waterfall. The trail through the forest was blanketed with autumn leaves. The kids enjoyed sailing their leaf boats in the stream until Michael accidentally slipped in the cold water up to his calves, prompting a quick exit. Upon our return to the hostel, hot showers beckoned while swans floated on Lake Windermere and the sun set on a lone fisherman casting his line.

SCOTLAND   7 November

Geography cares not about borders or names of countries. Our train passed from England into Scotland with only the residents knowing the difference. The scenery outside the windows remained unified in pastoral splendor draped in autumn colors. Farms, forests, cows, sheep and stone or brick houses with thatched roofs shared the terrain with the occasional ancient rock-walled church and kirkyard. Ambleside, England to Aviemore, Scotland was another all day venture with several train changes.

The Lonely Planet guide proclaims that the train trip from Perth to Aviemore is one of the most stunning segments in the world. The Scottish Highlands flowed past our train windows in a sea of olive green. With a touch of winter in the air, the

165

classic Scottish mist embraced the hills as we climbed north to Aviemore. Our place on the train was shared with a Scotsman who was about our age. We were to learn that the Scots are passionate about their country. He dove into conversation with the kids, beginning with the usual "Where are you from?" and "Where are you traveling?"

Bridget: "We are traveling around the world!"

Scotsman: "Wow! You are very fortunate that your parents are doing that with you." (Just thought we'd highlight that sentence.)

Bridget: "We've been to New Zealand and Thailand and Egypt and lots of other places."

Scotsman: "So what has been your favorite place?"

Bridget: "England."

The Scotsman winced and put on a face of mock horror. That was not the most politically correct thing to say in the moment. Bridget looked confused, so I tried to smooth the waters with a brief lesson in Scotland's muddy relationship with England. In spite of this innocent faux pas, the next two-hour segment on the train was particularly enlightening as he generously shared with us his country's history. We obviously needed acculturation. He pointed out significant castles, towers, and bridges as we passed and related their stories. Somberly, he gestured toward the small town where, a few years ago, a man went on a shooting spree in an elementary school. Nothing like that had happened before or since and he declared it the worst incident in his country's history. The result? The government banned guns and the Scots voluntarily turned in their weaponry. (We should be so lucky in the States.) In Stirling he noted the famous tower, with a spiral staircase to the top, which enshrines William Wallace's cutlass.

A bit of irony...Scotland only recently gained her governmental independence from England. While still considered a part of Great Britain, they initiated their own parliament and elected their "First Minister" (their version of president) in 1999. Our resident tour guide attributed this achievement to Hollywood. Upon the success of the American

166

film, "Braveheart," starring an Australian (Mel Gibson) playing a Scotsman (William Wallace), the Scots developed a bit of national fervor and pushed for independence during the 1990's. England finally relinquished. (An interesting footnote is that, during our week stay in Scotland, the First Minister resigned over a scandal about his misuse of funds. Their fourth minister in three years was elected by the parliament at the end of the week.)

Gentle Aviemore came upon us as the sun set through the stormy clouds on the horizon. The hostel was set in the woods, a short walk from the train station. Once we arrived we were greeted by a number of wild bunnies scurrying about. Bridget said that they were "the kind that make you want to hold them forever." After a long day of travel, this simple welcoming party was a sign of good things to come.

No matter where you are, the first snow of the season has something magical about it. We awoke to a winter wonderland of snow almost a foot deep. The whole town shared our excitement. Shops hurriedly stocked toboggans and shovels as we walked down the street. Wearing most of the clothes in our backpacks, our three and a half hour hike to Lochan Eileen that morning encompassed two lakes and a river on a mushy, narrow trail through trees still painted with orange, amber, crimson, and yellow hues. The fall colors against the dazzling white of the snow was a marvelous sight. As the snow continued to fall, cold gusts of wind sent clouds of glittering snowdust into our reddened faces (and runny noses), biting through our multiple layers of clothes. With a few occasional snowballs flying and the promise of snacks upon our arrival, we managed to make it to the lake visitor center.

Defrosting our appendages, we took in the simple nature exhibits and learned the history of the area as we waited out the storm. Over the past century, the Scots have been reforesting the area after logging took its toll. Now, a thriving forest encircles the pea-green waters of Lochan Eileen. On an island in the middle of the lake a tiny castle sits that boasts of a colorful past. Our return to the hostel seemed to go quickly as we enjoyed the winter scene and a warm stop at the folk art store on the way. That evening, the kids braved the cold once again, creating mittens out of plastic shopping bags and spending about two hours building various snow structures in front of the hostel.

Leaving Aviemore the next day, the train station looked as if it were a sight from a Norman Rockwell painting or a Charles Dickens tale. There is nothing like snow to turn even the plainest landscape into a work of art. The pedestrian bridge across the train tracks was a perfect vantage point to take in the mountains and valley blanketed in white. The consummate sight of fence posts with caps of snow completed the scene. On the trip from Aviemore to Edinburgh one masterpiece after another passed from our view, changing from snowy mountain forests to misty rocky beaches along the east coast of Scotland and the North Sea.

PHILOSOPHY 101: *Encountering the World*

Hostels are great places to meet people from around the world. Young and old from every continent have crossed our path. Germans, Japanese, Australians, South Africans, British, and Argentineans seem to be the main travelers from each of their respective continents, but there is diversity. At the same time, the world is pretty small. We also seem to keep running into people from Oregon. Next to us for dinner was a youthful couple from Portland, a field biologist and a sandal maker, who had been traveling the British Isles for about 3 months.

In the hostels people interact sometimes, sometimes they just keep to themselves. The bottom line is that, if you take a little initiative, you create an opportunity to learn about a different perspective of life and world events. As we prepared dinner our last night in Aviemore, three Scottish lads who were on leave from their posts in the British Army compared the recent American tragedy to the 60 years of "troubles" in Ireland. In Norway, I spent an interesting morning discussing our respective country's recent experiences with a woman from Israel. For her, a uniformed teenager with machine guns on every corner is a way of life. While it in no way lessens the horrible loss of life in the U.S, our experience of terrorism pales in the face of those who experience it on almost a daily basis.

In Verona, Italy a man from Iran struck up a conversation with me about terrorism. He had escaped the repressive policies of his country and had been trying to find a new home for the past ten years, but few countries would have him, until he came to Italy. In his broken English, he wondered aloud why the most powerful country in the world would want to destroy Afghanistan, one of the poorest countries. He strongly believed that the U.S. was framing Bin Laden so they could indiscriminately use their power to show off their weapons to sell to other countries. The U.S. military industry seems to be a popular topic for conversation to many travelers. In the end, we both agreed that terrorism and wars are horrible and that no loss of life is justified.

In general, it seems that travelers tend to have more liberal perspectives of the world. Is that because liberals like to travel more, or because traveling develops a liberal perspective? I can easily see how anti-western attitudes develop, however. At this point, we have traveled in so many cities in the world and have seen a franchise such as McDonalds or KFC in just about every one. I guess there is something to be said for western money creating jobs in these countries, but I wonder if they are better off. We made a pledge to not patronize any franchise on our travels. Yet, every McDonalds or KFC we have seen has been absolutely packed with people. It is obvious that they are popular places to go in every country. I cringe though, as I see mom and pop restaurants close by with few or no people inside. We embarked upon this trip to encounter new people, perspectives, foods, and environments. Are these cities beginning to lose their uniqueness?

The Edinburgh hostel was set among other two story homes stacked side by side in a large neighborhood. Yet, it had a pleasant feeling with old wood paneled walls, fireplaces aglow in the hallway and sitting room, and a touch of history on every wall. Hostels have all been so different around the world. Up six flights of stairs, our window offered an aerial view of the city.

Edinburgh has always been famous for its castle, university, and theater festival. Now she can add to her distinctions the birthplace of "Harry Potter." Our whole family has enjoyed each novel, but Clare has taken the prize for most devoted fan. She has collected newspaper clippings about Harry from around the world. She was distraught that we would be leaving the continent the day the Harry Potter movie was to open in England, November 16th. As luck would have it, our timing was perfect to take in the long anticipated movie on its preview weekend just blocks from where the book was penned.

Rather than zipping around to tourist attractions, we chose to simply enjoy the streets of Edinburgh. We took time out to join in a candle light prayer vigil for peace at St. John's. As in Dublin, the citizens of Edinburgh were displaying their concerns about the war in Afghanistan. On our long walks through the cobblestone streets we were rewarded with Scottish bagpipe music, a sprawling park below the castle, the hustle and bustle of holiday shopping on High Street between the castle and the palace, and a number of cathedrals along the way. One church had recently installed a resplendent stained glass window dedicated to the writing of poet Robert Burns and there were a number of markers in the city recalling moments in his life. As big cities go, Edinburgh was charming and beckoned us to return again.

ENGLAND   11 November

Our final adventure in Great Britain was a full day in windy, icy London. Having not prepared for the chilly conditions properly (our windbreakers were keeping warm on our beds in Alton), our whole day adjusted accordingly. We began by walking a good distance from the train station, past Big Ben, Westminster Abbey, and over to Buckingham Palace, arriving just in time for the 1:00 p.m. changing of the guard. Unfortunately, the winter schedule meant that the changing had occurred an hour and a half earlier. All was not lost, as the queen was home (her flag was up), so we waved. She didn't return the courtesy, nor invite us in for tea, however, as she was somewhere inside the palace confines and must have missed us.

One of our main objectives for the day was to see "The Lion King" at the Lyceum Theater. We stopped by a "half price" ticket booth only to discover that "half price" meant $40 per person. Ouch! Not within our meager budget as a family of five. The matinee started at 2:30, however, so we headed over to the theater, hoping to get cheap stand-by tickets. No such thing. We had one of two options: buy standing room tickets for $15 each for either the matinee or evening show or skip it. Inevitably, part of the family wanted one thing, part wanted another, and the rest couldn't decide. The next twenty minutes were spent struggling through tears and steadfast opinions to come to some sort of compromise. Meanwhile, the matinee had started, so at least that eliminated one option. We postponed a decision until the evening, when we could determine if we had enough energy to make it through the show.

By the time that was decided, our noses were frozen so we bought an all day bus pass and saw London through the windows of the top of a warm double decker bus. As the sun was setting, we got off the bus to walk through Kensington Gardens to see Princess Diana's former palace. What was very cold became very, very cold. After quickly looking at Diana's home and the Elfin Oak Tree (an oak tree carved with elves) we ducked in the gift shop to defrost. Once the feeling partially returned to our bodies, we bravely marched out again in search of the International Girl Guide/Scout House. As you might expect of us at this point in our travels, when we arrived at the spot I remembered from my college days, the nice lady at the desk of the new Girl Scout Office said that the International House had moved a mile or two away. Back to the warm bus. It was getting late. If we wanted to make the evening show we had to decide between trying to visit the Scout House or Kings Cross Station (to see the now famous platform 9 3/4). With Harry Potter fresh in their minds, the train station won out easily. Three fourths of the way there we were mired in rush hour traffic and again had to decide between the station and "The Lion King." This time, the theater took precedence (after all, they had heat!). We jumped off the bus in the stalled traffic and ran to the theatre for another "just in time" arrival.

Thankfully, after all that craziness, "The Lion King" was spectacular. I was amazed at our children standing for three hours without a single complaint. London theaters are wonderfully cozy, so we had a great view. The show was absolute magic. Fantastic scenery, costumes, music, choreography, and such a versatile stage. There was just enough drama and comic relief to keep the kids' rapt attention and weave in a few laughs. It was all the more special because we had spent two weeks in East Africa and a great ending to our time in the British Isles after a challenging day.

TRANSPORTATION INVENTORY (so far)

12 boat rides (ferries, etc.)	3 Tuk-tuks (motorcycle taxis)
11 Plane rides	3 miniature train rides
27 Taxis	1 aerial tram
14 shuttle bus rides	683 miles walking
103 Train rides	1 ox cart
39 Bus rides	41 miles on bicycle
23 Subway rides	176 miles in a jeep
2700 miles in rental cars	2 miles on water bikes
1 cable car	4 miles in row boats
1 Elephant	8 miles in a white water raft
851 miles in a Bedford Army truck	

Five and one half months after we set off, I was getting a real sense of being almost done, even though we had almost three months remaining. As we were about to arrive on our last continent it felt like the final phase of our trip. Yet, we expected the last phase of our trip to be the most challenging. To begin with, we were all a bit anxious about Guatemala, due to its tumultuous history. In addition, we actually had a specific purpose other than traveling around and soaking in different cultures. Our first month was devoted to learning Spanish and the next month and a half primarily devoted to doing service. We would be staying put for at least two weeks at a time, rather than moving about, so different relationships with people in these countries would evolve. It promised to be a unique and memorable time.

"Is it not pleasant
to learn with a constant perseverance and application?
Is it not delightful
to have friends coming from distant quarters?"
Confucius

LIMITATIONS
OF HIGH SCHOOL SPANISH

GUATEMALA   17 November

O ur fourth and final departure from Alton, England was
a 10:00 am flight to Frankfurt, Germany. It was one of
three flights in our quest for Guatemalan soil. In the
first true act of increased security in the airports, I was
randomly selected to be "padded down." The female officer
was very good-natured about my outburst of laughter (because
it tickled) as she searched me for dangerous items. In
Frankfurt, on the other hand, the whole family stood in a very
long line. Each and every passenger was searched, scanned
with a wand, and padded. These extra measures contributed to
our departure for Mexico City being delayed an hour.

As crazy as it may sound, because Lufthansa (the German
based airline) was our main carrier for the world trip, our
flight to Mexico City had to originate in Frankfurt which
meant that we flew right back over England. We continued
over Ireland, the East Coast of the U.S. then down to Atlanta,
the Gulf of Mexico and finally Mexico City. The plane from
Mexico City to Guatemala was delayed nearly two hours,
causing us to arrive at our final destination around midnight,
almost 24 hours from when we had started. We were just

174

awake enough to remember to filter the water to brush our teeth before landing in bed at our hotel.

The next morning we rode the city bus to the bus terminal, where we would get tickets for our six-hour ride from Guatemala City to Huehuetenango. Now you may have visions of the local Greyhound bus depot, typically a bit grimy, with those chairs with TV's on them in the waiting room, gum stuck to the floor, a ticket office behind glass, and a string of vending machines selling junk food. Scratch that. The bus depot in Guatemala City was a hole in the wall tucked in between small shops and piñata stores with gigantic colored paper figures.

The depot consisted of a desk with a smiling man sitting amidst a pile of papers in a space the size of a small bedroom. In fact, when we inquired "¿Donde esta el baño?" he directed us to the back of the office where there was another room with his mattress on the floor and the toilet nearby. Let's just say that there was no chart on the wall with hourly checkmarks showing that they had cleaned the bathroom. Piled all around the office were boxes and bags wrapped in twine that the locals drop off to send to relatives, etc. We bought our tickets and decided to spend the hour and a half wait walking the streets of the city.

Old American school buses and tour buses never die. They just end up on the streets of third world countries. Ours was an ex-school bus from Illinois that was very beat up. In one old tour bus the seats either didn't go back at all or were permanently stuck in the reclining position. There must have been a hole in the floor under my seat, because exhaust came up into my face every time the bus driver shifted gears. The tires were bald, garbage rolled around the floor, and this was the expensive shuttle. The "chicken bus" goes more often, but stops every few blocks and crams more people either in or around the bus (in between the chickens, hence the name). They are very good at making the most of their space.

As we left Guatemala City, we witnessed the vastness of the country's capital. Nestled between El Salvador, Honduras, Belize, and Mexico, Guatemala is Central America's most populous country with 13 million people. The city is quite expansive to accommodate the one and a half million people who live there. Guatemala is basically a clean city, but very run down, obviously still feeling the effects of about 40 years of war. Because it is a region prone to earthquakes, there are no tall buildings.

As soon as we left the borders of the gray cement city, we entered an indescribable landscape. Cast in the light of an orange sunset with gathering clouds, the passing scenery had a mystical feel to it. Forests of evergreens combined with flourishing tropical plants to cover the hills. We never saw the same species of tree twice. The topography of this volcanic region is mountainous without the craggy peaks we are used to in Oregon. Tall pyramid-like volcanoes rose from the valleys while terraced villages and farms, reminiscent of Thailand and Malaysia, were busy with the routines of daily life until the last traces of light retreated.

Huehuetenango, our objective, is a small city in the north of Guatemala. Before heading into South America, where we would be doing service in Peru, we wanted to learn as much Spanish as possible. Through friends of friends, we had decided to begin our Spanish training with Abesaida, a Guatemalan woman in her 50's who would provide us a home, language classes in the morning, and opportunity to explore Guatemala during the day and weekends.

Our panic threshold had steadily risen since we left Oregon; so at this point, it took a great deal to get us riled. This was an important mental state, because we arrived in Huehuetenango hours later than expected. It was very late at night and by the time Steven called Abeseida and got directions the only taxi available had left. The bus driver kindly dropped us off on a dark street in front of a school (which was closed for the night). Standing in the dark, contemplating our next move while thoughts of Guatemalan guerillas rolled through our subconscious, I smiled at our calmness. We walked down one street looking for some signs of life and found none.

176

Fortunately, "Huehue", as the locals fondly refer to it, is a small city and Abeseida was well known. Perhaps we were also not the first students to get lost? We started walking in the only direction left unexplored and found owners of a tiny café who kindly guided us. Finally heading the right direction we bumped into Evelyn (Abeseida's daughter) who was sent out to look for us. Two blocks later, gentle smiles softened our initial awkwardness as our teacher and her family greeted us.

We were all tired and couldn't understand most of what was being said and asked of us, but Steven grasped 2/3 of it. In an effort to impress our teacher he made a weak attempt to communicate using his high school Spanish:

"Mis niños estan muy casado."

Translation: My kids are very married. He had meant to say "cansado" which means "tired." Acknowledging a few confused looks, Steve realized his mistake, and explained what he meant. The laughter was a nice icebreaker. After scrambled eggs, beans, and tortillas we gratefully went to bed.

Huehue was also the temporary home of dear friends from Portland, Oregon, who were spending a year in service to the community. We had been communicating with Chris and Suzy over email about which buses to take to get to Huehue and we were eager to spend time together. Since they had given us directions, they were patiently awaiting our arrival in another part of town. It was no surprise that we missed them but even after we had arrived, eaten and gone to bed they were still trying to find us. Chris ended up sitting outside the house from 10:30-11:00 p.m. hoping to see us.

Sunday morning held a joyous reunion with Chris, Suzy, Gabriel (5), and Julia (3) as we attended mass together at the town's cathedral. What a blessing to have their friendship and presence. They speak Spanish very well and know Huehue as well as they know Portland, Oregon. Suzy's nursing skills were in high demand at the clinic for pregnant women while Chris supported the work by writing grants. Each day after classes we looked forward to time with them walking through town, taking the children to the park, teaching and playing new games in Spanish with all the children at their home or just sitting and sharing life stories.

We decided to come to Huehuetenango and stay two weeks for a number of reasons. First and foremost, we wanted to learn Spanish and Steve had met Abesaida a couple of times when she visited Oregon. He said she was very patient with him as he spoke Spanish with her, which made him think she would be a good teacher for us as a family. Second, Chris and Suzy would be living and working in Huehue for a year, so we could enjoy time together with them. Lastly, Guatemala has always had a reputation for being a colorful and mystical country with a rich Mayan history. Its recent past of civil war and stories of guerrillas killing tourists certainly made us nervous about going there, but numerous sources assured us it would be a safe place for the family, as long as we didn't go off to the jungles.

PHILOSOPHY 101: *Language*

As parents, we were determined that our children and we would not be like most Americans, knowing only their native language. As we have traveled around the world, it is humbling how many languages people know. Besides our initial travels through New Zealand and Australia, just about every person we have met speaks a minimum of two languages, often three or more. In Oregon last year, I taught mathematics to seventh grade students in a local school with Spanish speaking students. It made me acutely aware of my need to have a stronger grasp of Spanish for my work with future teachers and students.

Both Toby and I have been through the American standard two years of a foreign language. Ask anyone on the streets of America about their two-year experience and jokes are sure to follow. It is ridiculous that we don't teach kids at a younger age to learn another language. You learn an awful lot about a people, their culture, and their perspective of life, as you understand their language. In the classic film "The Gods Must Be Crazy", the African tribe in the movie has no word in their

178

language for the concept of possession. A linguist that my mom knows researched cultures and found that the English language seems to be the only language that has words for the concepts of fault and blame. Language often defines how you see the world. As we learn Spanish, I hope that it brings with it a deeper understanding not only of communication, but a different worldview as well.

We didn't know what to expect in Huehue. Our first impressions however, held true: the people were forthcoming, but the city was run down, polluted, and dirty. Suzy told us that seventy percent of the rivers in Guatemala are polluted to the point of being classified as dead rivers, as they have no remaining life in them. There appears to be a general attitude that dumping trash anywhere is an acceptable practice. As the buses go by in the street, you inevitably have to duck as someone tosses yet another plastic bag or old chicken bone out the window. People seem to think nothing of trashing the place. It is dangerous to come to a country with a western perspective and want to change things "for the better." Nevertheless, it is clear to us that the current cultural mindset there regarding care of the earth could benefit from a new way of thinking.

I could imagine living in so many of the other places we have visited in the world. Huehue was not one of them. It was not the third world poverty that was an issue. We visited many places on our trip where people live on the edge of survival. Instead, it was the cement, plain architecture, diesel-spewing buses, and the tremendous amounts of trash everywhere that was disheartening. Even the presence of such charming people could not override the physical appearance of the town. Guatemala is a gorgeous country. Guatemala City is relatively clean. Unfortunately, Huehue seems to be an uncared for holding ground for her community.

Yet, Huehue certainly has character. Because Guatemala is so prone to earthquakes, there are virtually no buildings over two stories. Similar to Egypt, Guatemalans appear to build

179

their homes with the potential for additions—that is, they build them with one story but leave enough rebar showing on the top to add a second story when they can accumulate the resources. On the rooftops of Huehue, vicious, barking dogs pace back and forth as a form of security. No need for "armed response" there. Generally, dogs roam everywhere. Steel bars surround every house. You certainly get the impression that security is a priority. Aside from one real grocery store, and the plastic grocery bags which have made their way into the waste stream in the past ten years, there is very little evidence of western influence: no McDonald's, KFC, or Pizza Hut.

The occasional cow can also be seen in vacant lots or meandering down the street. On our many walks, it paid to be looking at the street so we could dodge those piles contributed by the neighborhood animals. Pedestrians do NOT have the right of way, so "he who hesitates is squished." We kept reminiscing about the spacious and inviting sidewalks of Paris. In Huehue, they are anywhere from five inches to five feet above the street and six inches to three feet wide. You must pay attention to the occasional support wire or post sticking out of the middle of the pavement (regardless of width) or face the consequences (pun intended).

On the home front, the Spanish was very challenging for us all, particularly for Bridget and Michael. Abesaida was an excellent teacher for Steve, but was not as accustomed to teaching children, so they often got frustrated. Not having studied Spanish since high school (27 years ago) I completely shared in their frustration during my class time with Steve. My sensitivity for ESL students at home was greatly heightened. It took a few days to find combinations of student/teacher that fit ability and educational levels.

Thus, the days fell into a pattern. Steve and I rose at 6:15 to begin the day with a hike in the nearby foothills. Back to shower and have breakfast with the kids, wash the clothes on the "pila" (a cement wash basin) with a bucket, hang them to dry up on the roof terrace, classes for four hours, a late lunch, a walk to Chris and Suzy's to play and visit, then dinner with Abesaida's family before bed. It was always a joy to spend

180

time with Chris, Suzy, Gabriel and Julia; not just because we could all speak English, they are truly wonderful people whom we grew to love. With each passing day we learned a little more Spanish and felt comfortable enough to linger at the table for after meal conversations.

Our first hike up the mountain, however, was a bit more than we bargained for. As we climbed, the sounds of gunfire and explosions came from every part of the city behind us. Our nerves were frayed as we quickened our pace up the mountain. What about the kids? The thoughts of guerillas returned to the forefront of our minds as we reached the peak and looked down. Small puffs of white smoke rose from pockets between the beige buildings below. Nobody was running anywhere. It actually seemed pretty calm. After about a half-hour, the commotion subsided.

When we returned, we learned that it is a tradition in Huehue to explode fireworks on the morning of someone's birthday. Each morning from our perch on the mountaintop we were greeted by firecrackers and cherry bombs as the birthday celebrations began for somebody. Actually, lighting fireworks for just about any reason seemed to be the rule. Add to this explosive atmosphere the ever-present guards with big shotguns in front of every bank, and it is no wonder we were a bit jittery now and then.

As in Malaysia, Thailand, and Egypt, hot running water is not a common luxury in Guatemala. It took us a few brain-numbing showers and advice from Chris to master the water heating unit in the showerhead. The presence of an electric heater with water passing through it seems to go against everything I learned in Scouts about safety. This uneasiness was later justified as I got a good jolt when I stretched my hands up trying to direct the meager stream of water.

The other daily excitement was the electricity going off intermittently. The day before Thanksgiving it was off all day as we merrily prepared some of the feast over at Chris and Suzy's house. We had a tremendous time laughing, talking and cooking together when the lights suddenly came on at 5:00, which was quite fortuitous since the sun sets at 5:30. It

181

was short–lived, however, and we did the rest of our work by candlelight, then borrowed a flashlight to walk home.

Back at the house there had been no electricity or water all day so Abesaida was unable to make a typical dinner. We were thrilled to have just sandwiches since we didn't know if we could handle eggs and beans six days in a row. Five straight days had already created quite an intestinal cloud in each of us. Our host family must have different digestive fortitude that we could only appreciate from afar, as we spent time there and tried not to offend.

I had not even remembered Thanksgiving was approaching until Chris and Suzy suggested sharing it together. This event became a turning point in our relationship with Abesaida and her family as well. One of our hopes for this trip was to gain new perspectives about our lives. Thanksgiving has been a very special time to share with friends at home. Here, "El Dia de Gracias" took on added significance as we shared traditions with our old and new friends in Guatemala.

Following Spanish lessons on Thanksgiving Day, Chris, Suzy, Steve and I took over the kitchen at our house. Chris and Steve did an admirable job on the biggest bird we have ever cooked. Suzy borrowed a guitar from their house. I was in heaven playing for the first time in months. Suzy led us all in a thoughtful prayer, sharing what we were thankful for, and a song. Somehow we managed to seat fifteen people at a table built for eight. The tight squeeze added to the family atmosphere. The evening concluded with calabassa and manzana pies (squash and apple) and fun hand games we shared from Sweden. By bedtime, our friendship had grown considerably. In particular, our kids had become the playmates of Abesaida's children, Pati (about 26) and Andrea (8). From that day on, they played games every afternoon and evening, merrily mixing Spanish and English as they went.

After the meal, Steve, Chris, and I headed to the kitchen to clean up. Because they do not have running hot water, I needed to keep heating water on the stove to wash dishes. Arnoldo, the father of the house, said "Just leave it, Kata will do it in the morning." Kata is their housekeeper and cook.

Nevertheless, we could not in good conscience leave our huge mess for her to clean up. "We made the mess, we will clean it," I told Arnoldo. Once again, it was difficult not to overstep cultural boundaries. We often felt uneasy with the way Kata was treated. She was so humble, quiet, and hard working with always a smile for everyone. I wished I spoke well enough to chat with her and tell her how much her work was appreciated. She sat on a little stool in the kitchen to eat, only after everyone else had eaten his/her fill.

Chris related a heart-rending story to us as we washed the dishes. He and Suzy had lived with Abesaida for the month of October, so they got to know Kata well. She is a single mom with a fifteen-year old daughter. She works very hard to make ends meet and provide for herself and her daughter. While she is only 38, she looked as if she was in her late 50s. At the age of two or three her parents died and she was farmed out to relatives. Her brother and sister abandoned her and went to America. They have never called or written. She started working at the age of six, missing out on developing literacy in school, and has basically been on her own ever since. She works for Abesaida and her family seven days a week. Suzy and Kata share the same birthday so Suzy gave her a thoughtful gift. Kata was overwhelmed with tears saying, "But I have no money to buy you anything."

One night, when Chris and Suzy had dinner with Abesaida and her family, the meal was a tasty chicken dish. At the end of the meal, Chris was full, but he considered eating the last bit in the pan because it was so good.

"Does anyone want the last of the chicken, or should I save it for Kata?"

Abesaida said, "No, she is not eating."

Chris turned to Kata sitting on her stool in the kitchen, and asked "Why aren't you eating, Kata?"

"I am fasting for the little children of America, that God will keep them safe from terrorists."

In fact, her entire church was fasting for the children of America. Chris was so shocked and humbled by this statement, as was I in his telling it, that he suddenly had no appetite at all. Those who give out of their poverty are so much more blessed than those who give out of their excess.

We certainly had much to be thankful for. I started lingering long after dinner or sneaking in to the kitchen early in the mornings to clean up what I could before Kata arrived. Lacking sufficient Spanish I made it a point to greet her each day with a hug and kiss on the cheek. Some things can be conveyed without language proficiency.

PHILOSOPHY 101: *Competence*

I figured that these two and a half months would be challenging for us all, especially trying to learn Spanish. We have a purpose right now, unlike any other point on our trip, and there is a real sense of pressure. Each of us is responding differently to that pressure. I knew the most Spanish of us all, but I am a long way from fluent.

My friend Chris and I had a discussion the first day we were here about feelings of competence. For me, I usually feel pretty confident at home and at work. There are certainly times where I mess up and my self-esteem drops, but they are usually short lived. Over the years, I have come to the unfortunate realization that I am, in fact, human. I have had many opportunities to reinforce that perspective on this trip. I feel pretty down a few days at a time when our housing situation doesn't work out easily, we miss trains, get lost, etc. I feel like I am letting the family down by adding stress to all of our lives. Fortunately, I quickly have so many chances to redeem myself on this trip after a failure that this lack of confidence is typically short lived as well.

However, in Guatemala, it is a whole new ball game. Every day I am reminded that I am essentially illiterate in this country. I can't carry out sophisticated conversations. I am overwhelmed with the sea of words I get in response to one of my carefully crafted sentences. I am quickly learning what it feels like to have a lack of self-confidence for an extended period of time. When I carry on conversations in the safety of my classes with my teacher, she is quite patient and my sense

184

of inadequacy is mild. Once I set foot outside this haven, however, I immediately know where I stand—incompetent.

I have such a profound sense of the role of language in defining myself. As Chris said, he is a joker at home and here he can't make a joke in Spanish. So who is he? I make a living on my ability to think and teach. I can't even put together a sentence right now without stumbling along. When I was in seventh grade I had a mild stuttering problem. For a couple of years, I hesitated to say anything. Remnants of that disability pop up now and then when I teach and am not completely confident about what I want to say. This has shaped my personality as a somewhat quiet person. I need to think carefully about what I want to say before I say it.

Once again it is evident that language is shaping me as a person. Now I am starting from scratch, trying to make sense of what I hear and trying to participate. Unlike childhood, however, there are significant expectations for me to participate in society—to respond in conversations, to acquire food, bus tickets, and directions.

Two and one half months in Spanish speaking countries. How literate will I be by the end? How competent? Who will I be at the end of this challenging journey?

Our first weekend in Guatemala we decided to venture out to Lago Atitlan with Chris, Suzy, and kids. Bus travel in Guatemala was an unforgettable experience. Remember the college competition in the 50's to get as many people in a VW bug or phone booth as possible? Magnify that to the size of a school bus and you get the idea. Every inch was filled with gear and people of all ages and shapes. Invariably someone's bum was in your face. There is no concept of personal space. Bodies sit or stand anywhere and anyway. When it was time for someone to try to get off, I can only describe it as a baby coming down the birth canal and being pushed forth into the world, or the street, in this instance. Seats were in multiple states of disrepair. Yet, the people were all so kind. One very elderly woman held Bridget's sleeping bag in her lap for an hour trip between cities.

The drivers of these buses have no fear. They push those old jalopies to ridiculous speeds around the mountainous roads, usually taking up both lanes of the highway. They have tremendous confidence in their horns. "A blind curve? No problem, I'll just blast my horn and of course everyone will be out of my way!" Miraculously, this strategy actually works. At least we were fortunate enough not to witness it not working. This is particularly puzzling as some of the drivers (and their passengers) must have significant hearing loss due to the reggae or pop music playing at tremendous decibels over the speakers.

Also on each bus is an "ayudante" or helper. This guy managed to squeeze through the crowd on the bus to collect money, help people put gear on the bus, and advertise for riders as we rode through towns. He was never in the same place longer than a few minutes, appearing in one door and leaving out the back end or vice versa. In one instance, our guy loaded a large box on to the roof of the bus and then climbed back through the window of the seat next to me—all at 50 miles per hour. Imagine my surprise as I was looking out the window admiring the mountain scenery and a pair of feet, then legs swung in front of me. Ayudantes could easily hold their own against any stuntman in Hollywood.

Lago Atitlan is billed as "The Most Beautiful Lake in the World" and it certainly is one of them. Numerous volcanoes and mountains that tower above the water encircle the lake. One is still active, frequently puffing bits of smoke up into the sky. Our boat taxi delivered us from the city of Panachel on one side to San Pedro on the other. This was our first blatant taste of "Gringo price" vs. local price. I wondered if the assumption was: you are North American, you are traveling, therefore you must be rich. Suzy's excellent fluent Spanish kept us from being over charged a few times and helped us to get off at the right stops.

We enjoyed a fun weekend together, including an afternoon at the beach playing in the sand and swimming in the lake. I had a long conversation with two policemen walking the beach. They were extremely nice and very patient with my rudimentary Spanish. When Chris joined in the chat he inquired about their presence on this quiet strip of lakefront.

"So why are you guys hanging around here at the beach?"

"On the road right there we have lots of problems with people being robbed by machete wielding thieves."

Glad we took the boat! I had campaigned to walk around to the beach!

On Sunday morning in San Pedro there was an outdoor mass with indigenous people in their intricately colored traditional clothing. The procession for the Christ the King celebration involved over one thousand faithful around the town, ending in a pathway of flower petals that led up to the church. It was a brilliantly colorful affair, with people in their traditional Sunday best clothing. I think that the common assumption of people in the United States is that everyone in Latin America is Catholic. At least in Guatemala, this was far from the truth. There was a church on just about every corner of San Pedro in sizes big and small, using someone's house, an auditorium, or an official church. However, at least half of them were Pentecostal Protestant. This lends itself to a battle for airtime. While this Catholic ceremony toured the town, for instance, loud music and the sound of preachers over loudspeakers echoed down every street creating a dueling religions effect.

Traveling around as a family, high on the list of priorities was locating a bathroom at opportune times. The concept of a public bathroom is pretty foreign to most countries, particularly in the third world, and Guatemala is no exception. Women wear broad skirts that they can set down as a tent around them. Men and kids were frequently seen unloading their troubles on the side of the road or next to a building. The book Everybody Poops came to mind...I guess this has become a bit of a problem, however, because on the wall of the Catholic church, about 10 feet from the door, was a sign: "NO ORINAR AQUI", which, loosely translated means:

187

"DON'T PEE ON THE CHURCH." The eleventh commandment? Would the lightening bolt of God strike an offender? Like most women, I have always envied men for the convenience of their anatomy when needing to go and little guys like Michael seem to need to use a bathroom frequently. Discretion seemed to not be an issue in some places but it remained one with us.

One of our other outings was to the Zaculeu Ruins. These Mayan Ruins contain underground tunnels, remains of a king's pyramid palace, and a game stadium. Our expedition crew consisted of our family, Chris and his two kids, and three of the local children. After climbing all the ruins, we transformed the grassy plains into a cooperative kickball field and a stage for charades. Language was not a barrier for fun and camaraderie among Mayan history.

The night before we left, each of us was presented with a thoughtful memento. Early on the morning of our departure from Huehue we were touched that Abesaida's whole family got up to escort us to the bus stop. In spite of the challenges of learning Spanish for most of the family, we had grown to really enjoy Abesaida and her family.

Before heading on to Costa Rica, we decided to stay a night in Antigua. It was the original capitol of Central America for 200 years before being divided into its current several countries. After renting two rooms in a guesthouse run by a friend of Suzy's, we walked the streets of this bustling town. As evening fell, the three volcanoes peering down on the city were silhouetted in the sky. The lights of the central park were charming and the area full of interesting people to watch. It was bordered by an old church and a large stately building that had served as the capitol of the region. Four o'clock the next morning we rode in the back of a pickup truck for the hour drive to the airport and bid farewell to Guatemala.

188

The flight to Costa Rica from Guatemala, along the west coast of Central America, was fascinating as volcanoes and lakes dotted the landscape throughout. With this area being pulled and tugged between two continents, I can understand why they have so many earthquakes. A paradise of green, forested land with inviting beaches and turquoise waters passed beneath us. It seemed inconceivable that the three countries below: Nicaragua, Honduras, and El Salvador, have seen decades of war.

In contrast, Costa Rica has not had an army for 53 years. A national holiday on December 1st celebrates the abolition of the military. In 1948, the world was reeling from the pain of World War II. Costa Rica had just come through a two-month civil war of her own because of an election fraud. The decision was based on idealism as well as pragmatism. It is an isolated, mountainous country with basically no riches to conquer. The Minister of Security recognized that the Ministry of Education never had enough resources for its schools. The choice was between modernizing the armed forces or investing in their children's future. They chose the latter. Interestingly, the headline of that day's Tico Times predicted that Costa Rica would be the first developing country to eradicate extreme poverty.

In 1986, during Nicaragua's civil war, 250,000 were exiled here. The next year, Costa Rica's president, Oscar Arias Sanchez, won the Nobel Peace Prize for his plan for bringing peace to all of Central America. Ticos, as the locals are affectionately called, seem to blame the Nicaraguans for most of the country's social problems. Yet, it seems to be a parallel myth that in the United States most of the people on welfare are African-American. The reality here and at home is that most of the people at the margins of society are in the majority race. The same Tico Times reported that less than 10% of those in poverty are Nicaraguans.

The two major investments during our trip were our safari in Africa and our education in Costa Rica. We decided upon two weeks of informal Spanish training in Guatemala and two weeks of formal language lessons in Costa Rica. There are hundreds of Spanish schools to choose from in many countries. We had heard through our friends that Costa Rica was a safe and beautiful place. Through many hours devoted to the computer screen, Steve narrowed down the field to a few programs in San Jose that took families. ILISA's website was nicely put together and offered email addresses of families who had come to their program. In conversations over the net with these families, it was clear that ILISA had a solid program that would meet the different needs of our entire family. From the moment we arrived, we were treated with hospitality.

Most language programs offer home-stays in the country to help you practice your Spanish. Zeidy, the head of our new family welcomed us into her home. She was a single mom with three daughters. The eldest had a one-year-old son. It is the culture of Costa Rican as well as Guatemalan families that the children live with their parents until they are married. To the children's delight, the family had just been given a miniature Doberman Pinscher. Many hours were spent playing with the puppy as well as cleaning up fresh droppings around the house.

Zeidy spoiled us with delicious vegetarian versions of traditional Costa Rican cuisine. Most mornings we had gallo pinto (a beans and rice dish) with liquados (fresh squeezed fruit juices). In the evenings, dinner often included picadillo (tasty chopped up veggies), and platanos (fried bananas) for dessert.

As the school was very far from her house, our first order of business was to figure out how to get back and forth safely. San Jose, the capital of Costa Rica, is not a pedestrian safe city and our walk included two dashes across highways just to get to the bus stop. Nothing like an adrenaline rush to start your day! On Saturday, Zeidy and her daughter Julie trained us in bus system etiquette. Every bus has a different price,

190

depending on its route, in spite of the fact we always went the same distance. Classes started at 8 a.m. so we decided to bus in and walk the three miles home. Over the two weeks we were in Costa Rica our route home was never the same twice. We continually sought safer paths, so we experienced many different neighborhoods in San Jose.

It was the "low season" in the year and the events of 11 September also contributed to a relatively small student body at ILISA. Thus, we were each educated in classes ranging from one to four pupils per teacher. The facility is light and airy and the staff and teachers superb. I, for one, have never so looked forward to going to school! Some of us had classes outside in open-air classrooms surrounded by native plants and trees. In spite of predictions of hot and humid weather, it was wonderfully cool throughout most of our stay. The ever-blowing breeze orchestrated awesome cloud patterns that brought weather changes reminiscent of Oregon. During each week at ILISA, the school organized cultural activities after classes ranging from how to make arroz con leche, to dancing Salsa, to learning about coffee production.

To help your geography skills a bit, Costa Rica is nestled between Nicaragua to the north, Panama to the south, the Caribbean Sea to the east, and the Pacific Ocean to the west. We thought we had a lot of rain in Oregon but we learned that, on the Caribbean side, Costa Rica gets ten feet of rain annually.

Our weekends were devoted to exploring Costa Rica's treasures. The first weekend adventure was a trip to explore Manuel Antonio, a wild jungle preserve right next to pristine beaches. After a four-hour bus ride from San Jose, we enjoyed an evening swim in the temperate waters of the Pacific Ocean. The next day we hiked into the preserve. It is impossible to characterize the astounding diversity of plant life all around us. Palms, ferns, and trees of all different sizes and leaf patterns surrounded us as we walked the tropical paths. We delighted in the slow and methodical movements of sloths, the fascinating eating habits of iguanas as they slurped up flowers

191

in the sand with their long tongues, the haunting call of howler monkeys, and numerous brilliantly painted butterflies. It was an odd sensation, and such a relief, to be engrossed in the jungle life then suddenly come to a clearing to see the vast ocean before us with a magnificent, rugged volcanic coastline among white sandy beaches. Costa Rica's coast is like Hawaii without all the development and high prices.

Right on the shoreline, a dozen or so Capuchin monkeys are considered pests by the rangers, but playmates for the tourists. They are more than willing to violate the "don't feed the monkeys" rule, whether people hand them tidbits or they manage to swipe something from someone's picnic basket. The small primates look cute from a distance but when seen eye-to-eye they have a menacing scowl. Knowing that humans are suckers for their cuteness and tiny stature they have developed schemes less aggressive than the black kites of Africa but just as effective. It is not uncommon for two monkeys to distract a group of tourists while three or more raid unprotected beach totes for wallets, sunglasses and watches. I'm not sure about where the monkey black market would be for valuables.

With heat and humidity the likes of Hawaii in August the clear, refreshing ocean water was relief beyond description. We could have stayed in it all day. The weekend ended all too quickly and we were back in our classes on Monday.

Our final weekend in Costa Rica we ventured out to the Monteverde Cloud Forest with two of our classmates, Billy and Ayesha. Four Quakers from the United States were jailed in 1948 for opposing the draft. After serving time in prison, they were in search of a country that honored their perspective of pacifism. They found Costa Rica, a country without an army, and bought the uninhabited land of Monteverde in 1952. For twenty years, they were the stewards of one of the most extraordinary rain forests in the world. The oxcart roads that lead to Monteverde are not much better today than they were then. The locals continue to oppose road improvements because they want to protect the forest from over tourism. In

1972, the Tropical Science Center of San Jose took over the protection of the land from the Quakers.

At one time, Costa Rica was almost entirely forested. Deforestation is currently their prime environmental problem, with over two percent being lost each year. While Monteverde is well funded and protected by international organizations (only 120 people are allowed in at a time), national parks are still being logged illegally because the government can't afford to protect them. If you have ever seen the advertisements to sponsor an acre of rainforest, this is one of the beneficiaries. Rain forests cover about 7% of the earth's surface, but are thought to contain over half of the world's species of living organisms. After walking through this incredibly diverse environment, I can certainly believe it. In the Monteverde gift shop there was a t-shirt in Spanish and English: "Only after the last tree has been cut down, the last river has been poisoned, and the last fish is dead, will we come to realize that we can't eat money."

The rain forests are the jewels of Costa Rica. Ticos have a very popular saying, which I think is the only way to summarize Monteverde: "Pura Vida." Pure life. Pure wildlife of ferns, moss, lush plants, huge trees, and vines so long it was impossible to distinguish if they were roots growing down or vines growing up. Where was Tarzan? On more than one occasion Billy and Steve were very tempted to leave the well-made paths and try swinging.

We spent all of Saturday swimming through an ocean of green. The rain forest was true to its name, and it rained almost our entire hike. We were engulfed in a magical world with thousands of shades of green. The occasional spot of color, such as the orange and red of the bird of paradise plant, stood out starkly in this green world. It reminded me of advertisements in which everything is in black and white except for the Gatorade drops or the one person in color. While we spent a significant amount of time searching in vain for the multicolored Quetzal bird, we did manage to see an unimaginable variety of hummingbirds and an impressive display of the codependence of plant life. The trails, built of cement blocks and tree stumps, were the best maintained that I have ever seen, given the swampy conditions. Natural springs come right up out of the ground in some places while the bridges help you to cross rivers in others.

The adventures continued with the hike to the suspension bridge that puts visitors 100 feet above the forest floor, right up into the canopy, over a mighty canyon and river. Just as we left the main road we heard a resounding crack that echoed through the hills. A large tree fell across the path we had just occupied. Nature is constantly building up and breaking down. Thankfully we did not become part of the breaking down. At one point in the hike we stood at the top of the Continental Divide. Engulfed in clouds, however, we could not see the promised view of the Atlantic and Pacific Oceans. Winds blow over 80 mph in this forest moving the clouds with ferocious velocity. We were literally inside the fast moving clouds most of the morning. The cool, windy and wet weather was absolutely invigorating.

In the afternoon we visited a butterfly garden. The tour was given by a young psychology student from Canada. She was backpacking through Latin America for a year and ran out of money. This volunteer job offered her room and board in exchange for leading tours. After two weeks she already sounded like a life long expert on bugs and butterflies. Highlights of the tour:

1. **The rhinoceros beetle**: huge with a long claw coming out of its forehead that helps it chop off the heads of rival beetles.

2. **Spicy beetles**: they help cure asthma and have a bit of spiciness when eaten. (We passed on the opportunity. Ayesha, our biologist friend, had already regaled us with tales of her eating florescent green ant butts in Australia, which have tremendous amounts of vitamin C. She sampled the beetles and said they were not as spicy as advertised.)

3. **The Chaga Bug:** found in Central and South America, it kills more people than AIDS, malaria, and Dengue Fever combined. It is dark gray with six legs, a ridge like

194

hump on its back, with a long straw-like mouth, and is about two inches long. While people sleep, it bites like a mosquito, sucks blood, and then defecates on the wound. The protozoans in the poop enter the person's blood stream and ultimately lodge in the heart where it takes about 30 years for them to multiply enough to explode the heart. Gross! Needless to say, the kids were freaked out. Once again, the tour guide was no help…

Our kids inquire with hope of reassurance:

"Do they have those bugs in Peru?"

Tour Guide: "Only in really poor areas. Where are you going next?"

"A really poor area."

4. **Leafcutter ants:** It is fascinating to watch these little guys carry bits of leaves ten times their size across branches and into their underground homes. They don't eat the leaves, but pack them in a corner where they feed a fungus that the ants eat. The indigenous people use the soldier ants to close cuts by placing them on top of a wound and taking the head off. This causes the feet to grab and close the wound like stitches.

5. **Butterflies vs. Moths**: Moths use twigs and leaves to construct a cocoon while butterflies simply spit silk. When inside, the caterpillar breaks down into a fluid form of cells that rearrange into its adult form. We each got to name and release a butterfly into the gardens. Some of the butterflies were as big as your hand with bright colors and intricate patterns.

By Monday we were back in San Jose for goodbyes to our host family and classmates. Sleeping bags in hand and daypacks on our backs, we braved the traffic for the last time and caught two buses to the airport with plenty of time to check in. We proceeded to sit for four hours because our plane was delayed for two hours.

•   •   •   •   •

Before diving into stories of our final continent, we thought we'd stop for a moment to reflect on an important topic for our family: bathrooms. Someone, somewhere, must have studied toilet practices around the world for a college thesis. It would certainly be valuable literature for traveling parents. If not, here is a head start based on our hierarchy of toilets around the world.

BASIC DESIRABILITY RANKING SYSTEM

★   A structure exists
★★   It is open
★★★   It has a toilet, not just a hole
★★★★   It is free of charge
★★★★★   It is not flooded
★★★★★★   It has toilet paper
★★★★★★★ It is clean with no bugs

DETAILED REALITY RANKING SYSTEM			
Location	**Country**	**Tips**	**Etiquette**
1) Next to the truck	Tanzania	• Stay close to the truck--just in case a lion approaches.	Guys in front, girls in back
2) Tree or bush	Anywhere there is a tree/bush and not too many people	<u>Trees</u>: Stand far enough away from the tree that you don't get splashed. <u>Bushes</u>: Check for poison oak!	The tree is for privacy not for watering! (In Guatemala, privacy is low on the priority list.)
3) Pit toilet- -a hole in the ground with a shack around it	Malaysia, Thailand, Egypt (economy grade)	• Take a deep breath before going in. • Learn how to squat while simultaneously swatting flies. • Try to open and shut the door without actually touching it.	Squat low and aim straight, the next patron will appreciate it. Muslim rule: use your left hand to wipe.

4) Raised pit toilet in a shack: the hole is higher due to the cement built up around it	Malaysia, Thailand, Egypt (premium grade)	• Squat anyway, because it is too nasty to sit on. • Aim is a bit easier here. • Handkerchiefs are handy to have to cover your nose	Try to keep noises to a minimum, as the hole goes through to the stall next door…
5) Toilet seat in rural surround-inks	Peru Paraguay	• That bucket next to the toilet needs to be filled and poured in to flush.	Wash your hands as you fill the bucket.
6) Toilet seat in uncertain environs, i.e. gas station or train station	Most places	• Bring extra TP to place around the seat or wipe it clean. • "That will be 50 cents please."	People are waiting! Speed it up!
7) Basically clean toilet with limitations	Guatemala Parts of Costa Rica	• For high quantity, plan for multiple flushes and/or try to go in spurts	Bad plumbing in the whole country: don't throw the TP in the toilet but in the basket.
8) Clean toilet	First world luxury	• Count your blessings! • Read manual on how to use bidets ahead of time.	• Lift the lid and don't pee on the seat! • Put the lid back when finished.

General tips: In all cases, BYOTP (Bring Your Own Toilet Paper). It doesn't hurt to have a few moistened toweletts handy as well. (We saved these from airplanes for later use.) An easy alternative is a small bottle of sanitizing soap. Keep change handy: it costs money to go in just about every toilet in the world (tourists/gringos usually pay double). While we did not patronize American franchises overseas, the occasional McDonald's is handy now and then…it is just a matter of overcoming your guilt for not buying anything while using the facilities.

One interesting profession around the world is the toilet attendant. Not much room for career movement here, but a job nonetheless. There are different responsibilities and different approaches to doing this job. Some attendants are very pleasant, greet you with a smile, and take pride in their work (the bathrooms are spotless and you never have to scrounge for T.P.). Others sit with their feet up on a desk watching television and smoking a cigarette while the restroom looks like it was hit by a cyclone. I can always tell which women have children; they are sympathetic to pregnant women in desperate need of a bathroom **now** and are familiar with the side-to-side dance of a child who has waited too long to let his/her parents know that "I need to go!"

The levels of responsibility vary and can basically be summed up thus:

1. The attendant sits behind a caged desk like a banker, you pay and he presses a buzzer to unlock an electronic passage.
2. The attendant leans against a table with a bowl for money. Toss in your coins and she indicates with a nod which stall you may use.
3. There are pay locks on the doors and the attendant has his own "office" holding the tools of his trade, his TV and his cell phone. His sole purpose, as the toilet police, is to keep the stalls stocked and watch out for tourists who, in protest of high prices to pee, will hold the door for the next customer so they don't have to pay.
4. The turnstile is another pay-and-enter barrier which gives the attendant the power to choose who will enter for free and who will pay. Often a sympathetic attendant would instruct Michael and Bridget to simply crawl under for free.
5. The toilet is a run down old shack where the attendant sits on a stool, takes your money and gives you four squares of T.P. These toilets are in the countries where it is not uncommon for the tourist to be suffering from the reaction to foreign water or cooking methods. Sometimes four squares are just not enough. Fortunately, we learned to

198

always carry extra but there were times we let our guard down, especially in wealthier countries where we expected it would be provided. One incident stands out. In Salzburg, Clare and Bridget needed to use the public toilet. There was a long line and a grouchy attendant who was chain smoking and choking up the place. She grabbed Clare's money, refused to give her change and then to add insult to injury Clare was shown to a stall that had no T.P!

In all countries it seems that one of the perks of being a toilet attendant is the power to charge different prices at will as they try to ascertain what country you hail from and how badly you have to go. Never has the law of supply and demand been stronger.

AWARDS FOR BEST ENGINEERING
Toilets have all sorts of interesting engineering. In one place in Italy, when you push a button the toilet makes a loud noise and sanitary paper is rolled onto the toilet seat, like a train on a track. Then there are the laser toilets usually in airports. Somehow they know when you are finished and flush on their own. (I don't think they are that smart because they always seem to flush just when I am about to sit down. I hate that.)

Notable in this commentary of bathrooms is the "Space Toilet." In modern cities such as Barcelona and Paris, you will occasionally see one of these space capsules on a street corner. Imagine you are on the bridge of the starship Enterprise. To boldly go where no man has gone before, you put your 10 francs in the slot and the door slides open (complete with techno sounds) while a gentle, sanitizing mist dissipates, revealing the toilet stall. We had the misfortune of needing to use one of these now and then…notes from Steve's journal…

• • • • •

DATELINE: November in Barcelona, Spain

The kids are about ready to explode so we need to find a bathroom fast. Just below the castle on the hill is the Space Toilet. As much as we hate spending money on a toilet, we are in a desperate state. Toby deposits the pesetas in the slot, and she and the kids all cram into the one room suite. The hydraulic noises announce that the door is closing. Meanwhile, I stand outside waiting. An old man limps over to me and says in Spanish,

"Psst. Hey buddy, come here," sounding like a guy who is about to sell me some watches.

"No, thanks," I say, not being in need of any additional souvenirs.

"No, really. Come here," he says slyly with a bit of a wink.

I reluctantly follow. He walks around the food stall as if he has contraband around the corner and he shows me a small toilet just outside the food stall.

"It's free!" he whispers.

There is that uncomfortable moment as I assess whether I really need to go to the bathroom versus whether I am going to hurt his feelings for turning down his secret. I opt for passing on the potty offer, and tell him

"Thanks anyway, but I don't need to go."

He looks a bit hurt that I didn't take advantage of his kindness, so I feel guilty. Meanwhile, the space toilet grunts and groans and Toby and the kids emerge from the capsule. We head off for more adventures as I give the old man a little wave goodbye. I guess rebels come in all shapes, sizes, ages, and causes.

"The service we render to others
is really the rent we pay for our room on this earth.
It is obvious that man is himself a traveler;
that the purpose of this world is not
'to have and to hold' but 'to give and to serve.'
There can be no other meaning."
Sir Wilfred T. Grenfell
Canadian Doctor, Humanitarian, and Author

PERPSECTIVES ON POVERTY

PIURA, PERU   17 December

We had planned for our travels in Latin America to have a significantly different twist to them than the rest of the trip. Here we had specific objectives, unlike our exploration-oriented first five months. The month in Central America was focused on learning Spanish. When we entered Peru, our intent was to provide service to others. During our trip, it was extremely important for us to weave in time devoted to giving rather than receiving. We tremendously admire friends with children, like Chris and Suzy in Guatemala, and Jeanine and Mark in Brazil, who have dedicated their families for one to four years of service. Not prepared for that duration of commitment, we wanted to work for at least three weeks in a different culture or cultures, doing whatever we could for people in poverty.

This simple thought was incredibly more complicated in practice. Steve searched for over six months trying to find an organization to facilitate our desire to volunteer. As it turns out, there are a tremendous number of groups that are geared to providing that assistance. Most of them can be found on web sites. Unfortunately, there are also a number of obstacles for a family of five. Not many places are willing to take children. Those that are will only take them if:

1) they are very young (i.e. 1 year old)
2) you are willing to stay at least one year
3) you are willing to pay big money for the organization's coordination of work.

Each of these requirements proved to be an unending source of frustration. In spite of many bleary-eyed hours searching the Internet Steve had little success.

Sharing his thwarted efforts with friends, one conversation proved to be fortuitous:

Steve: "...and so I am getting very frustrated. I can't believe how difficult it has been to volunteer to help someone."

Julie: "Why don't you just contact some priest in some third world spot and tell him you want to help out?"

Steve: "I hadn't thought of that."

Julie: "As a matter of fact, I have a friend from college who is a priest in a poor town in Peru. I just saw him at my 20th college reunion and got his email address."

The rest, as they say, is history. Steve contacted Father Joe in Piura, which is a small town in northern Peru and asked if he needed any help.

"There are always opportunities to help the poor, Steve."

He offered his rectory as a place for us to stay as we worked with the community. Success!

Getting to Piura was not without the usual comedy of errors. The flight from Costa Rica left two and a half hours late, putting us into Lima at night. The airport tourism desk guided us to a suitable, cheap, next-to-the-airport hotel that included a shuttle and breakfast. At four the next morning, we feasted on one roll and a bit of warm milk then jumped in the van for the early flight to Piura. Being experienced travelers at this point, we arrived at the airport in plenty of time and decided to split up. I stood in the long line to pay the airport tax, while Steve and the children went to pick up the tickets. Reaching the front of the line, the teller informed me that I had to have the tickets in hand to pay the tax. I glanced quickly up to Steve, who was deep in conversation in Spanish at the airline counter. We had hit a small snag in our finely tuned operation.

Throughout this trip we made reservations for planes, hotels, and tours. Unbelievably, every one of them worked out just as planned. For the first time, our preparation ahead of time failed us. The airline staff informed us that the reservation we had secured for the flight to Piura was not sufficient.

"Yes, you have reservations, but you don't have seats."

Jerry Seinfeld has a great comedy routine on this very subject. He describes the scene as he is at the car rental desk trying to pick up the car he had reserved:

"I see. You know how to make a reservation, you just don't know how to hold the reservation. And that is the important part, the holding. That is where I come and you have a car for me."

So at 5:30 a.m., they had our reservation, just not a place to sit on the plane. Steve tried his best at the airline counter:

Counter person: "Our next flight is at 12 noon."

"Okay."

"We do have four spaces left on the waiting list for the 7 a.m. flight."

"Okay. But there are five of us."

"Sorry."

"We'll take the four places."

We hoped for the best, and prepared for the worst. Steve foolishly asked if I wanted to take the kids on ahead. "Are you crazy? Your Spanish is better than mine! We are sticking together!" Thankfully, at 6:30, we got the word that they had enough spaces for all of us. Steve secured tickets, I paid the airport tax, and we ran for the plane. No time to check in our luggage, so everything came with us, including all those now-forbidden pointy items (scissors, pocketknife, etc.). With the customary five minutes to spare, we jumped into our seats,

203

spaced throughout the plane. A cup of juice calmed our nerves as we sailed over the Andes' snow-capped, rugged peaks, jutting above the clouds. I wished we had time to visit there!

Landing in Piura, we walked from the plane to the terminal. A large group of people in red shirts were yelling and singing in Spanish on a balcony overlooking the tarmac. Being last off the plane, we wondered who was receiving this attention. No one was returning the enthusiasm. Drawing nearer we heard them a bit more clearly. "Steve, Steve! Somos de la iglesia de Padre Jose! Bienvenidos a Piura!" (We are from Father Joe's church! Welcome to Piura!)

With that enthusiastic welcome, we entered the Santisimo Sacramento (Blessed Sacrament) community with open arms. Fr. Joe's parish in Piura is in the northern corner of Peru, about two hours from the border of Ecuador. It is basically in the middle of the desert surrounded by sand and not a thing on the horizon but the horizon line. A blessed evening breeze typically brought a refreshing end to the hot, dry, or humid days. A trip to the shower revealed an apparatus with only one knob—the cold faucet. Another country without hot running water, but here the cold showers were a welcome relief.

PHILOSOPHY 101: *Harmony?*

I am simultaneously extremely anxious and looking forward to Piura and the opportunity to serve others. I want so much for us to truly work for the community and not simply be tourists of poverty. Our aspiration here is to put our hands and selves to use for others. I don't exactly know what that means at the moment. I am praying that it will be significant, not just for us and our well being, but that our efforts improve the lives of people who need support in Piura.

It is such a delicate balance doing service. Is this for selfish reasons? In a way, we want to use the experience to educate our kids about the importance of giving our time to help others. Also, it feels good to serve others and people appreciate what you do for them. Maybe it even relieves some guilty feelings about our advantages in life.

On the other hand, we truly want to give unselfishly and unconditionally, expecting absolutely nothing in return. If it is a difficult task and no one will know we did it, is it still worth doing? I hope each one of us can respond to that situation positively in our time here, for in my mind, that is surely the litmus test of service.

There are many emotions involved in providing service to the poor. Part of the reality is that we have so much more than we need and they need so much more than they have. We don't want to go into Piura with an attitude that we have everything to give and nothing to receive. What gifts, talents, or beauty will we receive from them? Can we give and receive harmoniously?

Standing at 6'2" Fr. Joe looks like a pro-basketball player towering above every citizen in Piura. His soft-spoken manner and dedication to the poor remind me of St. Francis, while his beard and long locks hint of Jesus. After graduating from Notre Dame, his primary goal was to go to a third world country and do all he could. Ten years he has been there now and the fruits of his labor are apparent. Santisimo Sacramento serves 33 outlying villages and the city, approximately 33,000 people.

This parish is open to the community and seemed to be occupied 24 hours a day. The church basically performs all the functions one would expect of agencies or social service groups: drug and alcohol rehabilitation, jobs and job training, food, clothing, shelter, education, and medical, dental, psychological and natural medicine care. Thus, his paid and volunteer staff is kept incredibly busy all day, every day.

Living upstairs in the parish house, we had two brick walled rooms with cement floors and access to a kitchen overlooking the rest of the church proper. Mosquito nets adorned our beds after our first night of providing a feast for the "sanguros." The parish community did their best to make us feel at home by stringing a row of Christmas lights across one wall and bringing up a tiny plastic Christmas tree for the kitchen, complete with a manger scene. We were also invited to use the stair tower to watch sunsets, listen to music, or just sit and view the city (which we did often).

Our days developed a routine as we kept insisting to Father, "We came here to work." His home parish in Edmonton, Oklahoma had recently sent two semi-truck sized containers full of donations (including a new Ford van). Although our assignments varied, each day we spent hours sorting, bagging and delivering clothes, toys and food to the impoverished villagers. One day we all tore down and began to build a new home. The kids worked along side us in the heat, dust and sand all morning. After lunch Steve and I returned to the work site with the crew while the kids were kept busy at the parish bagging toys and panetone (Italian Christmas loaf).

As in other poor countries, the people construct their homes out of whatever they can find or afford. The house we tore down, which was about fifteen feet square, had served the twenty-five residents for seven years. It was made of cardboard, plastic bags, tree branches, reeds, cane, bamboo mat walls and thin metal sheet roofing. We replaced this with sturdy bamboo poles, cane mat walls, and thin plywood front walls, with a new roof of thin cement-like material, all put together with wire and nails. The floor is just sand. Manuel, the foreman for the project, told us that the estimated life of this new home would be approximately four years and cost a few hundred dollars to make. Working until 6:30 that evening we finished a little over half the house.

I felt very grateful and a bit guilty the next day as Steve and I were asked to do the prison run instead of going out to complete the house. It was brutally hot that day, anything but house building weather. The children worked all morning preparing hundreds of buttered rolls to accompany the four-foot tall barrel of luke warm chocolate milk to be delivered to the prisoners. They stayed behind and sorted clothes while we headed out to the prison. Fr. Joe said that it isn't Christmas for the people of Peru until they have had chocolate milk and bread.

Our trip to the prison took us through the Universidad Nacional de Piura (the public university), which we noticed was in great need of repair. After the university the paved road turned to dirt and another poor village of reed and mud huts appeared. Peru has 45,000 miles of roads, but only about 15% are paved. Immediately following the village was the incongruous sight of a lush, green, private cemetery with gorgeous trees, grass and flowers. I said to Ginet (a young social worker who is Fr. Joe's right hand employee) that the dead live better than the living. I guess my Spanish was accurate enough to get my meaning across because she laughed at the comparison and said, "That's true!"

The prison appeared to be in the middle of a barren desert. It was a desolate area with no trees. Had they cleared them or don't they grow out there? It was very low security compared to Los Angeles and Salem prisons. They are so poor that they cannot afford to put prisoners in uniforms. Most of the guards were only distinguishable by t-shirts and baseball caps. Prisoners wear their own clothes and hair is varying lengths, not shaved as Steve and I have seen in the U.S. Inmates in LA wear numbered, color-coded coveralls, which readily labels the severity of an offence. Ironically, due to poverty, the inmates of Peru maintain their identity and dignity.

We walked from place to place inside the prison stopping to distribute the chocolate milk and rolls. The men, from murderer to petty thief, eagerly waited in line for this once a year Christmas treat. Each man at the Piura prison had a cup, bowl, pitcher or dirty old pot—anything metal or plastic that would hold liquid or food. Some looked gross but it was all a man had. My guess is that is the only means of receiving meals. We were touched at how they looked after each other-- lending a cup or bowl to another inmate or getting bread for someone else. They did not have the hollow "dead man walking" look I have seen on prisoners in the States. Instead they were alive, jovial and grateful.

Grateful does not begin to describe the reception at the villages each time we made a delivery. The truck was loaded with huge sacks full to bursting with donated items. The presence of the church's truck rolling and honking through the village often made people drop everything to run and see what had arrived. We entered the school, church, or designated home where women had lined up in the hot sun waiting. A big blue tarp, not much cleaner than the sand floor, was stretched out on the ground and we began dumping piles of clothing. The women were invited in 5-10 at a time, depending on space, and the organized chaos began.

Each searched the piles for a set number of pieces, usually about six. Sometimes they paid one sole (about US $0.25) per item, other times it was free. Paying or not, the women hugged and kissed us and thanked us for their treasures. They often trusted me with their sleeping babies while they dug through the piles of clothing. On one hot morning, I cuddled an eight day old infant and wondered if her life would continue in this cycle of poverty or would she one day get an education and a career. How much personal sacrifice and perseverance does it take for a child such as this to advance from this day forward, overcoming all the obstacles, until they rise out of poverty?

Steve learned a quick lesson as we did our deliveries on the first day. We stopped by a house for one of the staff to check on a family. The rest of us all politely waited in the car. One little boy who lived there came up and asked pointedly, "Why are you not coming into my home?" Steve interpreted his question as "Is my house too poor for you rich Americans to come inside?" From that point forward, he made a point of going in with the staff each time we stopped at a house. He became our representative, being introduced to the family who lived there as "the people from the United States who are helping us." Kisses on the cheeks, hugs, and "mucho gusto" (I'm very pleased to meet you) were common rituals in the poorest to the nicest of houses, communicating that we had relationships with each person we helped, and that they were not simply someone to give things to. They were honored to have us in their homes. Human contact was just as important as stuff.

Christmas in Peru means chocolate milk, panetone, Las Posadas, and fireworks. Panetone is a cross between a fruit loaf (the one with florescent pieces of fruit that is the brunt of many Christmas jokes in the United States) and a big round loaf of sheepherder's bread. It is a tradition somehow borrowed from Italy.

Five days before Christmas we celebrated Las Posadas. Joseph, a pregnant Mary, and a burro led the people on the traditional walk through town. At occasional points, Joseph and Mary knocked at a door, and we all sang Spanish Christmas carols. Many were American favorites with Spanish words, so we could almost follow along. At the end of the singing, Father Joe would inquire whether there was room at the inn: "Hay Posadas?" Upon hearing the inevitable "No" we would walk off to another home, ending at the church, with Joseph and Mary taking their places in the live manger scene among the cow, burro, goat, lamb, chickens, and turkeys. The evening concluded with a few more Christmas carols and a community gathering.

There was no mention of Santa Claus and gifts are not really exchanged. You may see an occasional Christmas tree, but the main focus of the season is the Holy Family and the birth of Jesus. Christmas Eve came upon us quickly. Midnight mass began at 10 p.m. with joyous music and a lively beat. An uproar of cheer echoed in the church as Father Joe entered and declared "Jesus is born!" The cheers rose once again as he picked up the live "baby Jesus" from the manger scene at the front of the church and raised him high in the air. Christmas morning, our children awoke to a present from us, a simple finger harp from Kenya and a small toy from Santa in a stocking (each child had hung one of Steve's socks—they were clean).

I'm sure that all of you, throughout your lives have had what I call "booster shots" or God moments. It is a feeling that results from reading or experiencing something that momentarily stops you in your tracks, and makes you remember, refocus, and re-learn what is truly important in life. The play "Our Town", the book "Living, Loving, and Learning", the movie "Forest Gump", a brilliant sunset on the ocean, the sun rising over a snow-capped mountain, waterfalls, and a child's hand in yours are a few of mine. They are the hiccups of life that cause you to stop and think, "I want to hold on to this feeling."

I had numerous booster shots on the world trip, but none so sustained as being with the people of that parish, and working daily among the poor. The children struck me the most. There were thousands of them in each pueblo. As in Africa, they have nothing to play with but what nature provides. Then we loaded up the truck and made our deliveries, handing out donated new and used balls, stuffed toys, dolls, puzzles, and little plastic toys from fast food restaurants. The children were thrilled with anything.

Given that we were on our trip and had limited space, expectations were low for numerous presents, as can be the usual American custom. That year there was no shopping stress and no real focus on gifts. Instead, we seemed to be focusing a lot more on others...particularly the people of the villages. I wondered if our children were a bit disappointed not to have gifts to open from their relatives. However, on one of our walks, Bridget and Michael said that they really enjoyed Christmas in Peru. They just missed their relatives. We all did. Our Christmas morning consisted of writing down what we wished for each other. I can't say whether it will have a profound and lasting impact, but the simplicity of this Christmas was refreshing.

There are some incidents that I think will have a lasting impact on all of us. Steve is a wiz with bicycles so we offered to spend an afternoon repairing and cleaning up all the donated children's bikes and scooters. Just before Christmas we loaded the truck for delivery. There is not a more joyous sight than the look on the faces of those families when they received one used bike for ten kids to share. The boys did not complain one bit when all that was left in their size was an obviously girl's bike (pink and purple with "Barbie" written on it.)

That same afternoon we returned to the church, regrouped and headed right back out to help with a Christmas gathering in another village. Pulling up to a small, dusty church we skirted the ever-present, mangy, truck-chasing dogs and rearranged the rickety wooden benches on the cement floor. The 150 children were invited in to sit down. Each had brought his/her own cup or glass from home to receive the coveted chocolate milk. The mothers remained in the doorway watching as the children were led in prayer, songs and then served chocolate milk and buttered rolls. With an abundance of rolls Clare and I were able to serve the mothers outside as well. Finally, the children were given a little toy and that was it. In all of maybe twenty to thirty minutes their Christmas came and went.

From the back of the truck, we continued through the pueblo distributing the rest of the toys. One tiny little girl of maybe 3-5 years ran after the truck for a good 200 yards trying to get a toy. When she finally got to the driver's side door she was ecstatic to receive a simple gift. Just as we were driving away, an older girl suddenly grabbed the toy from her and the little girl was trampled. As we pressed on, her mother led her home in tears. All of us were very upset at the injustice. Was it better not to give anyone anything if you can't guarantee something for everyone?

At our next stop we told Ginet (our driver) what had happened and she drove around the village back to the area. Twenty minutes later, Clare and Bridget spotted the little girl outside her shack with her mother, still crying. Ginet gave her a tiny plastic doll and she clutched it to her cheek as if it was a precious puppy. Her smile was jubilant, but did all that previous effort and pain justify the end result?

The whole incident seemed like a metaphor for life: it can be completely unfair and arbitrary. With not enough for everyone we first tried to give to the youngest children and only when there was not a large group. Some children ran for blocks sucking in exhaust and dust, receiving nothing for their

211

efforts, while one lad just standing by the road with his father was given a toy. The distribution was sporadic as our driver had to constantly assess the safety issue. Once too many kids started gathering, we had to move on. In the States we are taught that you can achieve anything if you work hard enough. Success was entirely random there, not tied to how far you ran barefoot through gravel.

There was occasional fighting as some kids grabbed toys away from others. Yet, there were also times where one or two toys were delivered to a large family and they immediately shared together. A small girl could not run fast enough to get to the truck, so an older child brought her a toy. On the other hand, many kids came up to the truck with one hand behind their back hiding what they had already received. Is it greedy to want two toys?

What a set of conflicting emotions! I handed a little girl a new stuffed animal wrapped with a bright red bow and she glowed with excitement. The boys ran from the truck cheering with their new balls. What a tremendous power we had to give joy to children in such a simple way. Still, as we drove around the village, hundreds of kids came running to the truck. In spite of the fact that we gave out thousands of toys, there were not enough to go around. Before we came, they had no expectations of presents for Christmas, as do children in the States. Had we raised some kids' hopes only to dash them? Is that a worse deed than bringing joy to the thousands of children we did manage to give a toy? This was mental turmoil.

During our time in Piura we tried to offer our services in any way possible. One of the first questions that Father Joe asked of us was what strengths did we have to share with the poor? At the time, it was not a very easy question to answer. However, each of us seemed to find our niches. I brought my hair cutting scissors to one larger village and cut hair for two hours while everyone else facilitated the clothes distribution. This was a challenging task in more ways than one, as one lady's hair was full of lice. Steve created an entire web site for the parish. The kids eagerly hugged and played with all of the

212

staff, providing nice breaks from the work now and then. We all helped with house demolition and reconstruction. I hope that our efforts were valuable.

Father Joe is very sensitive to not becoming the eternal Santa Claus of the city. Having the resources of generous churches in the United States behind him, he is unique in Piura. He takes great care to provide just enough support to keep families off the edge of survival, while not diminishing their need to find work. In our occasional evening chats, he related his philosophy of the importance of self-respect and dignity. These come from being able to provide for your family. He initiated a program called Family to Family in which 450 families in the States have sponsored 450 families here. At $25 per month, a family will not starve but have their basic needs met so they can focus on establishing a consistent source of income. As they say, a hand up is more dignified than a hand out.

Hard work made the days fly by. On New Year's Eve the church was packed for the 11 p.m. mass. The music was upbeat and so was Fr. Joe. The New Year began, as mass was ending, to the serenade of fireworks exploding in the sky all around us. Outside, small bonfires lit up the street in the traditional burning of an effigy. Earlier in the day we had passed by many vendors who were selling "los muñecos" or stuffed figures of bad people from the past year. Former Peruvian President Fujimori (who resigned due to corruption) and Osama Bin Laden were favorite characters to torch this year. There were a few Bill Clinton and George Bush muñecos as well. They burn the effigy to represent all the bad things that happened in the past year that will be erased to start the New Year with a fresh slate.

The people of the parish hugged and kissed us with the greeting "Feliz año!" We were so fortunate to be in their company. A group of us went up to the tower to watch the night sky and showers of sparks below. Bridget and I found the North Star and prayed for peace.

PHILOSOPHY 101: *Harmony Part II*

I have often worked "for" the poor in soup kitchens, delivered clothes or food, built homes, etc. Knowing how much I have in relation to how much most of the rest of the world has, compels me to give of my time and resources to those who need support.

Now this is not meant to be an essay on how humanitarian I am. On the contrary, my experience in Peru has shaken my perspective a bit...I entered this community in Piura with the unconscious assumption that I was going to help "those poor people." In essence, we have done just that. For the past two weeks, we have built houses, delivered food, clothing, and toys to people in very poor villages. However, there has been a significant twist. The "we" part.

Each day, a group from the church worked with us as we delivered and built. But then, something simple and momentous happened. We stopped by one of their houses. It was in the same village where we were helping other people with the same dirt floor and the same bamboo walls and tin corrugated roof. At the end of the day, they return to their homes here. I had made that unconscious assumption that "we" church people were out helping the poor. In fact, the "we" was the poor. The group of people that we were working with were every bit as poor as the people we were helping. In my mind there was an emotional realization that there is an important distinction between working "for" and working "with."

Intellectually, I have always known this is an important perspective. Emotionally, and on a deeper level, however, that awareness was not truly present within me until now. These are not people who are some entity somehow outside of me, but next to and within me. I wonder if people such as those who work in the Peace Corps or other long-term service domestically or internationally have that denouement, that feeling of internal transformation, in which "them" becomes "us." The people I am working with are my friends, my companions, my fellow helpers, the poor. What a gift in personal formation I have received from them this day! What an important metamorphosis in viewpoint!

Courtesy of Steven, Santisimo Sacramento began 2002 by entering the technological age. He worked tirelessly for three days with his digital camera and laptop computer creating a parish website for them. The website is in English, because the purpose is to let people in the States know about the volunteer and donation opportunities to help this community in Piura. After all the energy it took to find a suitable service situation for our family, we thought it would be good to smooth the way for future workers. Father Joe will also add a Spanish component to communicate with people in his parish that have access to the Internet.

Our time in Piura ended with a couple more hot days sorting and bagging clothes in the shade of the clothes room. After saying goodbye to everyone we could find at the church, we hopped into the back of the pickup truck, along with seven of our new friends, for the ride to the airport. Father Joe surprised us by bringing another six friends, who had been working, to see us off. Through many tears and longing questions of "When will you come back?" we bid our farewells. As we walked back out to the plane, a sea of people waved from the balcony once again—people who had been transformed over two and a half weeks from strangers to dear friends.

One of the most frustrating aspects of traveling around the world was airport protocol. Besides the usual hassles of standing in lines and going through customs, we were met with the inevitable airport taxes or unexpected border visa requirements. This was one expense we had not accounted for in the trip budget. Either the airline industry or the country is certainly getting rich off of tourists. In the airport, one person was typically in a booth collecting wads of money and giving you a stamp on your airplane tickets. U.S. airlines usually include taxes in the price of tickets, so we never think about it.

215

After continually racing to airport automated teller machines or moneychangers at the last minute, just so we could fork out extra cash, I think I prefer to remain ignorant. They don't take credit cards or traveler's cheques, just cash. All told, we paid almost $2000 in airport taxes and tourist visas to enter and leave countries. Not that the following is overly fascinating, but it caused us such angst each time we went to the airport, that we feel compelled to add it to the story. Here is the final tally of our lament.

Country	Charge	Type	Total
New Zealand	$22 each	Exit	$110
Australia	$40 each	Visa	$200
Singapore	$15 each	Exit	$75
Malaysia	$40 each	Exit	$200
Thailand	$12 each	Exit	$60
Egypt	$15 each	Visa	$75
Kenya	$40 each	Visa	$200
Tanzania	$50 each	Visa	$250
Guatemala	$20 each	Exit	$100
Costa Rica	$14 each	Exit	$70
Peru	$29 each	Exit	$145
Brazil	$45 each	Visa	$225
TOTAL			**$1710**

We flew to Lima for a quick night's stay before our 4 a.m. wake up call to catch an early morning flight to Cuzco, Peru. In 55 minutes we went from sea level to 11,207 feet. Talk about a head rush! Walking through the streets of Cuzco, we fought headaches and dizziness as we adapted to the high altitude. The locals drink "mate," which is a tea made with coca leaves, the plant responsible for cocaine. The hotel offered us some on our arrival: "We highly recommend this to you to help you adjust." It is a mild form of the drug that is supposed to expand your lungs, but we decided to manage on our own.

Cuzco is a large, antiquated city surrounded by mountains and greatly benefiting from being the gateway to Machu

Picchu. It is an odd combination of thriving tourism business and poverty. There are colorful plazas, a well-kept train station, and an old cathedral. Yet, enormous pigs scrounge through garbage heaps on the sides of the road, poor homes abound, and many people beg on the sidewalks. Enjoying a city is difficult when poverty lurks around every corner. Guilt pangs hit on a regular basis because we had money but couldn't possibly give to every needy person on the way. A few coins in a cup now and then did little to ease our troubled hearts.

In Cuzco we were treated to lightening, thunder, and rain accenting the refreshingly cool weather—quite a welcome contrast from the heat of Piura. Clare, Michael and Steve ventured out to the Incan museum to view a simple but interesting exhibit about the local native history. That evening we feasted on a three-course meal at the vegetarian restaurant, Govindas for $0.75 apiece. It was an odd experience to trust Lonely Planet's write-up, walk in, sit down at one of four tables and be served food without seeing a menu. Dinner was great and we even left with food for the next day's lunch.

Our primary reason for being in Cuzco was to catch the train that would take us to Machu Picchu, an Inca ruin and one of the most fantastic sights in the world. The tourist trains were old, clean, very organized, and the attendants kind and helpful. PeruRail must be extremely proud of their trains. The windows shine as if they know tourists are here to see their impressive country. One train was an hour late leaving so the staff brought everyone crackers and tea as an apology. This was a far cry from many trains we had ridden in the world, which often stopped for two hours in the middle of nowhere without an explanation.

The trip to Aguas Calientes, the jumping off point to Machu Picchu, demonstrated the awesome geological diversity of Peru. We began by zigzagging up the mountain from Cuzco then passed richly producing orchards, terraced farmlands, madly rushing muddy rivers, and snowy mountain peaks. Evidence of the Incan civilization could be seen throughout the trip in the form of an ancient bridge across the

217

river, fortresses, and remains of other buildings, and agricultural areas.

At this point, our accommodation strategy changed significantly. Throughout the first two thirds of our journey, we made reservations or called ahead for rooms to be sure we had a place to stay for the night. When we got to Latin America that deteriorated into walking out of the train station and allowing ourselves to be barraged by the mob of hotel sellers. This strategy or lack thereof resulted in significantly more stress but much cheaper lodgings than we might otherwise have acquired.

I guess this was a symbol of our evolution as a traveling family. We were much more willing to go into a situation without knowing every detail in advance than we would have been at the beginning. It was a bit more nerve wracking, but certainly engaged us with the people more than racing to our lodgings immediately after arriving in town. When we arrived in a new city we chatted with the people about which were the riskier parts of town or which place would be a more strategic location so we could walk to the things we wanted to see. Of course, getting all this wise information was not so easy when ten people were shouting at you that their place was better, but that was the idea anyway. In the end, they offered deals instead of the usual rate, so we did save a bit of money. The customary formality was that they showed you the room first before you decided, but every room we saw was just fine. Then again, "fine" is a state of mind. Half the time, the reality was that sinks were falling off the wall, there were no toilet seats or toilet paper, no shower curtain, cracks and holes in the walls, curtain rods bent in half and curtains falling down, and beds with a crater in the middle. At least there were relatively few bugs.

Aguas Calientes is a minute tourist village that basically exists because of Machu Picchu. It is nestled in the midst of the Urubamba Valley, with green mountains rising all around. You can only reach the town by train or by foot and there were no cars to be seen. With our new accommodation strategy, we managed to find a quaint, nicely furnished hostel to drop our stuff, then headed out for a walk along the train tracks to a nearby waterfall. The kids complained vigorously throughout, as they had not been in their walking groove for almost a month. At 3:15 p.m, the first return train to Cuzco rushed by a few feet from us, the wind drowning out their complaints, and causing us to have second thoughts. The path gradually faded away until the only way to walk was on the tracks. As the rest of the trains heading back to Cuzco were due to start coming by, we decided to relent and returned to town.

The streets of Aguas Calientes were filled with restaurants and multi-colored handicraft vendors. Hand-woven tablecloths of green, magenta, and gold lay next to piles of t-shirts, flutes, small figures, and other replicas of Incan treasures. Walking back to our hostel, we were accosted at every step with restaurant crusaders vying for our patronage. Menus were thrust before us or people would call out the delicacies or deals waiting inside their doors. We settled for pizza.

A twenty-minute bus ride at 7 a.m. the next morning took us to the famed, spectacular Incan city of Machu Picchu. Hiram Bingham, discoverer of the ruins in 1911 described it in his book Lost City of the Incas (1948) as a city, "perched like an eagle's nest on a cliff-ringed mountain saddle." Ever since we saw a picture of this mystical mountain city on a poster, we wanted to visit. I've never seen so much meticulous thought put into the construction of a city. Granted, the Incas had some brutal sacrificial practices, but their sheer genius in architecture and agriculture must be appreciated. The entire city had breathtaking views from every possible angle.

Every detail was purposeful and religious in nature. Three windows or three steps signify the three worlds of heaven, earth, and the nether world. Light shines through particular windows during particular seasons to illuminate objects in temples. Stone carvings of condors or the surrounding mountains artistically adorn structures. The Incas were very interested in the stars, so they had observatories created with spiritual significance. The sun temple was constructed so well that no mortar was needed between the perfectly carved stones

219

to make its walls. Bingham observed that "no pin could penetrate through tightly fitted blocks."

Photographs of Machu Picchu always include the miter shaped peak of Huayna Picchu in the background. This mountain can be climbed by registering at the head of the trail. It is not one for the faint of heart, as the steps are the same steep and narrow ones the Incas created 600 years ago. Confident that our kids could make it, we set off. Half way up, the altitude and steepness took its toll and Clare and Bridget refused to take another step. Michael and I continued the journey while Steve stayed with the girls. I was so impressed with Michael's determination and energy to get to the top. It was a precipitous, difficult climb and the altitude made even the most athletic looking hikers huff and puff. He was a determined little hiker, easily the youngest on the trail, insisting on reaching the peak. The 360-degree view from the top was well worth the effort.

One of the highlights of the city for the kids was "the slide." This was a stone slide that may or may not have been meant to be a slide by the Incas, but many people go down it anyway. All three of our brood and Steve enjoyed whooshing down. Fortunately, only Michael walked away with a ripped seam for a souvenir. Thanks for that sewing kit Mom, it was indispensable!

The bus ride up was scenic so we decided to walk down the road, get a bit more exercise, and let the kids choose how they wanted to spend the money we saved in bus fare. The eight-kilometer walk became more exciting when we discovered a series of stone and wooden stairs in between the switch backing roads. We gained a bit of company when a little Incan boy dressed in traditional costume raced the buses down the mountain. If the child wins, he boards the bus and asks for money to celebrate his defeat of modern technology. In somewhat the same spirit, our kids treated themselves to Incan ice cream and soda with some of their bus fare money.

As the trip began to wind down, we were more cognizant of getting little things here and there as mementos or presents for loved ones at home. Space was at a premium, so only the

220

smallest items could be acquired. We dashed around the handicraft stalls for a while and then sought out food for the trip back to Cuzco. We found an out of the way market where the real locals shop ("Gringos, here?" and much better prices) and stocked up on fruit and bread.

The four-hour return trip turned into an impromptu show by our children. Our fellow passengers delighted in their creative antics and hand games. We were so impressed with the confidence they had to share stories about our travels, in English or broken Spanish, or lead people in silly games. Steve and I could have never anticipated what this whole adventure would do to their imaginations. They were so used to spending hours upon end riding or waiting for trains, buses or planes that they invented ingenious games and improvisations which invariably ended up entertaining all those around. They often were the icebreakers in our relationships with other people. On this trip, I ended up speaking Spanish for two hours with two members of the Colombia Symphony Orchestra who had joined in with the children during their mime skit.

Back in Cuzco late at night with pouring rain, we took a shuttle to a different hostel close to the train station from which we would depart early the next morning for Puno. It was so early in the morning when we boarded the train that no stores were open to buy food. Facing a ten-hour train ride with three apples, a little bread and some mandarins, it was going to be a very hungry day. Once again, a little miracle saved the day in the form of a mechanical delay. An attendant announced that we would depart 1 1/2 hours late. Steve jumped off the train, ran all over town and was back in 45 minutes with plenty of edible surprises to sustain us. The train left just as he returned.

The glorious ride to Puno followed a huge, furiously rushing, muddy river most of the way. I don't know how they rate white water rapids, but this must have been on the top of the scale. Half way through the trip, we encountered a rockslide that had occurred shortly before our arrival. Quickly, most of the train staff jumped off and started pulling huge rocks off the track. An hour later, we managed to ride very slowly over the dented track and continue on our journey. At one point we reached an elevation of 14,147 feet (almost as high as Mount Whitney, highest in the continental U.S.) but we were well acclimated by then. PeruRail actually reaches 15,800 feet on another track, making it the highest railroad in the world. Puno sits at 12,500 feet and hosts the world's highest navigable lake--Lake Titicaca. By 7 p.m. we were settled into another hostel and had arranged a great tour for the next day.

One unexpected delight was constantly reconnecting with other travelers who seemed to be on the same agenda. Thus, as we boarded our shuttle the next morning we smiled at familiar faces we had also seen in Cuzco, Aguas Calientes, and Machu Picchu. Their presence made the 2 1/2 hour boat cruise out to the main island fly by as we all shared stories, jokes, magic, and brainteasers.

Lake Titicaca is massive, covering 3,200 square miles, with 60% on the Peru side and 40% on the Bolivian side. Over 25 rivers contribute to it. However, its true wonders were the floating islands, about one half hour by boat from Puno. Made entirely of a six-foot deep reed bed on top of one foot of peat moss, the Uros live about 10 families to an island and subsist on fish from the lake and fruit from the mainland. The island we visited had been much larger but three years ago two groups of people weren't getting along so they simply cut the island and let half of it float away. We could see the other island just a stone's throw away. Every two months the reeds must be replenished. Standing too long in one place will cause water to seep up and soak your shoes. It's a strange sensation to walk on the squishy surface--like living on a waterbed.

The totora reeds are used to make their island, huts, medicine, soap, canoes, and are eaten for food. We tried a bite and it tasted a bit like celery. Imagine living on six feet of celery. The inhabitants drink water directly from the lake, a bit of a dicey prospect when you listen to their history. In the

222

past, they had two methods to deal with their dead family members:

1) put the body in a reed boat and push it off into the lake to float away, or
2) tie a rock to the body, toss it and let it sink.

Now, the body is rowed to a cemetery on the mainland.

While they appear to be very traditional and living primitively, solar power is their source of electricity for stereos and TVs inside their small huts. Between five and seven people live in a one-room house with no furniture. As with many Peruvians, the Uros Indians are great craftspeople and the tour boats supply them with ample customers. They live in traditional native dress and will let you take their picture for a price.

Next stop was Isla Taquile, a large natural island of 2000 residents. Docking on the western side of the island we headed to the east side, gradually hiking to the top, about 500 feet up from the lakeside. At 13,000 feet it didn't take much for everyone to get winded. Our Peruvian guide stopped and showed us a bush that was all over the island. Taking a handful of its tiny leaves, crushing them in our palms, and then breathing in the aroma filled our lungs with precious air. It sure did the trick! Any time I felt sluggish as we walked, a quick breath of those fragrant leaves would instantly open my lungs.

The people of the island live by a three-code ethic: don't lie, don't steal, work hard. All day long the women spin and the men knit. Every minute their hands are busy. Married men wear a solid colored red hat. The single men wear a half white, half red hat. When a couple contemplates marriage, they must live together for 2-3 years to see if they want to get married. If the woman decides to commit, she signifies this by cutting her long hair and giving it to the man who then makes it into a belt. People of Taquile must marry from the island.

All in all, it was a fascinating experience, great hiking, and fun conversation with our companions from Bavaria, Switzerland, Romania, New York, and Oregon. The boat returned us by 5:30 p.m. and it was time for dinner in Puno.

Best of all, we did not have a 4 a.m. wake up call the next day! Instead, we were able to walk around Puno the next morning and explore the outdoor markets, pedestrian streets, and Catedral de Puno.

An hour-long taxi ride in the afternoon put us at Juliaca airport in plenty of time for our delayed flight to Lima. As this was our fifth time in Lima airport we considered advocating for a frequent departure tax card. Having paid it so many times couldn't they comp us just once? An 11:30 p.m. flight to Brazil landed us in São Paulo the next morning.

*"The world is a book,
and those who do not travel read only one page"
St. Augustine, philosopher*

NIAGRA FALLS
IS A KITCHEN FAUCET

<u>BRAZIL</u>   9 January

With almost 20 million people, São Paulo is an enormous city—the largest in South America. It was founded in 1554 by two Jesuits and now accounts for almost half of Brazil's industrial production. Brazil, as the fifth largest country in the world, is slightly smaller than the United States, and takes up almost half of South America. Interestingly, it got its name from the Portuguese word for the reddish color of brazilwood, which is used to make violin bows. Brazilwood was an important export in the 16th century, but now Brazil is the world's largest exporter of coffee and sugar.

A massive immigration in the 19th century gave Brazil a fascinating diversity of people. Walking the streets of São Paulo, it was very difficult to identify a "Brazilian" as they come in all shapes, sizes, and skin tones. Besides the native population and the Portuguese, who were the first immigrants, there are Italians, Germans, Syrians, Lebanese, and Japanese. Five million African slaves were brought to the country before slavery was abolished in 1888.

Our aversion to big cities prompted us to taxi from the airport to the bus terminal for a ride to Curitiba (with five of us, a taxi was cheaper than the bus or subway). As Steve gathered the bus tickets, he came to the unfortunate realization that Portuguese and Spanish are not similar enough for us to

225

survive on Spanish. The old stereotype about rude Frenchmen that we never saw in France was played out instead in São Paulo. Lacking fluency in Portuguese, he found that anytime he tried to speak to Brazilians in Spanish, they instantly gave him the cold shoulder, a shake of the head, and a harrumph implying, "Oh, those tourists again!"

Undaunted, however, he managed to secure the tickets for the next bus, which was (of course) in five minutes. We raced to the platform, jostling our bags through the terminal, and made it just in time to collapse in our seats. After all of our travels, we were exhausted and slept for the 6-hour bus ride. When we got to Curitiba, our original plan of checking out Paranagua (one of the most scenic spots in Brazil, according to Lonely Planet) dissolved due to a lack of time so we decided to go straight to Iguazu Falls. A 10-hour overnight ride placed us in Foz do Iguaçu (the Brazilian spelling) by 6:30 a.m. After securing a cheap hotel, washing clothes in the sink, and rigging our bungee cord clothesline it was time to explore the Brazilian side of the falls.

The awesome camera footage of these falls in the movie "The Mission" inspired our trip here. Imagine Niagara Falls and about every other waterfall you have ever seen. Multiply that amount by three or four and you have a sense of the magnitude of these waterfalls. Now combine this immense amount of falling water with a lush jungle background and you've got the picture. When First Lady Eleanor Roosevelt visited Iguaçu Falls she commented, "It makes Niagara Falls look like a kitchen faucet."

As we walked the trail along the waterfalls, around every corner another unbelievable outpouring of water from the jungle-covered mountains surprised us. At the end of the trail was the largest of the falls. It is impossible to convey the majesty and the enormity of water that gushed forth, but we will never forget the feeling or that mighty roar. The best part of the Brazil side was a catwalk that went out over an area at the base of one fall. Standing with our faces to the wind and the mist, we relished the cool water on a warm day. I closed my eyes and stood there until I was soaked. It felt so delicious.

We returned to our hotel in Foz do Iguaçu to wait for Steve's cousin, Heather. She was in the second year of her Peace Corps assignment in Paraguay, our next stop. We decided to meet in Foz do Iguaçu so that she could enjoy the falls with us and escort us back to her small village in Paraguay. Steve walked the streets to find pizza and when he returned, Heather had just arrived to enjoy it with us. It was a wonderful reunion as we exchanged stories of our mutual experiences well into the night.

Early the next morning we joined a tour of the Argentinean side of the falls given by our hotel manager. The Brazilian side is for looking, but the Argentinean side is for doing. The tour was an all day combination of walking, taking the park train, and a boat ride to the island. The pouring rain was great weather to keep all those other tourists at bay while we enjoyed the falls. Great hikes and trails brought us up close to the falls: over, above and below. The contrasting peacefulness of the trees, butterflies, and birds on the trail belied the powerful water cascading off the nearby mountain. The engineering efforts to construct catwalks through the jungle and on top of the waterfalls were mind-blowing feats of daring and ingenuity. Our guide saved the best for last—a platform literally right over massive horseshoe shaped falls. We were drenched as we walked up to the erupting mist. It felt like we were going over the falls. Millions of gallons of water rushed over the edge. Mind-boggling.

On the way back we stopped at the confluence of the Parana and Iguaçu Rivers which allowed us to view all three nations at once: Paraguay, Argentina, and Brazil. Each country has a stone pillar painted in the colors of its flag. If you could hang glide from one to the other it would form a giant triangle over the rivers. Once again it makes you think about the invisible borders that people draw to say, "This is ours, that is yours," but nature could care less.

"Hope is the last thing that dies in people;
and though it be exceedingly deceitful,
yet it is of this good use to us,
that while we are traveling through
it conducts us in an easier and more pleasant way
to our journey's end."
Francois, Duc de la Rochefoucauld, French Philosopher

PARAGUAY   13 January

Our time in Paraguay turned out to be an important part of the trip for our family as we lived in the impoverished conditions of Heather's village. Beginning with a long walk from the bus drop off, along the hot dusty road to her home in Mboiy, it became clear that this experience would be different from any other. The heat was so oppressive and the bus rides from Brazil had been so long that, initially, our only solace was reminding ourselves that we only had eleven days to endure that climate before we headed back to the United States. However, the pure joy of being with Heather and her unflinching "can do" attitude quickly helped to ease us in to our new temporary home.

Her four-room house, which was about 20 feet on a side, was made of thin sheets of plywood. The world outside could easily be seen through the many cracks and holes in the walls. Shutters closed over the non-glass, non-screened windows at night or on rainy days. Her thatched roof proved to have a few leaks in it when the rains came, but two sheets of corrugated tin protected her bedroom over the thatching. The dirt and brick floor needed continuous sweeping, as dust, leaves, and small plums were constantly brought in from outside on the soles of our shoes. Electricity had been a recent addition to the village, so bare bulbs lit up two rooms at night. Running water at the street corner was also newly acquired, due to a Peace Corps project three years earlier. Frequent runs to the spigot for water to drink, cook, wash dishes, and bathe was everyone's job. Many trees surrounding the property provided welcome shaded relief from the oppressive heat as well as limes, guayabas, and an interesting whitish fruit whose name escapes me.

In this small pueblo of 500 people Heather's house was not the worst, nor the best. There were varying degrees of comfort depending on one's profession. Teachers are relatively well paid by the government and enjoy job security. Even though they had been working without a salary for the past four months it was easy to tell their houses. They were the ones with a satellite dish next to their stucco or brick house. There were two or three of these in the area. Still, these houses were very simple, typically one story homes with the same glassless windows and brick or cement floors. Every yard was tidy with plants usually adorning the front of the house, communicating a true pride in their surroundings. The rest of the houses were extremely simple and small structures in assorted states of decay.

Our first night proved to be the most challenging. There is something about the night that brings out the worst in a place sometimes (and the best: the fireflies reminded us of Vermont). Heather's home took the prize for the one with the greatest amount of bugs on our travels. Actually, we firmly believe that there were more spiders in her home than there are in the entire state of Oregon. So many species of spiders and ants in one area! Thousands of crawling insects lived in the crevices, spider webs decorated every corner and beam, and moths, gnats, and other mysterious bugs continuously fluttered throughout the house. Clare was especially petrified by the airborne creatures of the night and shrieked and swatted as she made her way for her bed, crying uncontrollably. Michael and Bridget equally conveyed their nervousness through a stream of tears:

Michael: *"We're not staying here!"*

Steve: *"What do you suggest we do at 10 p.m. at night and no more busses anywhere until tomorrow?"*

Michael: *"I don't know! I just want to go home!"*

Bridget: "I'm scared of all these bugs!"

While Steve and I had equal concerns and uneasiness, we tried our best to comfort them. This was truly a scene from some horror movie. Had we crossed the line as parents? Was this just too much for our kids? How traumatic would this be for them? Heather found an old mosquito net that we draped over their bed. Unlike our tents in Piura, this one didn't even come down over them but its presence, and a fan blowing, slightly calmed their nerves as they settled in.

All three slept sideways on the one twin bed in the house, with legs draping over one edge. Heather thankfully had two more bed frames (four pieces of wood with chain mail stretched across) on which to toss our sleeping bags. Steve and I shared one and she had the other, saving us from braving the floor. In the middle of the night Steve felt something crawling on his forehead. Instinctively, he reached up and swatted it. A few seconds later, the tickling sensation returned and he reached up to brush away the remaining legs. Shortly thereafter I nearly leaped out of my bag as a huge moth tried to fly up my nose.

Needless to say, we all had the jitters by morning. Heather said, "You get used to it." She was right, of course, but with each passing day I admired her tenacity more and more as she faced this time commitment with enthusiasm. I also can't express deeply enough how amazed I was with our children. After that first night of terror, not another word was said about the bugs. Remarkably, they simply adjusted and went on.

Clare: "I guess we just got used to it."

Bridget: "Well, we didn't really get bit by anything, so I wasn't as afraid later."

Michael: "I don't know. I didn't think about it after that first night."

After a couple of nights, they even no longer needed the mosquito net as their security blanket. On our last night, we all admired one particularly large moth as we settled in for the evening. When the lights went out, however, it began zooming around the room like a stealth bomber. Heather and I finally got up, grabbed an empty yogurt container and a piece of paper and performed the moth relocation routine. You get used to it.

Unfortunately, we mistimed our stay with Heather and she was called away to Asuncion for Peace Corps training for four days right after our arrival. In the end, this may have been a positive development, as we needed to fend for ourselves for a little while. Before she left, we discussed a few projects to keep us busy in her absence. We decided to paint the inside and outside of the house, put up a structure to shade her garden, and run pipes from the street to the back shed so she could have running water at her outdoor sink and bathroom.

Her "bathroom" was actually a three-sided brick-walled box located off of an old shed. The absence of a roof gave a new definition to "sky light" especially when nature called in the middle of the night. The presence of the stars was a comfort to us when surrounded by the wild natural sounds of the area. She had a real toilet, but no tank or plumbing so we had to haul water to flush.

Steve decided to create a shower for Heather inside this structure. Of course, when it rained, a real showerhead was a moot point. In the true Peace Corps tradition, Steve was trying to help Heather improve on her present way of bathing which was to stand in a bucket armed with a cup. By the time he was finished Steven had run underground pipes to a showerhead (cold water only of course) mounted just above the toilet. There was one flaw in the previous design that Steve could not change. When it did rain, the bathroom still flooded with 3-4 inches of water due to insufficient drainage and a floor that did not tip toward the little drainage hole.

Our chosen projects served to give us a focus on accomplishing something and we were exhausted at the end of each day. Working sunrise to sunset the time flew by and Heather was back before we knew it. She was thrilled with the transformation of her humble abode and genuinely grateful, bringing in all her community friends to show off the work.

Oddly enough, she said that our presence in the village helped to dispel a few myths about Americans. Seeing us working hard every day in the heat and humidity was quite contrary to the TV/movie impressions of well-off Americans who sit around in offices making lots of money or in huge homes with their plush sofas and the remote control. It also made her seem more natural to them, namely that she has a family. The presence of a white woman living alone in that environment goes against all their cultural norms. Women in Latin American countries that we have visited could not leave the house until married. This was one of her biggest obstacles to overcome in order to be accepted and thus carry out projects to improve their lives. We so take for granted the acceptable boundaries for men and women friends in the States. What we know to be a polite "good morning" at home may be misconstrued as "flirting" in their society. The Peace Corps strives to work within a culture's mores, not change it. Heather worked very hard her first year to earn the trust and respect of the community, and seemed to be gradually achieving it.

On one hand, we were "visiting" poverty, living in poor conditions with very little money, because we could not change it when we got to Paraguay. Needless to say, they didn't take traveler's cheques or Visa anywhere. This forced us to plan out each meal carefully, buy exactly what we needed and no more. We needed to make the money we had last until Heather returned with more. The situation made us very aware of people's experience of not knowing when the next check is coming. Of course, the significant difference was that at any time we could decide to leave. They didn't have that option.

On the other hand, living in this simple, rustic way fulfilled every fantasy I have ever held of being in the Old West (a la "Little House on the Prairie"). Hauling water, walking the dusty, sandy roads daily to the tiny stores for food, enjoying fruit fresh from the trees, washing clothes in the bucket and even riding the horses with the neighbor children all rounded out the experience. Steve was a

232

carpenterial wizard working with only a hammer and saw while building everything from scraps of woods he found. Nails were pulled out of any old piece or place where he judged they were no longer of use. The constant presence of roaming cows, oxen, horses, pigs and chickens completed the picture.

One morning we were invited to milk an ox. It's a lot harder than it looks. Michael and Bridget showed exceptional skill in this area, getting a good stream going into the cup. Steve and I struggled at it, providing great entertainment to the woman of the house who reached in and shot a thick stream about two feet long right into a small cup without hesitation. We were justly humbled.

PHILOSOPHY 101: *Progress?*

When is development progress? Clearly, getting water and electricity to people's homes has eased their situation. Yet, there seems to be a struggle here, a tension between the old and modern ways as there is almost anywhere. Ox carts roll down the road carrying groceries, a pile of dirt, or a new dresser made by the carpenter. People are riding horses or walking down the dirt roads to their work or a shop. At the same time, motorbikes and pickup trucks go racing by at a completely different pace.

I'm confident that if I asked Evangelico, one of Heather's neighbors, if he wanted to buy a motorcycle, he would laugh and ask "Why?" He is comfortable in his ways and pace of life. His daily horse rides to put his few cattle out to pasture and get them back again round out his day. Evangelico's needs are met. He has a loving wife and he enjoys his routine. He has a nice, simple home by Paraguayan standards. Does he need the Peace Corps and Heather's services to improve his life?

At the other end, as seems typical around the world, the teenagers and 20 somethings are driving a faster paced life. They are the ones with the motorbikes rather than the horses. Are they going somewhere? Racing into a brighter world or

233

temporarily pushing the envelope before settling down with a family? Young families don't seem to have the luxuries of faster vehicles. They ride their ox carts along the dusty road just like everyone else.

And so, I struggle to define progress for this community. Do they need to rise to western standards of living—a two car garage, 2.1 kids, two incomes, two TV's, and two weeks of vacation a year? Is progress for Paraguayans a satellite dish in the yard? Is that when you have really made it? At home in the States, the media continually tries to convince us that we need a little bit more in order to have "made it." We never seem to quite be there until we have the home theater system, the newest car, or fastest computer. Evangelico stands in defiance of that drive for more.

Perhaps Heather's efforts to move people out of poverty and into stability is enough. When you have enough resources to not worry about taking care of your family's needs then you can be at peace. Then there is the matter of clearly defining what you need versus what you want. Progress is peace within. Evangelico seems to have made it to that place.

In the final analysis, it was the heat and humidity that put a bur in my stocking. It's so hard for us, as driven, hard-working Americans to accept the "tranquilo" lifestyle of sitting around for the hot hours of the day, drinking terere (similar to iced tea) and just being with people. The custom to drink terere is unique to Paraguay and is really at the heart of the culture. They fill up the "guampa" (a kind of mug) with pre-crushed herbs and then use the "bombilla" (a metal straw with a strainer on the end) to drink. The water poured into this guampa must have lots of ice to be refreshing, so people everywhere have their trusty thermos nearby and are always ready to top off a guampa. Depending on your ailment, you can also put natural plant remedies in to the pitcher of water. Heather talked often of her "terere moments" of just relaxing and chatting with people. After the first week, we were fortunate to have a couple of "terere moments" with the neighbors ourselves (even if we didn't drink the terere). We struggled a bit with the language together, but it was good to just be with each other.

Relationships are very important in this small village. When you want to borrow eggs, you don't just go over and ask for a couple of eggs. You chat for about half an hour first, mention you could use some eggs, and then chat another half hour before excusing yourself to get back to work. "Oh, don't forget the eggs." On one hand it is a prohibitive tradition when you want to get things done. On the other hand, it makes you slow life down and focus on people rather than needing to accomplish more in your day. When you don't have money to buy books, TV's, music CD's, or other items that Americans typically enjoy, you tend to spend more time with people and develop richer relationships. Perhaps there are some lessons to be learned from "poverty."

Living in these conditions was a challenge in many ways and not so difficult in others. Yet, as Heather shared on one of our early morning runs, it's one thing to temporarily live in poverty, because we have another reality to return to someday. It's entirely another to make it your permanent way of life.

Other highlights of our stay were eating mangoes Paraguayan style, watching Heather at her job, and hearing her radio show. Heather was a beekeeper. It is a fascinating job and thrilling to see in action. The kids were treated to being her "smokers" as she worked with the hive. They took turns getting in bee gear and pumping the smoker, which calms the bees. When the bees smell smoke, they think their home is on fire, so they don't focus on protecting it from predators, but on preparing to leave. It was exciting for them to get a close look at the queen bee and the whole operation. Honey fresh from the hive sure tasted good! While Steve was moving in close for a few pictures, a bee caught wind of him and angrily chased him across the field for about a hundred yards. Clare sat in a chair nearby and enjoyed watching the chase.

Once a week Heather hosted a radio broadcast with all the professionalism of a seasoned DJ, speaking mainly in the local language of Guarani, although people in town know both

Castellano Spanish and Guarani. In between music selections, she informed the listening public of classes she would be teaching and group meetings. During our stay she also interviewed a not-yet-famous professor from Willamette University in Oregon about his family's trip around the world.

The Peace Corps has been in Paraguay for thirty-five years. With time it has learned valuable lessons about demonstrating rather than trying to force change. Heather worked hard to demonstrate new ways of doing things by simply doing them herself and inviting people to observe. She grew new crops, used strategies for raising the yield, made homemade shampoo or her own soy milk then shared with her women's group, beekeeper's group, or anyone who happened by. It seems to be a more subtle way of teaching and more lasting when someone shows the initial interest.

Our time with Heather was an excellent way to end our world travels, one that I hoped would have lasting effects on us all as we headed back to a life of ease in the United States.

PHILOSOPHY 101: *Fare-thee-well*

Have we become too good at saying good-bye? It struck me as we said goodbye to Heather's neighbors that we might have become too callous with our departures from new friends. With tears welling up in their eyes, this family said so many heartfelt things about their sadness because of our leaving. "Come back!" they pleaded in Spanish. "You have a wonderful family. When will we see you again?" There was truly a deeper connection with them than I had realized. The father had graciously helped me install the piping for Heather's water system and we taught card games to their kids. Yet, I didn't feel the same depth of emotion that was clearly in their eyes and words.

Is it us who have changed? We have said goodbye to so many new friends on this trip. Every place we have gone, we developed short-lived relationships, either for the day, as in a train ride, or for a few of weeks, as in Piura. So many people that we will never see again. Have we done a disservice to our kids by conditioning them to say goodbye easily? What is a relationship when we have insulated ourselves for frequent good-byes? Does that impact the willingness of our hearts to go deeper?

I recall Michael's reflection as we were leaving Thailand..."Do you know what the hardest part about traveling is? Making friends with wonderful people and then having to leave them." Does he still feel that way or has he developed emotional shields? I decided to ask him.

"Michael, how has it been for you to say goodbye to people as we have traveled?"

"Well, it was sort of easy to say goodbye to people like those guys we met on the boat on Lake Titicaca. It was kinda hard to say goodbye to those kids at Heather's house in Paraguay that we played with a lot. They were so nice and fun to play with and we will never see them again."

That made sense. Maybe it's just me.

On the other hand, is it them? Are they so unused to new faces in their community that it is a moving experience for them to connect with others? Is their community so stable that relationships are always long lasting and they don't know how to relate any other way?

Well, whatever is going on, I do miss that family. They said that they needed to find a good Paraguayan man for Heather so she wouldn't leave them. I will remember their good hearts and warm smiles.

SO NEAR YET SO FAR: 23 January
    Heading Home

The collective universe must have known we were finally on the last leg of our journey. A number of situations transpired to keep us praying, "Please, God, just let us get to the airport." Heather's village normally has rain every two or three days, which relieves the humidity and helps the crops. After eight days we hadn't seen a drop. Neighbors were voicing their concerns and we tried to help by praying, singing

237

rain songs, and hanging out laundry. Our biggest fear was that the rain would finally hit on Wednesday morning as we were trying to leave the village. Being only sand and dirt, the roads become impassable when it rains. The buses would not run. We could literally be stuck in San Blas without a way out!

A blessed storm finally raged through late Monday afternoon, cooling off the pueblo. The journey home began at 4:30 on a dry morning on what promised to be another very hot day. Walking in the dark to meet the bus we all reminisced with Heather about our stay and the trip in general. I had the same feelings that morning as I had when we left the States back in June: excitement and apprehension.

Two long bus trips placed us in Ciudad del Este just before noon. In one of Heather's Newsweek magazines, courtesy of the Peace Corp, I read that the "tri-border area" we were entering between Brazil, Paraguay, and Argentina is suspected of being a major artery in the terrorist network. According to Newsweek, thousands of Lebanese and Muslims live in Foz do Iguaçu (Brazil), Ciudad del Este (Paraguay), and Puerto Iguazu (Argentina), some of whom authorities in the United States believe are supporting Hizbullah, Al Qaeda, and Hamas. I could understand some of the concerns. There were basically no border controls between Paraguay and Brazil as we just rode a bus right past the border without any inspection on our way into Paraguay.

Heather told us that the Peace Corp volunteers are currently forbidden to be in Ciudad del Este. Tourism dropped sharply there after the U.S. made their concerns about the area known, prompting major Muslim leaders in the area to complain that they are being unjustly accused of supporting terrorism. Around the world this sensitive issue is affecting Muslim people. Just as a very small percentage of Americans are involved in racism and hate crimes, a very small percentage of Muslims are involved in terrorism. Many are being harassed without cause in the quest to stamp out the evil element. From our perspective, we certainly want to be safe and protected, but we have met many wonderful Muslims on this trip and would not want them to be unjustly accused. (No

238

more than we would want to be associated with the wars on Afghanistan and Iraq.) This is a very difficult time for the leaders of the world in finding the fine line between safety and civil rights.

With this new background information fresh in our minds, we were slightly nervous reentering this border area, but we encountered no outward signs of danger. Once on the edge of Paraguay, a city bus from Ciudad del Este would deliver us across the border back to Foz Do Iguaçu in Brazil. Due to construction traffic on the bridge, this one-mile ride took three hours. At one point the bus driver turned off the bus, jumped out and went to a restaurant for lunch while we sat in the bus in traffic for nearly two hours. We seriously considered getting off the bus and walking across the border but it was extremely hot, sweat was pouring down our faces, and we did not want to deal with border inspections.

Neither did the circus of people who jumped on just before the border.

For the first two hours on this bus there had been four other riders and us. Just blocks before the checkpoint, the bus was bursting at the windows with would-be vendors who had gone in to Ciudad del Este to take advantage of the low prices and lax laws of this drug town. They bulk shop for major items to sell over the border in Brazil. Everyone seemed to know each other as they lugged their huge parcels on and off the bus. An hour in the bus shoulder to shoulder in 100 degree heat, inching forward for about three blocks, and we were drenched in sweat with no shower ahead of us for two days.

Once over the border, we slowly became the only people left on the bus and assumed that the bus was going to head to the central bus terminal. It didn't. As we made our way out to the edge of the city, the kind driver let us stay on until he had looped back around to the central business district and pointed out a place for us to change money. It was pouring rain and I was getting a little concerned as we didn't know what time the bus to São Paulo departed.

Upon obtaining the needed Brazilian Reais from a moneychanger, away we went to the terminal by taxi. Or tried

239

to. His engine kept struggling and finally died less than half a mile from our destination. We coasted out of traffic, the meter kept running but the car didn't. After letting the engine rest a while he tried again. The kids and I prayed fervently in the back seat. Visions of us missing our plane back to the States kept taunting me. Our driver cranked up the engine again, we drove another block and then it died. For the third time he coaxed his car into action and we made it as far as the intersection to the terminal. I was ready to jump out and run through the downpour but didn't want to offend him.

As if in a slow motion movie his Ford inched toward the drop-off curb, we exited, paid him, and he popped the hood. Quickly, Steve secured bus tickets to São Paulo. The good news was there were five seats left. The bad news was the bus left in fifteen minutes. Dinner the day before had been our last meal, but time was short so we purchased some fruit, crackers, yogurt and chicken at the terminal café and rushed to our seats. The bus pulled out at 4 p.m. and all went smoothly until 10 p.m. when we pulled into a rest stop and were told to change buses. No problem. Ours had been slipping gears, it was out of drinking water, and some kid had puked in the bathroom without cleaning it up.

By 9:15 the next morning we arrived in São Paulo, Brazil. We had been traveling on buses for twenty-nine hours. That must be some kind of Guinness World Record or at least worthy of Ripley's Believe it or Not. Incredibly, the kids were great throughout the travels. Hard to believe they could endure that much time on their bums without complaining. At last, it was time to stretch our legs before a nine-hour flight that night.

Jeanine, Mark, and their two children are long time friends who live near us in Portland. They decided to commit four years of their lives to serving the poor in Brazil. Our timing was right. They were in São Paulo for two weeks of orientation just as we came to complete our world trip. We arranged to meet at a park for lunch and celebrated the beginning of their new life and the end of our travels. It was wonderful to share our last moments on the road with such inspirational friends.

The flight to New York was thankfully uneventful. How does one begin to re-enter the U.S. after such a sojourn? We were famished, so the first order of business was to find food; New York bagels from a street stand. An unexpected discovery was the Museum of Native Americans, a recent tribute to this country's indigenous people. Spending time there connected our native people with those the world over whose histories and lives we had recently seen. Then we officially wrapped up our world tour with a visit to the site of the World Trade Center. All around the city were memorials to those who had lost their lives in the tragedy. What struck me the most was a single bicycle locked to a light post. Covered in flower memorials it stood there still awaiting its owner to come unlock it and ride home. I don't know why that singular sight caught in my throat. Maybe because I bicycle everywhere. I wonder if it is still there, untouched, still waiting.

The vast space where the towers once stood in the midst of a crowded city was an eerie, emotional place to reflect on all that had transpired over the past eight months. A large part of our trip was colored by the events initiated at that spot. Thankfully, we had spent that time making friends in so many different countries and developing an understanding of the many cultures and perspectives of living life. For us, at the end of our trip, we realized that the only true way to avoid anger and bloodshed in the world is to build relationships with people, appreciate each person's uniqueness and work to meet people's basic needs. There is so much beauty in the surroundings and the people out there. As Steven so aptly observed aloud at the end of this journey, we are all more similar than we are different. All over the world I have seen people just wanting to survive, love their children, and see them grow into happy, compassionate adults.

Since our tickets ended in New York, we decided to spend time nearby, back in our former home, Middletown Springs,

241

Vermont. It was the perfect place to slowly begin the re-entry process. We spent time with friends and got re-acquainted with things like clean American grocery stores: 1,420 varieties of cereal, perfect looking fruit, people ready to assist you, magazines and newspapers shouting out the latest gossip while you stand in line. Colors assault your retinas down every aisle. Brilliant white lighting blinds your senses. Overload. It wasn't easy readjusting to the U.S. "standard of living." Thankfully, Vermont has a welcoming, gentle pace to it. After a week of de-processing, it was very hard to leave, but it was finally time to head west.

We had begun our world trip without a way home. Knowing the tickets ended in New York we had several options in mind for getting back to Oregon.

1) purchase a used car and drive home.
2) take the train across the country.
3) use the frequent flyer miles we had generated during the trip to get free plane tickets home.

Being seriously in debt at this point, option three won easily. However, the flight home was easier said than done. The last leg of the journey was a bit more complicated with the atmosphere in the U.S. very different from the one we had left.

Red flag #1: We secured tickets three days prior to flying.

Red flag #2: We returned a one-way rental car from a different state.

Red flag #3: Unlike his identification, Steven had a full beard from months of not shaving.

Red flag #4: We had been out of the country for over seven months.

Red flag #5: We had no luggage to check, only sleeping bags and small backpacks.

Red flag #6: We had one-way tickets.

Red flag #7: We were flying to Portland, Oregon via Kansas City and Los Angeles.

Is it any wonder that we got to know the security staff at every checkpoint along the way? We were searched thoroughly five times. I am still searched every time I fly. (Is it because of the *Abraham* in my last name?)

After leaving Vermont at 3:00 in the morning to drive to New Hampshire, we arrived in Los Angeles sometime the same afternoon. A five-hour layover permitted us to see some of our family and celebrate our niece's third birthday before flying into Portland at midnight. An overnight with friends and then a ride home landed us back in Salem on Sunday. The children were in school the next day probably wondering if it had all been a dream.

"Children are messages
we send to a future we cannot see"
Neil Postman, Author, Professor of Media Ecology

EPILOGUE

I t is difficult to comprehend the totality of memories we have amassed now that we are back in Oregon. The pace of life can return much too easily, so we are consciously making choices about commitments of our time. What have we achieved by traveling the world for eight months?

At the very least, we attained our primary goal of spending time with Clare, Bridget, and Michael. Now that they leave every morning and return in the afternoon only to do homework and play outside with their friends we feel the loss of that 24 hour closeness. They are wonderful people and we thoroughly (well 98% of the time) enjoyed being continuously with them. As they proceed to grow older and develop independent lives, we will cherish memories of that constant contact. For now, we can only make a special effort to share dinner each night and not get so busy with our lives that we miss opportunities to play and spend time together. We need to find those "terere moments" with our children as our Paraguayan neighbors taught us.

In that spirit, Steve, the children, and I have somewhat different reflections on what has transpired these past eight months. I'll begin with Michael, Bridget, and Clare's perspective. One year since our arrival home, we asked them what they remembered and what they learned. Here are their streams of consciousness…

Michael (age 7):
I remember getting huge ice cream cones in (Lucca) Italy after we had walked around like crazy. We would usually

244

never get those at home. There was a train that kept going forwards and backwards as it went up the mountain (in Cuzco, Peru). Also, there was that train in Norway where the brakes caught on fire. I liked going on the plane to Singapore and doing video games (something else he can't do at home.)

I learned how to speak Spanish, kind of. The Maoris (New Zealand) shoot out their tongue when they are in battle to scare their enemies. When I was traveling in Peru I learned that a lot of people are poor in the world. There is a bug in Paraguay that poops in your wound and you die in 30 years. At this place near the big waterfalls (Foz do Iguazu, Brazil) there were three posts at this point where two rivers came together. Each one represented Brazil, Paraguay, and Argentina. In England there was a real Thomas the Tank Engine. Egypt was hot. In one of the pyramids it gets so small that the deeper you go the harder it gets to breathe. Thailand makes really good food and elephants let you ride on their backs.

People in Germany don't like to drive to Dachau because the concentration camp for the Holocaust is there. In Germany their chocolate was really good. There was this big church in France (Taize) and this guy who helped people in World War II. After the war he took care of the prisoners and he is still alive. People in Australia had really weird accents. In the showers in Malaysia, tons of ants crawled around and cats made lots of noise in the roof. Sometimes there were thunderstorms. Geckos were everywhere. We had to take this awful medicine in Africa in case we got bit by a mosquito and we didn't see a single mosquito. St. Clare in Assisi was waxed so her body wouldn't dehydrate. When there was this big earthquake (at St. Francis' church) the parking lot fell through and they found tons of graves where poor people died, and where they hid St. Francis' body.

All they ate in Guatemala was rice and beans. At a park there were tons of slides of different sizes and it was really fun. There were cockroaches in Costa Rica and all they ate was rice and beans (the people, not the cockroaches). In the trees there were sloths and lots of monkeys. At the butterfly

245

farm you got to let out butterflies. We learned that you can use red ants for stitches. When we went to Norway we didn't know that there was a Royal Wedding going on. It was funny because these sailors had their bayoneted rifles and when they stretched or put their rifles on their shoulders, a guy who was walking by almost got stabbed in the face.

Bridget (age 10):

The Maori stick out their tongues. Seeing seals. Getting cold and going back into the rental car with the heat on. Kangaroos. Those two people (Ross and Thelma in Australia) and how, when we first got there, they left us stuff that was really good. Swimming in the pool in Singapore when there was thunder and lightening. Don't chew gum and don't spit. Singapore Airlines was the best plane with TV's and video games. Don't point in Malaysia. Riding elephants and going through the rapids (Thailand). My favorite food on the whole trip was in Thailand. Egypt. Yech. The big pool. We could see the pyramids through our windows. Never go to Egypt in summer. People beg you to buy their stuff. I remember hyenas in Africa. Don't get drunk and go outside in the Serengeti. Keep the zipper of your tent zipped. The people were nice and always said hello. We got to see friends in England where we got to do normal things like go swimming. We were just part of their family and got to help them celebrate their first Halloween party ever.

I liked Norway. Behind our hostel we had this gigantic mountain. One day I woke up and said to my mom, "Let's go climb to the top". And so we did. I was really angry the day before and it helped me get my anger out. When we got to the top, it felt so good, but it was very cold. There was a warm restaurant at the top. People rode a tram to get there. But I felt really good because we climbed it and they were lazy. We stood at the top for a long time and looked all over Bergen. It was a really pretty place. I want to live there. After the long cold climb down, it was nice and warm and toasty in our hostel. The next day we walked for miles and miles and got gigantic sandwiches and ice cream. We saw the Royal Wedding. The prince was marrying a commoner.

I liked Switzerland because we went to the International Girl Scout house. There are only four in the whole entire world. We did the Girl Scout Challenge. The worst parts were when we had to dunk our heads in freezing cold ice mountain water in a stream and wake up at four o'clock in the morning to climb a mountain. One of the challenges was to lead a sing-a-long at the campfire. We used up the whole box of matches until the last match lit the fire. At the very end we deserved our badge. In Germany we saw Juliane and Dachau. Hitler was a very bad person. We saw a movie where all the people were lying in a ditch. It made me cry. I liked Lourdes because I got holy water. We got in free to the Louvre in Paris and I saw the Mona Lisa. We also saw the Eiffel Tower. I like seeing famous things. I wished we could have gone in the Leaning Tower of Pisa.

I didn't like Guatemala because it was unsanitary and I got a very bad sickness. The people were very nice, but the place wasn't very nice. I liked my Spanish teacher in Costa Rica. It was very pretty there. It was clean and beautiful. I liked our host family's dog. It was fun to celebrate Christmas in Piura because we got to hand out presents to people who were poor. It made me feel sad because I have so much stuff and they don't. We were giving them all these ugly dolls, and they still loved them. I liked Paraguay because our cousin Heather was there. They spoke Guarani. I liked painting Heather's house. What I didn't like about Paraguay was that it was too hot. I liked Iguazu Falls because it was really neat. Lots of mist flew into your face. I was sad sometimes because of all the people we saw in Third World countries. They didn't have much.

Clare (age 12):

In New Zealand one day Michael was playing with his gum and it got all over him and the rental car. Seeing deer on farms was not normal. They were treated like domestic animals. The bubbling mud in Rotorua was cool. Kangaroos in a cemetery were weird (Australia). Being at the beach and knowing that across that ocean was America. Singapore. The heat. Swimming with coconuts floating in the pool. In Malaysia we went snorkeling and we saw this huge fish. It kind of scared me. That big komodo dragon on the island. Riding on the elephants in Thailand. It was so scary! All we had was a rope to tie us in. Hearing about black dogs that they sacrificed in the village when they built a new house to get rid of all the spirits. I liked the lodge that we stayed in. It was out in the open with nice places to sit. The pool in Cairo was huge! The history about it. There is such an immense time span between then and now. The train was like a little miniature apartment.

I loved hanging out with Mary Kate and their kids (England). Having a Halloween party with them for the first time in their lives because they don't celebrate it in England. It was cool being in Netherlands, because that is where one of my friends was born. Riding bikes on the dikes was neat. You hear the story about how the kid holds up the dikes with his finger and then we got to ride on them. It was like being part of the story. We got to be in Anne Frank's house and walk where she walked before she died. I had just studied all that stuff, and I was actually able to see it.

Seeing the prince get married to a commoner in Norway. Walking in the church and seeing all the decorations. The trolls looked like my math teacher. Seeing the Holmdahl's house that was in their family for 300 years. Rowing in the boat on the lake next to their house out to an island. Being with Juliane again (Germany). After seeing her in our country we got to see her in hers. I used to be obsessed about reading about the concentration camps. Actually being in the place (Dachau) where they say birds have never again flown over it because of the evil there was spooky. It was amazing that a 17 year old with a machine gun was in control of 200 people. In school we have chaperones for every ten kids and we don't even listen to them. How can one person control 200?

Going on our Sound of Music travels (Austria). The castle with the bishop with interesting humor with water. It was a bit of welcome back to reality because after seeing all the death

248

and evil it was nice to see something good. Watching a famous American in a coffee shop in Hungary (Eddie Murphy) filming a movie. The Girl Scout house was cool because we did the challenge (Switzerland). And it was a challenge! Dunking yourself up to your neck in melted snow is no mean feat! We were able to speak in English! I got rashes in Taize (France). We got to go in the Louvre for free because the workers went on strike. The leaning tower of Pisa and eating all that good pizza (Italy). Usually we only get pizza about once a month. Here we got it for every meal! (Italian pizza is a wafer thin crust with tomato sauce, garlic and herbs. Cheese is not standard; it is a topping to be ordered separately. A far cry from the Americanized version!) The flag performance in Assisi was cool. The dead body of my patron saint (Saint Clare) was kinda gross.

Seeing all those animals up close in Africa. Especially watching Daddy's reaction when the lion roared at him when he got too close trying to take a picture. The big truck we traveled in. We got to see elephants and stuff. They were all out in the wild, no fences. They were real. It was a weird feeling, like I was being the one stared at rather than the staree. All those people were so nice, so kind. We sing songs in Swahili in choir, but it is not the same as hearing people speak it. In Guatemala, it was hard because Abesaida didn't really speak English. It was neat hanging out with our friends in Guatemala and seeing how they would be living for a year. Going to the lake where there was floating pumice rocks. In Spanish immersion school (Costa Rica) they could speak English so it was easier.

Peru was an interesting place to spend Christmas. I spent it riding around in a pick-up truck giving presents to kids who wouldn't be getting anything. I've read about Las Posadas, but we did it! These people have nothing and we have everything. We've got insulation, fiberglass, and wood. They have tin and pieces of cardboard boxes and bamboo for houses. It was kind of like all those people in Dachau who were starving. Without the guns, they were still hungry. It was neat being able to speak with them and have them understand me and me understand them (in Spanish). Playing in those big rooms of clothes. Watching them burn paper mache people in effigy (on New Year's Day) was weird. It was cool being with my cousin in Paraguay. We hardly get to see her in Oregon! Painting her house was fun. She has a bidet for a planter. She had to walk to a water place to get water, but we were able to build plumbing for her. Seeing the bee keeping was awesome. It was a shocking reality check that people don't always like Americans. It was unreal to hear about the attack in the United States while we were traveling.

Toby:
I went on this trip with no agenda other than to show our children the world and give them a global perspective of life. Hopefully, the result would be a compassionate respect for people of all cultures. Had it not been for Steven's tireless efforts we would not have gone. I was content to travel a different continent each summer rather than all at once. The thought of going that long, all around the world and with three children took on a challenge of its own. People thought we were crazy. I've never been one to do anything on a dare but the whole idea started to feel like a self-imposed dare; could we survive this?

Frequently Asked Questions
What was your favorite country? Impossible to answer. It is difficult for me to separate a country from the people, natural geography, or situations we encountered. On each of these levels positive and negative impressions were formed.
Would you do it again? Hard to say now that it's over. I think it came down to something I felt I needed to do. There are places I'm glad we experienced but I've no desire to ever return. I went with an open mind and attitude ready to listen to what God might say along the way. What thoroughly surprised me was the feeling I got returning to the States. I didn't experience classic culture shock so much as a strange numbness. Easing our way back with a week in Vermont made a significant difference in the re-entry process. The pace of life

there is less frenetic than typical America and more closely matches the feeling of places we had become accustomed to on our travels. People live simply and are content with less of the trappings of American life. Friendships and spontaneously spending time with each other are very important. A traffic jam consists of cows crossing the road and cell phones do not double as earrings. In short, less is more.

Back in Salem, neighbor children were taller, businesses had closed, two houses had new residents, and trees had grown significantly. All were evidence of the passing of time. Still, I felt in a time warp with a head full of memories, experiences and new friends around the world. After being back for a year I truly wish that we had sold our house before leaving so that we could return and make a completely fresh start. As it was, returning to the same home, it felt as if we never left. This was a huge disappointment to me. I wanted to hold on to the lessons and experiences from our world trip.

How does it feel to be back? Weird. Normal. Indescribable. How do I explain to others that we didn't just travel? We hosteled, we stayed in run down shacks, had to survive on very little at times, shared the life of the poor and worked among the poverty stricken. It's like trying to answer the question, "How was your trip?" There is no quick reply.

I can say, a year later, that for a long time I felt as if I didn't belong. Memories of my childhood, when my father returned from a year in Vietnam, resurfaced. (He had served in WWII and Korea but Vietnam was probably the most traumatic, or at least "the last straw".) He was constantly telling us to turn off the lights, don't waste water, food, anything. . . that we had no idea how lucky we were. He was right. We didn't have any idea of the affluence and relative ease of our lives compared to most of the world. This trip gave me first hand experience into his frustration with us. I find myself saying and thinking some of the same admonitions. On a very small scale, I began to relate to the war veterans who return to their lives but are forever changed.

Have you adjusted back to normal life? Yes. No. I don't think I ever will again. Before we left we were proud of our

251

efforts toward a simpler life-style: one tiny car, a big organic garden, clothesline, bike riding, recycling, and composting everything. It was an earnest effort to live light on the earth and not waste resources. Now our house feels huge and cavernous, excessive. I look forward to moving to a smaller home in a smaller community.

I scrutinize "wants" from "needs" even more and I am thrilled to take a shower with hot running water. Frequently when I turn on a faucet I remember hauling large pails of water in Paraguay or watching the little girls in Tanzania carry the huge buckets on their heads for miles.

The only way I can explain this dualism is comparing it to when you lose someone you dearly love in an untimely death. It is not his fault. It's unfair. You feel the loss very deeply but you eventually get on with your life. Still, his life and death remain in your mind and heart to surface occasionally to make you stop and think—oh, yes.

It's the same for me now. I go about life here in Oregon but the very recent memories of other realities are just beyond yesterday whispering---oh, yes. It's like putting on an old skin that no longer feels right. I have friends who live in mud huts. I know how it feels not to have all the comforts of modern life. I have seen poor children running barefoot after a truck thrilled to receive a broken toy. Is it all sheer luck, where we are born, to whom and when? We lived the poor life for days or weeks at a time but we always had an out. We were only volunteers and visitors who were blessed with a chance to walk in someone else's moccasins for a while. Memories can fade with time. I wish to hold on to these.

The disparity between the U.S. and the rest of the world is incomprehensible. I don't understand how an actor can receive $1 million for one episode of a sitcom or an athlete can be paid several million per year to play a game. What makes them more deserving than a teacher in Peru or a laborer in Thailand? Life, it seems, is not only arbitrary but unbalanced as well.

Ignorance is truly bliss. Growing up I was always the eternal optimist filled with an unflinching hope in humankind.

252

It seemed the more I learned about the way the world worked—or didn't—the more disheartened I became. How could we, as a human race, permit such degradation of our earth, turn a blind eye to child abuse, the poor, the elderly? Why is there so much war?

By traveling all over the world, even in the face of 11 Sept. (especially because of 11 Sept.) my faith in human beings was restored. Strangers and angels came to our aid in every country just when we needed them most. The bad news is there are a few rotten eggs. The good news is that, (despite typical media coverage) loving, caring people far outnumber the bad. There is not a single problem that we have created for ourselves for which we do not also have solutions. I believe in the human race as a caring entity that will eventually unite for the good of our planet and its children. More than anything, this journey taught me there is an abundance of hope out there. Small, individual acts of kindness can make a difference in a life.

Are you doing anything differently? More than anything else, this trip was extremely humbling. In every aspect of our lives we have more advantages and more choices than any other nation we visited. We expect clean hot and cold running water, working electricity, flushing toilets with toilet paper provided. People can become immediately impatient and demanding when a product isn't perfect, a plane is late or a purchased meal is not up to snuff. Patience is a virtue that not enough people in First World countries possess. Traveling as we did was a good practice in delayed gratification and patience. We have always known that our choices, however small, affect the lives of other people. This trip made that fact all too clear.

To that end, I had this incredible urge to live differently somehow, in any possible manner. We gave away our clothes dryer. That is not such a sacrifice in the warm summer months and the clothes smell refreshing drying in a breeze. In Salem, it typically rains from October to May. Then, doing without a clothes dryer becomes a challenge and a daily reminder of our travels. We tried to live without a car for a month, but that was unrealistic. Neighbors helped bail us out with their "extra" cars until we found a car that we could afford and got decent gas mileage. (Unable to afford anything west of the Rockies, we found a used car on the Internet. I used our last one-way frequent flyer ticket to fly to Texas and drive it home. That trip itself reads like a sitcom.)

Perhaps the greatest outcome of the trip presently has been the writing of a show that we produced at the middle school where I teach. As we stood in the Peace Plaza in Dachau Clare whispered to me, "Mommy, we have to do a show about this." I pointed to the wall on which was written "never again" in all the languages of those who had perished there. "There's your title," I told Clare. Thus, "Never Again" was born. It is a wonderful show that deals with human rights and social justice throughout the world, throughout history.

Whatever happened to the miracle cross in Ireland? We experienced so many miracles, large and small on this trip. My favorite story of all is finding the Celtic cross for Zach in the Glendalough Youth Hostel. It was a story that remained unfinished until recently. Our return to Oregon in February 2002 coincided with the time that the necklace, if unclaimed, would have been sent to Sweden. I eagerly awaited some word that Zach had received it. When none came I tried to email the youth hostel in Glendalough. With Steve's expertise in finding his way around the super highway I finally got a message through to Ireland while simultaneously writing to Sweden again. It was a ticklish situation, rather like trying not to spoil a surprise party but still needing to know the whereabouts of the honored guest.

In the fall of 2002 two emails came within hours of each other. The first, from Ireland, was from the new hostel manager. His bittersweet story relayed how the young woman with whom I had left the necklace had gone home to Wales that December after our visit, complaining of headaches. She was diagnosed with cancer, an inoperable brain tumor, and died that winter. Prior to her death she had indeed kept her promise and sent the Celtic cross to the young lad in Sweden going through a very rough patch in his life. I was deeply saddened by the loss of this vibrant young woman whose conversations I had enjoyed during our stay. Gone? Life is so, so short.

My excitement at knowing that the cross had been sent to Zach was doubled the next morning when an email came from Sweden confirming that Zach had indeed received the cross and had been wearing it ever since.

One song sums up what I experienced in our travels. I share the lyrics here as a prayer for the world and a dedication to the man who wrote it, one of my favorite artists:

From *"I Want to Live"* by John Denver
For the worker and the warrior, the lover and the liar.
For the native and the wanderer in kind.
For the maker and the user and a mother and her son.
I am looking for my family and all of you are mine.

We are standing all together face to face and arm in arm
We are standing on the threshold of a dream
No more hunger, no more killing,
no more wasting life away
It is simply an idea and I know its time has come.

I want to live, I want to grow,
I want to see and I want to know
I want to share what I can give, I want to be,
I want to live.

Steven:
Toby and I engaged in writing the book as somewhat of a catharsis. We not only wanted to document our experiences, fun and otherwise, for our kids but process in our minds what was valuable in affecting our "ideas of living." Now that we are coming to the end of our writing, I think that goal was optimistic. Not the documenting part, but the profound changes in our lives part. At this point, about a year after the end of our trip, it is very difficult to identify major impacts.

255

Looking back ten years from now, what will we see about how this trip has influenced our lives? It may take quite a while to sift out the significant from the trivial. There are a few things, however, that do stand out presently.

As we were about to get on the plane leaving Piura, Peru, Father Joe commented that our kids had a great amount of self-confidence. He was impressed with how they were able to just dive in and speak with people from different countries about their experiences. I hadn't thought about it much until that moment, but our kids had developed quite a willingness to engage with people when they were thrust into new situations. In every country we traveled, Clare, Bridget, and Michael quickly established relationships with people, regardless of their looks and language. Of course, this flew in the face of parents' mantra to their kids: "Don't talk to strangers." Now that we have returned, when are strangers potential companions and when are they potentially dangerous? That one is a bit tricky.

Upon our arrival, a new fear pervades the United States. Who can I trust? Who might be a terrorist? What a horrible way to live day to day, worrying about other people, particularly those who may look different than us. One of the movies we have seen since our return to the U.S. was "Bowling for Columbine." It was a documentary that offered the theory that possession of guns in the United States is not the problem that led to atrocities like Columbine, but our society's state of fear. Michael Moore, the filmmaker, proposed that the United States is unique among countries in its anxiety.

Madison Avenue clearly uses fear in advertising…Don't be a loser, buy this _____ (fill in the blank: car, beer, clothes, technology, etc.) Don't be embarrassed in public! Buy this _____ (detergent, deodorant, wrinkle cream, etc.) Don't be afraid! Live in this gated community, buy this alarm system, get this gun. Our government now makes a regular point of telling us to be afraid of potential disaster. These fears were not part of the lives of the people we have spent the past eight months with. How does this impact the psyche of our children, ourselves?

Obviously, I want my kids to be safe, but I want them to be open to the goodness of the vast majority of humanity as well. I am proud that as a result of this trip my children now encounter people from other cultures and see possibilities for friendships. Powerful, but simple memories of our visit to the tourist office in Malaysia and laughing with a Muslim woman, living with Abesaida and meeting Kata in Guatemala, and our hike with the amiable Maasai warrior in Tanzania will live in my mind as reminders of the beauty of people. Will that sense of appreciation of others persist in spite of our fearful society? Our challenge as parents now is providing the right amount of prudence in situations to remain safe while maintaining an eagerness to connect and learn from others. I hope that we can continue to seek and appreciate diversity.

People often asked what our expectations were as we took this trip. One of my stock answers was "To see the different cultures and ways of living life in the world." Traveling all those countries certainly revealed unique customs, foods, and environments that were great to learn about. Yet, what truly struck me was not the differences, but the similarities. All over the world, people had families, kids played in front of houses, and people worked to support their families. Our kids have this book at home called Everybody Eats Rice. A child goes from door to door in his diverse neighborhood and finds that everyone eats rice, but with a different, cultural recipe. You can see it as everybody is different or everyone is the same. To me, on this trip, particularly in light of the recent atrocities in the United States, it was important to see how similar we are to everyone else in the world.

A second area of growth for our children is their creativity and imagination. Stuck on planes, trains, and buses for hours on end tends to bring out the best or worst in people. It is incredible that our kids rose to the occasion. Different characters and story lines were conceived and acted out, card games filled every spare moment, and opportunities to play

257

with new, friendly faces were seized. They loved to tell stories of the road, particularly about something stupid their father did. Whining was rarely heard during those times, as they seemed to say to themselves: "This is going to be long, so I'm going to make the best of it." What a great commentary on their fortitude as people.

On the other hand, when we arrived back in the United States and spent a week in Vermont old habits quickly returned. After church, as Toby and I stood socializing with a few old friends for about ten minutes, the kids continuously tugged at our sleeves saying: "We're bored! When are we leaving?" I guess it was too good to last. As drug rehabilitation programs know too well, when people return to their original surroundings after a long absence, the environment, which helped to form habits, continues to pressure them to return to old ways. Old habits of communication and habits of living full lives have returned to our family all too quickly. Can our kids sustain their creativity in the presence of their friends who have television and Nintendo based imaginations? Can we maintain loving relationships in our family and our lives in spite of the pressures of school and work? I hope so.

As for Toby and me, our consciousness of the world and issues of poverty and politics was pretty high before we departed. In a debriefing chat about our trip, a friend of ours in Vermont, also named Steve, said: "You guys already have a broad awareness of the world. This trip just filled in some details." That was probably a pretty accurate assessment, but there are an awful lot of details to fill in, and we certainly didn't get them all! Prior to the trip we had a good breadth of understanding. Our travels and experiences have served to provide us with much greater depth of understanding of the world's people, environment, and economics than we had before we left.

Poverty stands out in my mind as the most important experience of our trip. As a result of our working with and traveling around people in very poor situations, I had hoped that our kids would develop an understanding of first versus third world dynamics. At this point, they aren't ready or perhaps are not old enough to convey their thoughts on this complicated issue. It is difficult enough for me to lucidly explain my thoughts about our experience. Throughout our trip, I struggled emotionally when faced with people who were unable to meet their needs. Our family has so many resources beyond our needs that it was disturbing walking the streets of third world countries.

As I write this, Michael walks by and says "I'm hungry." What an incredible luxury it is to be able to say "Just open the cupboard or refrigerator and find something." Our modest home is the home of kings in many countries. Do our children understand their relative prosperity? Yes. This trip has certainly made them aware of the disparity between how we live and how much of the rest of the world lives. Does it impact their lives, their thinking? I'm not so sure. Peering into the cupboard, Michael yells out "There's nothing to eat!" Translation: "I have a particular desire for a particular food and it isn't here now". In spite of boxes and cans of assorted food filling our shelves, this is a common refrain in our home. What went wrong?

Rice and beans every day in Guatemala and Paraguay. Not a word of "nothing to eat". Somehow, we all realized then that we ate what was available. We had few options and that was okay. Now we have 1,420 varieties of cereal and there is nothing to eat...With the disparity in our living standards so clear in our travels, Ghandi's words "Live simply, so that others may simply live" often came to mind. As we now rebuild our lives here in the United States, it is our mental chant to organize our lives in a way that does not use up resources unnecessarily. We need to remind ourselves of the significant difference between our wants and our needs. In our home in Oregon, the overwhelming choices available to us makes this easier said than done. As parents, we struggle with the balance between preaching these ideas, consciously modeling them, and just plain hoping that somehow they will seep into our children's consciousness.

Is this too much to ask of kids? Shouldn't we just let them play and not weigh them down with the worries of the world? Perhaps. I am all for abundant playtime for everyone. It was not until college that I began to have a social consciousness. Yet, we so desperately want our children to become adults who are compassionate, sensitive, and aware of the world beyond their immediate reach. We pray that they might live their lives as if every act has global implications. My favorite guilt trip on myself is to think "If everyone in the world did what I am doing right now, what would happen?" If everyone lived simply then others could simply live. Pretty heady stuff for our children, but when do you sow those seeds of thought? I don't think us telling them "Eat that broccoli because children in India are starving!" has much impact. I hope their experiences on this trip, however, have provided those seeds of compassion.

One insight for me from this trip was that there are many kinds of poverty, many causes, and many ways to live it. As we were working with the poor in Peru we couldn't help comparing poverty there to poverty in Africa. In neither case do we claim to have a perfect understanding of the realities people face. However, based on our experiences and observations we formed opinions anyway.

In Peru, twenty-five people lived in a house made of cardboard, sticks, and plastic bags that was infested with roaches and other bugs. Thousands of homes, wall to wall in that area were basically the same. As we rode through the towns each day, men, women, and children simply roamed around town. Most men tried to find work, but brought home meager wages. There appears to be no hope of a better life. People appear to be resigned to the lives they lead. Their needs are basically met, but they all seem to be on the edge of survival.

In contrast, the Maasai of Tanzania appear to have their needs met. They are not necessarily satisfied with being poor, but satisfied with their lives. In their small villages they live out centuries old traditions of house building, farming, cattle

260

raising, and art work. By our standards, they have nothing. As their counterparts in Peru, they too live on the edge of survival. Yet, they seem to enjoy the lives they lead and have no desire to move forward into the "progress" of the 21st Century. Their eyes do not have the hopeless look of despair that you might see in the homeless in America or the streets of Piura, Peru. Obviously not all Africans can say that their needs are met, as thousands die every year. Yet, the Maasai are able to feed and clothe their children, live off the work of the land, and not seem despairing.

From these two experiences it was clear to us that poverty spanned two levels: poverty of resources and poverty of the spirit. Are your needs met? Are you at peace with your life? There are tremendous obstacles for the people of Piura to rise above their situation. The Maasai choose to preserve their culture and lifestyle of simple living. With approximately equal resources, the people of Piura seem very poor while the Maasai seem to have their needs met, both physically and spiritually. There are certainly hardships in both cases, but in the case of the Piurans, they seem to also have poverty of spirit. They have a sense of hopelessness.

What implications do these discoveries have for our family?

Well, I can attest to the validity of the saying that you only appreciate what you have if you leave it for a while. After traveling around these past eight months, I have come to appreciate many things about the United States. We can be thankful that we have our basic needs met, and, as a family, realize our relative wealth of resources. I hope that memories of our experiences will facilitate our discernment when it comes to considering our needs and wants in the future.

Perhaps equally important however, is addressing that poverty of spirit on two levels: our family and our world. In regard to our family, thanks to my parents and my education, I have the attitude instilled within me, and the means, that I can choose to strive for anything I want to. I'm confident and appreciative that my children will likely never have that sense of hopelessness that we experienced in the eyes of many

261

others in the world. In so many countries, people either don't have the attitude instilled within them or face obstacles that are insurmountable. In the U.S, there is always a way if there is the will. I see it as our responsibility as a family to take advantage of our opportunities so that we can create opportunities for others.

I'll conclude with a story and some thoughts that our friends Mark and Jeanine shared with us as they began their humanitarian work in Brazil.

Nine runners were in a Special Olympics race, eagerly anticipating the starting gun from their positions on the line. At the signal, eight of them leaped forward and began to race for the finish, but the ninth stumbled out of the start and fell down. Dejected, he began to cry. The others, hearing the cries, all paused and looked back, stopped, and returned to their fellow runner. Helping him up, they all locked arms and ran to the finish together, to great applause from the crowd.

In so many places in the world, particularly in the United States, there is a race for power and people are compelled to increase their "standards of living." Too often, that drive narrows our field of vision and we lose sight of those who are left behind. "Winning" necessitates someone losing. Whether in our own country or in the countries of the world, our travels have shown us that a great many people are "losing." We do affect the world and we are affected by it. Our hope is that this trip has been an opportunity for our family to stop and be aware of those around us. There is so much beauty in people and the earth that we miss in our drive for more. There are also so many needs in the world of which we are ignorant.

In my office at work I have a picture of the earth as seen from space. Every time I look at it, I reflect on the fact that there are no lines evident. "Imagine there are no countries. It isn't hard to do."(John Lennon) As a result of our travels, each of us feels a bit more connected to others in the world. There are less miles and fewer barriers between here and there. Now that we have returned to our home in the United States, we need to look around, remain conscious of our brothers and sisters throughout the world, and act in ways that ensure that all of us can cross the finish line together.

We began the book with a quote from Mark Twain challenging ourselves to "sail away from the safe harbor". In the end, we can be proud that our family took a significant risk and set sail. We began this final chapter with a quote by Neil Postman, "Children are messages into a future we cannot see". This world adventure was an attempt to shape that message and perhaps shape our children's future.

We end this book with another quote (if you hadn't guessed already, we like quotes…). Miriam Beard, an American author said that "travel is more than the seeing of sights; it is a change that goes on, deep and permanent, in the ideas of living." When a face across the oceans becomes a friend and when the uniqueness of a culture and way of living is valued, the world becomes smaller. That is at the heart of what we hope has happened within each one of us--changes in our ideas of living.

Peace be with you.

Post Script: in an effort to keep this book a reasonable length we have omitted many tales, web sites, how-to tips and the photographs of our trip. For those who wish to see and read more (e.g. how we acquired the world ticket and managed to fly all of us for a reasonable price) please visit the web site: www.sawtoothpress.com